Library of
Davidson College

Revolutionary Cuba

About the Book and Author

*Revolutionary Cuba: The Challenge of
Economic Growth with Equity*
Claes Brundenius

This comprehensive analysis of the economic and social revolution that has engulfed Cuba since 1959 is the first attempt to evaluate quantitatively the impact of the revolution on economic growth, employment, income distribution, and the meeting of basic needs. Dr. Brundenius draws primarily on previously unpublished statistical information that he collected on frequent visits to Cuba since 1973. He also places the revolution in a historical and comparative perspective with extensive references to the prerevolutionary era (1933–1958) and to two other celebrated development models in Latin America, post-1964 Brazil and Peru in the period from 1968 to 1980.

Claes Brundenius is a research fellow at the Research Policy Institute, University of Lund, Sweden. He is coeditor of *Development Strategies and Basic Needs in Latin America* (Westview, 1982). In the spring of 1983 he was on a United Nations assignment at the Ministry of Industry in Managua, Nicaragua, and at present he is a visiting Mellon Professor at the Center for Latin American Studies and the Department of Economics at the University of Pittsburgh.

To
Lena
Katarina
Tomas
Peter

Revolutionary Cuba:
The Challenge of Economic Growth with Equity

Claes Brundenius

Westview Press • Boulder and London

Heinemann • London, Kingston, and Port of Spain

This volume is included in Westview's Special Studies on Latin America and the Caribbean.

All rights reserved. No part of this publication may be reproduced or transmitted in any form or by any means, electronic or mechanical, including photocopy, recording, or any information storage and retrieval system, without permission in writing from the publisher.

Copyright © 1984 by Westview Press, Inc.

Published in 1984 in the United States of America by Westview Press, Inc., 5500 Central Avenue, Boulder, Colorado 80301; Frederick A. Praeger, President and Publisher.

Published in 1984 in Great Britain by Heinemann Educational Books, 22 Bedford Square, London WC1B 3HH, England. 175 Mountain View Avenue, Kingston 6, Jamaica. 27 Belmont Circular Rd., Port of Spain, Trinidad.

Library of Congress Cataloging in Publication Data
Brundenius, Claes, 1938–
  Revolutionary Cuba, the challenge of economic growth with equity.
  (Westview special studies on Latin America and the Caribbean)
  Bibliography: p.
  Includes index.
  1. Cuba—Economic conditions—1959– . 2. Cuba—Economic conditions. 3. Income distribution—Cuba.
4. Labor and laboring classes—Cuba. I. Title.
II. Series.
HC152.5.B79 1984   338.97291   83-12432
ISBN 0-86531-355-5

British Library Cataloguing in Publication Data
Brundenius, Claes
Revolutionary Cuba.
1. Cuba—Economic conditions—1959–
I. Title
330.97291′084   HC152.5
ISBN 0-435-98120-X

Printed and bound in the United States of America

10   9   8   7   6   5   4   3   2   1

Contents

List of Tables and Figures ix
Preface xv

Introduction 1

1 **Economic Growth in Cuba in Retrospect** 5

    Growth and Stagnation in Prerevolutionary Cuba 5
    The Sugar Economy: 1900–1929 7
    Depression and Recovery: 1930–1958 10
    A Permanent Crisis? 12

2 **Measuring Economic Growth in Revolutionary Cuba** 19

    A Note on Statistics and National Accounting
      in Revolutionary Cuba 19
    Index of Total Material Production, 1946–1961 23
    Index of Total Material Production, 1961–1968 26
    Index of Total Material Production, 1968–1980 27
    An Estimate of Cuban Gross Domestic Product,
      1958–1981 28

3 **The Economic Performance of Revolutionary Cuba** 41

    The Unfolding of a Revolution 41
    Socialist Upsurge in the Countryside 42
    Mounting Pressures Against Resources 45
    The Goods Famine of 1962–1963 and the Great Debate 49
    The Revolutionary Offensive and the 10-Million-Ton *Zafra* ... 54
    The Second Decade: Sustained Economic Growth 57
    The Fight Against Unemployment 58

      Mechanization of Sugar Production and Return
        to Material Incentives.. 60
      External Dependency and Structural Economic Changes 61

4 Basic Needs and Economic Growth........................ 79

      A Yardstick of Basic Needs 79
      A Composite Basic Needs Index for Cuba.................... 81
      Food and Beverages... 82
      Clothing 84
      Housing.. 85
      Education 88
      Health 90
      A Composite Index of Basic Needs Performance.............. 91

5 Distribution of Income and Consumption................. 105

      Income Distribution Before 1959 105
      Income Distribution in the 1960s........................... 106
      Income Distribution in the 1970s........................... 109
      Distribution of Consumption................................ 111
      Regional Differences in Income and Consumption 112

6 Cuban Growth and Equity in a Comparative Context 119

Appendix 1   The Development of the
Cuban Labor Force, 1970–1980 125

      The 1979 Survey... 126
      Unemployment 126
      Female Labor Force 128
      Educational Level of the Labor Force 129
      Estimate of the Cuban Labor Force, 1970–1980.............. 130

Appendix 2   Statistical Tables................................ 139

Notes 185
Bibliography 199
Index 217

Tables and Figures

Tables

1.1	Per capita production of raw sugar and apparent per capita consumption of certain consumer and intermediate goods, 1905–1909, 1925–1929, and 1945–1949	14
1.2	U.S. direct investments in Cuba, 1929–1958	17
1.3	Growth indicators of the Cuban economy, 1946–1958	18
2.1	Global indicators of the Cuban economy, 1962–1974	32
2.2	Indexes of Cuban industrial production, 1946–1961	34
2.3	Net domestic income at factor cost in 1953	36
2.4	Growth estimates, 1959–1961	36
2.5	Estimate of total material production at factor cost in 1962	37
2.6	Reconstruction of total material production, global social product, and gross material product, 1965	38
2.7	Estimate of Cuban gross domestic product at factor cost, 1958–1981	39
2.8	Growth rates of Cuban GDP and main components, 1959–1981	40
3.1	Land tenure in Cuba at the beginning of 1959	68
3.2	Land expropriations, as of May 1961	69
3.3	Collectivization of ownership of means of production and services in Cuba, 1961–1977	71
3.4	Economic performance indicators, 1961–1980	71
3.5	Some characteristics of the Cuban labor force, 1960–1980	73
3.6	Employment and mechanization in the sugar sector, 1957/1958–1980/1981	74
3.7	Cuba's trade dependency, 1946–1980	75
3.8	Commodity and partner concentration in Cuban exports, 1965–1980	75

List of Tables and Figures

3.9	Sugar exports, sugar prices, and commodity and partner concentration in Cuba's foreign trade, 1959–1982	76
3.10	Structural changes in the Cuban economy, 1961–1981	77
3.11	Gross investment by economic sector, 1962–1981	78
4.1	Indexes of consumption of food and beverages, Cuban and Canadian weights	93
4.2	Annual construction and estimated stock of dwellings, 1958–1980	95
4.3	Number of dwellings and shadow rents paid by number of rooms, 1970	95
4.4	Dwellings with basic facilities, urban and rural, 1953 and 1970	96
4.5	Basic needs indicators, education, 1958–1980	97
4.6	A comparison of average costs per student by type of education in Cuba and Canada, 1961	98
4.7	Basic needs indicators, health, 1958–1980	101
4.8	Estimated unit costs in health services, Canadian and Cuban prices	102
4.9	Composite basic needs index for Cuba, 1958–1980 (Cuban weights)	103
4.10	Composite basic needs index for Cuba, 1958–1980 (Canadian weights)	103
4.11	Comparison of per capita growth rates of TMP and basic needs, 1958–1980	104
5.1	Estimates of Cuban income distribution in the 1950s	113
5.2	Employment and unemployment, 1953	113
5.3	Estimated income distribution, 1962	114
5.4	Estimated average annual income by income groups, 1953 and 1962	114
5.5	Wage scales applied in Cuba between 1963–1979 and after 1980	115
5.6	Income distribution estimates, 1973 and 1978	116
5.7	Distribution of family expenditures by income groups and family size, Havana, November 1980	117
5.8	Examples of monthly wages in Havana, April 1979	117
5.9	Prices of rationed and liberated consumer goods in Havana, October 1980	118
5.10	Regional differences in income and consumption, 1978/1979	118

List of Tables and Figures

6.1	GDP per capita and growth rates, Cuba and selected areas/countries in Latin America, 1960–1982	123
6.2	Economic structural changes in Cuba and selected areas/countries in Latin America between 1960 and 1981	123
6.3	Levels and growth of per capita income by strata—Brazil, Cuba, and Peru	124
A1.1	Employment by economic sector and by occupational category, 1970 and 1979	131
A1.2	Employment by sector and growth of labor force and population, 1953–1979	133
A1.3	Total labor force, occupied labor force, and unemployed labor force by sex, 1960 and 1970–1980	134
A1.4	Unemployed as percent of labor force	135
A1.5	Characteristics of the female labor force, 1970–1980	135
A1.6	Employment of female labor force by sector, 1970 and 1979	136
A1.7	Educational level of the population and of the labor force, 1953 and 1979	137
A1.8	Labor force characteristics, 1970–1980	138
A2.1	Estimates of Cuban national income, 1903–1939	140
A2.2	Output of raw sugar, sugar income, and Cuban share of world sugar production, 1900–1958	141
A2.3	Growth estimates, 1930–1958	143
A2.4	Estimates of Cuban national income, 1939–1958	145
A2.5	Total material production at factor cost, 1946–1961	146
A2.6	Annual growth rates of total material production by branches, 1947–1961	148
A2.7	Total material production at factor cost, 1961–1968	149
A2.8	Annual growth rates of total material production by branches, 1962–1968	150
A2.9	Total material production at factor cost, 1968–1980	151
A2.10	Annual growth rates of total material production by branches, 1969–1980	153
A2.11	Output of transport equipment and machinery, 1958–1980	154
A2.12	Output of electrical equipment, electric power, and mining industry, 1958–1980	155
A2.13	Output of metallurgy and metal products, petroleum products, and raw sugar, 1958–1980	156

xii List of Tables and Figures

A2.14	Output of sulphuric acid, rayon tire cords, fertilizers, insecticides, herbicides, paper pulp, newsprint, tires, and matches, 1958–1980	157
A2.15	Output of construction materials and durable consumer goods, 1958–1980	158
A2.16	Output of nondurable consumer goods, 1958–1980	159
A2.17	Estimate of Cuban labor force and its distribution, 1962–1978	160
A2.18	Per capita consumption of food and beverages in Cuba, 1963–1971	162
A2.19	Prices of basic needs goods, Cuba 1977 and Canada 1961	166
A2.20	Estimated per capita expenditures on food and beverages, 1963–1980 (Cuban 1977 pesos)	168
A2.21	Estimated per capita expenditures on food and beverages, 1963–1980 (constant shadow prices)	170
A2.22	Estimated per capita expenditures on clothing, 1963–1980 (Cuban 1978 pesos)	172
A2.23	Estimated per capita expenditures on clothing, 1963–1980 (Canadian 1961 dollars)	173
A2.24	Basic needs indicators, clothing, 1963–1980	174
A2.25	Basic needs indicators, housing, 1958–1980	175
A2.26	Estimated per capita expenditures on housing, 1958–1980	176
A2.27	Enrollments by level of education, 1958–1980	177
A2.28	Estimated basic needs expenditures per capita in Cuba, 1958–1980	178
A2.29	Estimated distribution of wages and salaries in 1953	180
A2.30	Estimated distribution of wages and salaries in 1962	181
A2.31	Estimated distribution of wages and salaries in 1973	183
A2.32	Estimated distribution of wages and salaries in 1978	184

Figures

1.1	National income, sugar income, and sugar output, 1900–1958	15
1.2	World sugar prices, 1900–1958	16
1.3	Growth estimates, 1930–1958	17
2.1	The Cuban national accounting system	31
3.1	Total material production 1946–1961, actual and trend projection	69
3.2	Growth and composition of total material production, 1961–1981	70

3.3	Cuban terms of trade with the USSR and the West, 1963–1981	72
4.1	Index of per capita expenditures on food and beverages, 1958–1980	93
4.2	Index of per capita expenditures on clothing, 1958–1980	94
4.3	Index of per capita expenditures on housing, 1958–1980	96
4.4	The Cuban educational system	99
4.5	Index of per capita expenditures on education, 1958–1980	100
4.6	Index of per capita expenditures on health services, 1958–1980	102
4.7	Composite basic needs performance indexes, 1958–1980	104
5.1	Estimated income distribution in Cuba in 1953, 1962, and 1978	116

Preface

The Cubans are now celebrating the twenty-fifth anniversary of the revolution that overthrew the Batista dictatorship. What could then be more timely than an assessment of the impact of this revolution on economic growth and equity? I can still remember the atmosphere in Cuba in 1959 when, as a young student, I visited the island for the first time. Everywhere I went I was surrounded by enthusiastic people who told me optimistically about the brilliant future that they thought lay ahead. I have since then had the privilege of returning to Cuba several times, and during the last five years I have collected the information and data that have made this book possible.

Large parts of this book were presented in 1981 as a Ph.D. dissertation at the University of Lund, Sweden, under the title "Economic Growth, Basic Needs and Income Distribution in Revolutionary Cuba." This book is, however, an entirely revised, enlarged, and updated version of that dissertation, including several new chapters, notably on economic structure and dependency relations, the development of the Cuban labor force, and a comparative view of the Cuban performance in a Latin American context.

I am greatly indebted to a number of colleagues and friends for encouraging support and invaluable assistance in the preparation of this book. First of all I want to thank my many Cuban friends for their generous support and comments on earlier drafts of the book. I am especially grateful to Dr. Carlos Rafael Rodríguez, vice-president of the Council of Ministers and the Council of State, and to his assistant Miriam Fernández for their willingness to receive me on several occasions and to discuss the progress of my research. I am also much indebted to my many friends at the State Committee on Statistics for their advice and readiness to share statistical information with me, especially Dr. Fidel Vascos, minister-president of the State Committee on Statistics, José-Antonio López Pereda, and Ernesto Díaz. I have also benefited greatly from comments by Oscar Pino Santos, Santiago Díaz, and Eugenio Espinoza.

A large number of colleagues and friends outside Cuba have also been most helpful with comments and suggestions on earlier drafts. Above all I want to thank the following persons: Lennart Jörberg, Carmelo Mesa-Lago, Jon Sigurdson, Mats Lundahl, Olle Krantz, Tommy Bengtsson, Tom Alberts, Claes Croner, Charles Edquist, Dan Usher, and Susan Eckstein. A very special feeling of gratitude goes to the Swedish Agency for Research Cooperation with Developing Countries (SAREC), which has financed large parts of my research.

Finally, but not least, I am very much obliged to my wife, Lena, and my children, Katarina, Tomas, and Peter, for having had so much patience and understanding during critical moments of the preparation of this book.

Claes Brundenius

Introduction

Men make their own history, but they do not make it just as they please. They do not make it under circumstances chosen by themselves, but under circumstances directly encountered, given and transmitted from the past.
—Karl Marx, "The Eighteenth Brumaire of Louis Bonaparte"

The most difficult task was not the overthrow of Batista and the taking of revolutionary power. . . . The most difficult task is the one we are engaged in today: the building of a new country on the basis of an underdeveloped country, the creation of a new consciousness, a new man.
—Fidel Castro, addressing a rally on 26 July 1967

Latin America is a region of contrasts in practically every sense of the word: geographically, climatically, economically, and politically. It is a rich area endowed with abundant natural resources—minerals and other raw materials—and these assets have produced considerable wealth in the past, but too often only for minorities at home and abroad with little of the wealth trickling down to the masses.[1] In this respect Latin America is, of course, no exception to the rest of the Third World. On the contrary, it seems that this situation has been the general rule in the past.

During the 1960s, the First United Nations Development Decade, the international debate on the causes of and the remedies for underdevelopment was imbued with a spirit of optimism. The rate of growth of many Third World countries, and in particular of several countries in Latin America, had advanced at an accelerating rate after World War II, and studies by Simon Kuznets and others showed that the early stages of growth are accompanied by growing inequality (Kuznets's famous U-curve) but that, in the longer run, growing income would tend to be accompanied by narrowing income gaps.[2]

However, during the first half of the 1970s, the Second Development Decade, many scholars began to have second thoughts about growth and inequality in the developing countries.[3] Looking at several country experiences, we can see that there was no automatic trickling down to the poor as a result of high rates of economic growth. Even in Brazil, which often was cited as an example, the government in its second development plan (1975-1979) explicitly recognized that the poor had not benefited from the "economic miracle" of the end of the 1960s and the beginning of the 1970s and declared that

> the Government has rejected the position of waiting until the economic growth by itself solves the problem of income distribution, or the theory of "waiting for the cake to grow bigger." It is necessary, while maintaining an accelerated rate of growth, to undertake redistributive policies "while the cake is growing." The truth is that, on the one hand, growth may not solve the problem of adequate distribution of income, if left to the mere evolution of market factors. And on the other hand the growth solution, if left to itself, may take *far longer than social conscience will permit* [italics mine] in terms of the need to improve rapidly the level of welfare of wide sectors of the population.[4]

This change in development thinking in the ruling circle of Brazil, even if it turned out to be just paying lip service, was no doubt inspired by the many conferences and seminars held under the auspices of the United Nations in those years. There was a growing concern about the redistribution of income and assets and the need to implement development strategies that as a first priority would satisfy the basic needs of the large majorities. The International Labour Organization (ILO) arranged a number of employment missions to several developing countries, and these missions focused on the question of how to create more jobs. The ILO employment missions discovered what Gunnar Myrdal had already described in *Asian Drama*, namely, that "the real problem is that in order to be unemployed one has to be fairly well off; in order to survive there must be some income from another source."[5] At a famous symposium in Cocoyoc, Mexico, in 1974, Patterns of Resource Use, Environment, and Development Strategies organized by the United Nations Conference on Trade and Development (UNCTAD), the purpose of development was defined in these terms:

> Our first concern is to redefine the whole purpose of development. This should not be to develop things but to develop man. Human beings have basic needs: food, shelter, clothing, health, education. Any process of growth that does not lead to their fulfillment—or, even worse, disrupts them—is a travesty of the idea of development. We are still in a stage where the most important concern of development is the level of satisfaction of basic needs for the poorest sections in each society which can be as high as 40 percent of the population. The primary purpose of economic

growth should be to ensure the improvement of conditions for these groups. A growth process that benefits only the wealthiest minority and maintains or even increases the disparities between and within countries is not development. It is exploitation. And the time for starting the type of true economic growth that leads to better distribution and to the satisfaction of the basic needs for all is today. We believe that thirty years of experience with the hope that rapid economic growth benefitting the few will "trickle down" to the mass of the people has proved to be illusory. We therefore reject the idea of "growth first, justice in the distribution of benefits later."[6]

During the second half of the 1970s there was a steadily growing interest in the formulation of strategies that would stress income redistribution and satisfaction of basic needs without sacrificing growth. *Redistribution with Growth* (Thetford, Eng.: World Bank and Sussex Institute of Development Studies, 1974) focused on the question of how growth affects distribution and vice versa. Most contributors to this volume clearly saw that growth is a prerequisite for the eradication of poverty and for redistribution, but it was also becoming evident that economic growth in many developing countries reinforced existing inequalities.

In the wake of the debate that followed the publication of the World Bank–Sussex report, there were a number of studies of countries that—at least according to preliminary findings—had successfully carried through a growth-with-equity strategy. Examples of such countries were the Republic of Korea and Taiwan.[7] There has also been a renewed interest in the experiences of socialist countries in the Third World,[8] and it is within this framework that this book has been written.

Even in the 1960s Cuba had become an example of an alternative development model—at least for the Latin American leftist. In the 1970s, the Cuban experience with respect to the eradication of unemployment and mass poverty and the country's stress on redistribution and basic needs satisfaction again drew attention—this time the attention not only of the Latin American Left, but also of international agencies such as the United Nations.[9]

This book on the Cuban experience after the 1959 revolution is divided into six chapters: (1) a historical review of economic growth in Cuba since the beginning of the century until the fall of Batista; (2) a discussion of problems in measuring growth in revolutionary Cuba; (3) an evaluation of the Cuban economic growth record since 1959; (4) an attempt to measure Cuba's performance with respect to basic needs; (5) a presentation of various estimates of income distribution in Cuba, both before the revolution and at some points during the 1960s and 1970s; and (6) a look at Cuban growth with equity in a comparative context. Two appendixes deal with the Cuban labor force and present a number of useful statistical tables.

1
Economic Growth in Cuba in Retrospect

Growth and Stagnation in Prerevolutionary Cuba

As measured by real income per capita, Cuba could not be considered to have been a poor country on the eve of the 1959 revolution. It has been calculated that in the mid-1950s, the Cuban gross national product (GNP) per capita was 361 current U.S. dollars, ranking fourth in Latin America after Venezuela ($762), Uruguay ($569), and Argentina ($374).[1] Harry Oshima argues that the Cuban gross domestic product (GDP) per capita was no less than $430 in 1953 (basing his estimates on the census in that year), or just about the same as that of Puerto Rico and one-fourth that of the United States.[2]

And yet there is a "mystery surrounding the performance of the old Cuban economy": while the "total stock of capital thus grew at a slow, although unstable and unspectacular rate," real national income stagnated during most of the decades leading up to the revolution.[3] The reasons for this apparent contradiction were twofold. In the first place, Cuba's investment booms were, at least until the 1940s, highly correlated with export activities (sugar, tobacco, and nickel), which invariably had a temporary character. Second, and the main reason according to James O'Connor, there was underutilization of investments, and a misuse of them in industries where they were in fact employed. As evidence of the secular stagnation of the Cuban economy, O'Connor claims that real income per capita averaged $201 (in 1926 dollars) during 1903–1906, increased slightly to $216 in 1945–1948, and then fell to around $200 in 1956–1958.[4]

O'Connor's figures are based on Julian Alienes's real income estimates for the period 1903–1948,[5] updated to 1956–1958. Those estimates were based on four statistical indicators: public revenues, bank clearings, bank deposits, and value of exports. Alienes then related these figures to independent estimates of the 1938 national income that were based on sales and tax data. Assuming that the relation between the indicators and the national income in 1938 could be considered as fairly typical, he estimated the long-term series, and then, by deflating the national income figures, he arrived at real income estimates for the period 1903–1948.

In deflating for price changes, Alienes used an index of U.S. wholesale prices, which might sound adventurous, but he apparently opted for this solution because there was no available index series for wholesale prices in Cuba for the period in question. Even so, a report on the Cuban economy by the International Bank for Reconstruction and Development (IBRD) reproduced the Alienes estimates and found them to be legitimate, because there was a fairly good agreement between other price movements in the two countries (such as the cost of food) except during the two war periods.[6] It can be estimated that the cost of living in Cuba (as measured by the cost of food) increased by 114 percent in the period 1913–1918 compared with an increase in U.S. wholesale prices in the same period of 82 percent; in the period 1939–1945, the difference between the Cuban cost of living increase and the U.S. wholesale prices increase was even more accentuated—107 percent in Cuba compared with 37 percent in the United States.[7]

Alienes's estimates of Cuban national income 1903–1939 are reproduced in Appendix 2, Table 1, but I have also made a new, or alternative estimate of real national income by deflating the nominal values with the cost of food index instead of U.S. wholesale prices. The comparison shows that there is a rather close agreement between the two estimates of real national income in the years up to World War I, but then there are important differences. The new estimate would suggest that Cuba's real national income should be adjusted slightly upward for the 1920s and especially for the end of the 1930s. The general trend is the same in both estimates, however, implying a stagnation, or even a decrease, in per capita income in the latter half of the 1920s and in the 1930s. (It should be pointed out that although the estimates are given in Cuban pesos, they were more or less equivalent to U.S. dollars, particularly after 1915 when a new monetary system—identical with the dollar— was introduced.)[8]

The national income estimates in Appendix 2, Table 1, should, however, be interpreted cautiously. There are no reliable income statistics for the years before 1950, and the rather violent annual changes in real per capita income from time to time suggest that the statistical base of Alienes's estimates is rather shaky. But even if the nominal income estimates are correct, there is still the question of which deflator to use, as deflating by the cost of food index does not necessarily reflect the actual levels of personal consumption. Other sources, however, do suggest that per capita consumption of many goods was the same, or even lower, in the late 1940s compared with the late 1920s. In addition, Table 1.1 shows that there was an even stronger decline in the apparent consumption of intermediate products such as iron and cement. All these figures tend to support the claim that there were serious stagnation tendencies in the Cuban economy after 1925.

The Sugar Economy: 1900-1929

As Figure 1.1 and Appendix 2, Table 2, show, there was a real boom in the Cuban economy during the first quarter of the twentieth century as the output of raw sugar increased from 636,000 metric tons in 1901 to 5.3 million tons in 1925, and real national income more than doubled in the same period. But due to a very rapid growth of population, per capita income in the middle of the 1920s was just about the same as at the beginning of the century, about $200 in 1926 prices.

Two important features dominated the Cuban economy in this period. Sugar cultivation expanded with the growth of the latifundios (big estates) and the whole economy was penetrated and dominated by U.S. capital.[9] The conditions imposed upon Cuba by the United States after the War of Independence (1895-1898)—a war that was fought against Spain and not the United States—encouraged both phenomena. The Platt Amendment of 1901 gave the United States the right to intervene in Cuba for various reasons, "including the maintenance of a government adequate for the protection of life, property, and individual liberty,"[10] and the so-called treaty of reciprocity reduced the duty paid on Cuban raw sugar on the U.S. market while it increased the duty on refined sugar.[11]

U.S. dominance of the Cuban economy had actually begun long before independence,[12] and U.S. capital interests were consolidated during that country's military occupation of the island, which lasted—with some interruptions—until 1908. Up to that point, the *colonos*—an important group of small cane growers—had existed as an independent class,[13] but in the short span of two decades, the Cuban economic structure changed drastically. Although sugar had already become the main source of income by the turn of the century—ahead of other resources such as cattle, tobacco, and coffee—the increasing sugar prices on the world market (Figure 1.2) caused the rapid spread of sugarcane plantations all over the island.[14] By the end of World War I, Cuba's share of the world sugar production (including beet sugar) had increased to about 22 percent compared to 5 percent in 1901 (see Appendix 2, Table 2).

In addition to the traditionally strong Spanish interests in Cuba, particularly up to the War of Independence, there were also important

British investments on the island during the nineteenth century. The British interests included the famous El Cobre mine, one of the world's principal sources of copper during the first half of the nineteenth century; the Henry Clay cigar manufacturing combine; and after 1899, Havana Railways.[15]

During the first decade of the twentieth century, the growth of U.S. investments, which in quite a few cases replaced British investments, was impressive. This period witnessed investments by the United Fruit Company, the American Tobacco Company, and the National City Bank of New York; the formation of the Cuba-American Sugar Company; the completion of the Cuba Railroad; and the establishment of the Cuban Telephone Company.[16] Around 1900, U.S. capital in Cuba had totaled some $100 million, of which $45 million were invested in tobacco and only some $25 million in sugar;[17] by 1911, the total of U.S. investments had doubled to $205 million dollars, of which a little more than a third was invested in sugar.[18]

Between 1911 and 1927, U.S. sugar investments increased from $65 million to $600 million.[19] Prior to World War I, mill ownership was predominantly Cuban and Spanish, and U.S.-owned *centrales* (sugar mills) accounted for merely 15 percent of the sugar output in 1906.[20] In 1925, the U.S. share had increased to no less than 35 percent, and by the end of the 1920s, about two-thirds of Cuba's sugar production was under U.S. corporate control. This share fell to 55 percent in 1939, to 47 percent in 1950, and to just over 40 percent in the years before the revolution.[21]

The expansion of sugar production had very serious effects on the cultivation of other crops, especially coffee, since large land areas were converted into sugar plantations.[22] These sugar plantations not only took over land that had formerly been devoted to other crops, but large forest areas also began to disappear—just as they had once before at the end of the eighteenth century.[23]

The year 1920 marked the peak of the importance of sugar production in Cuba (see Appendix 2, Table 2). In that year, the price of sugar skyrocketed on the world market, and the sugar companies had more than $1 billion in revenues—more than all the crops had between 1900 and 1913. At the beginning of the *zafra* (the harvest period), the world price was already over 9 U.S. cents per pound, well above any previous recorded price, and the prices continued rising until they reached 22.5 cents in May.[24] This so-called dance of the millions created a sugar mania on the island. People rushed to borrow money to invest in planting still more sugar, and a wave of speculation and inflation swept the country. But prices soon went down to more normal levels, and the euphoria of many speculators came to an end. Indeed, the dance of the millions produced a devastating economic crisis, and it affected every segment of the population. The banking system totally collapsed, and U.S. interests gained control not only of more of the sugar production but also of the credit institutions.[25] Small planters were relegated to the tobacco growing areas or to poorer lands on the lower slopes of the mountains, and large sectors of the rural population, especially the *colonos*, were forced to work as *braceros* (cane cutters) on the plantations.

The shortage of cheap labor during the *zafra*, a result of a drastic decline in population during the War of Independence, gave rise to a flow of immigrant workers from the neighboring islands. It has been estimated that immigration contributed some 700,000 people to the Cuban population between 1899 and 1931, which resulted in a total population increase in this period of more than 30 percent.[26] Fifty-nine percent of the immigrants came from Spain, and 25 percent came from the Antilles, especially Haiti and Jamaica,[27] and the immigrant workers often lived in miserable conditions.[28]

O'Connor says that "during the first quarter of the century the very definition of economic growth was the expansion of cane cultivation and sugar manufacture,"[29] but the sugar companies no doubt built up an excess capacity during World War I—a capacity that did not correspond to the harsh reality of the 1920s when beet production in Europe rapidly increased to prewar levels.[30] In spite of falling sugar prices, however, the big *centrales* continued to expand production, which reached a level of 5.2 million tons in 1929 (see Figures 1.1 and 1.2).

Still, after thirty years of almost continuous expansion of the sugar industry, the country was—except for the *centrales*—as industrially underdeveloped as it had been at the beginning of the century.[31] In 1925, sugar processing accounted for about 84 percent of all the manufacturing output; the tobacco industry accounted for some 5 percent.[32] Total nonsugar manufacturing amounted to only 56 million pesos and employed only some 26,000 people, less than 3 percent of an estimated labor force of 1.1 million.[33] One of the main reasons for the retarded industrialization was the narrow domestic market for consumer goods. A small class of sugar farmers, mill owners, and local and foreign businessmen had an overwhelming share of the purchasing power, which they often used to buy imported consumer goods, and repatriated profits further diminished the local market.[34] In the latter half of the 1920s, there was a belated attempt to diversify the economy through tariff protection, but the attempt was in vain. The 1929 crash on Wall Street had catastrophic consequences for Cuba because its economy lacked any defense mechanisms.[35]

Depression and Recovery: 1930-1958

The protectionist measures adopted by the U.S. government in 1930 (the Hawley-Smoot Tariff Act) sent the price of Cuban sugar plummeting downward to a low of 0.93 cents per pound (see Figure 1.2). Sugar income was reduced to a level approximating the level thirty years earlier, and real income per capita in 1932 was only half the prewar level (see Appendix 2, Table 1). Unemployment burgeoned, and living conditions in general deteriorated. Polarization and class antagonism led to revolutionary struggles in 1933. These culminated in the overthrow of the Gerardo Machado dictatorship, but the revolutionary government was short-lived and was soon replaced by a government that was more docile to U.S. interests.[36]

The Roosevelt administration abrogated the humiliating Platt Amendment in the spirit of the Good Neighbor Policy, although the United States kept the Guantánamo base. In spite of this apparently new U.S. attitude toward Cuba, however, the island's economy became even more linked to the U.S. economy than before. Cuba was assigned a sugar quota of 28 percent on the U.S. market by the Costigan-Jones Act of 1932, whereby a maximum of 22 percent of the total quota was permitted to enter as refined sugar—a ratio that remained roughly the same until 1960 when Cuba was deprived of sales to the United States altogether. The quota of 28 percent was substantially lower than the Cuban quota in the past, but on the other hand, Cuban sugar was now sold at U.S. market prices, which were usually above the world market price and were also more stable. At the same time, a number of U.S. products were given preferential treatment on the Cuban market.[37]

In the 1930s, there was a trend toward disinvestment in sugar, and the book value of U.S. investments in sugar stagnated between 1936 and 1958 (see Table 1.2). As a matter of fact, only one sugar mill was built in Cuba after 1926.[38] However, the decline in sugar investment between 1929 and 1936 in particular was, according to the U.S. Department of Commerce, less the result of disinvestment than of financial readjustments resulting from the 1929 stock market crash, which heavily affected the value of almost all U.S. holdings in Cuba.[39]

In 1929, U.S. investments in Cuba had ranked first among that country's investments in Latin America, accounting for 26.5 percent of all U.S. direct investments in the area,[40] and almost two-thirds of the total invested in Cuba up to that point was in sugar mills or other agricultural assets.[41] By the outbreak of World War II, this share had fallen to 43 percent, and on the eve of the 1959 revolution, it had fallen to 26.5 percent. Some of the *centrales* were sold to Cuban *hacendados* (plantation owners), and others were simply dismantled.[42] By 1952, there were only 161 sugar mills left in Cuba compared to 184 in 1926.[43]

Although U.S. interests in Cuba had been concentrated in sugar production, there had also been an early interest in the mineral deposits of the island. After the closing of the El Cobre mine in 1918 (Cuba had been the third largest copper producer in the world in the early nineteenth century), the major producer of the ore was the Matahambre ("Hungerkiller") mine, which was developed by Cuban business groups after the deposit had been discovered in 1912. In 1921, the mine's operations were taken over by the American Metals Company, which maintained control until 1943.[44] During World War II, the need for secure supplies of strategic nickel led to a 1942 decision by the Roosevelt administration to develop the Lovisa Bay deposits in Cuba.[45] The nickeliferous iron ores of Cuba are considered to be among the largest nickel reserves in the world, and although the process to recover the nickel was difficult to develop, the effort to do so was successful shortly before mining operations started in Nicaro.[46]

The Nicaro plant was operated on a fee basis for the United States between 1943 and 1947 when the plant was closed down. As a result of the Korean War, the plant was reopened in 1951, and a few years later, an additional $64 million were invested to develop the nearby Moa Bay deposits. This project was based on an acid leaching process whereby cobalt is separated and received as a by-product,[47] and the refining process was to be performed by Freeport Nickel in the United States. However, the Moa Bay plant started operations in 1959, and the plant had been operating only for a short time when all its operations were taken over by the revolutionary government.[48]

After World War II, there was also an increase in U.S. investments in the nonsugar manufacturing sector (see Table 1.2). It could be estimated that U.S. subsidiaries were responsible for about 20 percent of total manufacturing sales in 1957, although there were large variations among the sectors, ranging from 90 to 100 percent in sectors such as rubber and chemicals (paper, pharmaceuticals, detergents, and cosmetics) to about 10 percent in sectors like food and beverages, textiles and leather.[49]

Judging from the total loss claimed in 1970 by U.S. individuals and companies active in Cuba before the revolution, U.S. capital was omnipresent in Cuba at the end of the 1950s.[50] Even if the total claim of $3.3 billion is exaggerated (as a matter of fact, that sum is more than three times the official book value of U.S. investments in Cuba in 1958), it provides overwhelming evidence of U.S. penetration of practically every corner of the island. Of the total, $689 million (20 percent) were claimed by sugar companies; $443 million (13 percent), by public utilities and communications companies (primarily the Cuban Electric Company);

$348 million (11 percent), by banks and financial institutions; $345 million (10 percent), by mining companies; $248 million (8 percent), by forty-two manufacturing companies; and $186 million (6 percent), by petroleum companies.[51]

According to Alienes, the Cuban economy reached a trough around 1932 or 1933 but had recovered by the second half of the 1930s. But if there seems to be little doubt about the economic trends during the first quarter of this century, there are divergent views on what happened in the second quarter. There are four independent estimates for the whole, or fragments, of this period as shown in Appendix 2, Table 3, and partially in Figure 1.3. Alienes's estimates of real national income in Cuba embrace the period 1930–1948. His war period estimates (1939–1945) have been criticized by the IBRD mission and are probably exaggerated for the reasons mentioned earlier. Jorge Pérez-López has constructed an index of industrial output in Cuba between 1930 and 1958, covering mining, manufacturing (both sugar and nonsugar), and electricity and gas.[52] There is reasonably good correspondence between the Alienes and Pérez-López indexes for the 1930s, although the depression was deeper and the trough came one year later according to the latter estimate. Both indexes indicate that the economy had more or less recovered by the outbreak of World War II.

But what happened during the war is an enigma, and the estimates vary considerably. The IBRD mission revised the Alienes estimates for 1939–1948 (although refraining from making any estimates at all for the war years) by deflating the monetary national income with the official cost of living (food) index—instead of the U.S. wholesale price index used by Alienes—and the difference is striking.[53] According to Alienes, real national income in 1945 was 71 percent above the prewar level, and the IBRD estimate indicates that the increase was merely 21 percent. Another, more recent, estimate by Jorge Domínguez suggests that the real income level was the same in 1945 as in 1939 (although there were violent ups and downs in between).[54]

A Permanent Crisis?

Many authors have claimed that the Cuban economy was heading for a serious crisis before the revolution, in spite of relatively rapid growth after World War II. As a matter of fact, some people even think that there was a permanent crisis and that the levels of production, even in the nonsugar manufacturing sector, were doomed to stagnate.[55] The figures in Table 1.3 tend to support the claim that there were serious stagnation tendencies in the Cuban economy after World War II, at least after 1952 (when a record 7.2 million tons of sugar were produced). Real national income increased at the rather moderate rate of 3.4 percent, or 1.4 percent per annum—(which was moderate in relation to other countries in Latin America at the time), and Mesa-Lago has estimated that the per capita rate of growth was as slow as 1 percent during 1950–1958.[56] It is true that nonsugar manufacturing expanded through import substitution at a sustained rate of more than 5 percent after 1946, but if all productive activities are considered (that is, agriculture, industry, and construction = total material production),[57] there was a clear slowdown after 1952 and a stagnating, or even negative, per capita trend.

The important substitution that took place after the war was a slow process, however, considering the low initial levels of output. It has been estimated that as late as 1957, 45 percent of the capital invested in Cuban industry was accounted for by sugar plants and 20 percent by mining activities.[58] Only 35 percent of the capital was invested in the remaining industrial sectors—of which a tiny 0.2 percent was in the machinery industry—and many of the industries, such as the textile and chemical industries, depended heavily on imported raw materials.[59]

But the structural problems facing prerevolutionary Cuba were not limited to slow growth and a low level of industrialization. As additional problems, Mesa-Lago mentions the excessive dependence on sugar, high levels of unemployment and underemployment, and wide differences in the standard of living between social classes and especially between urban and rural areas.[60].

The sugar industry was old and its machinery in many cases was completely obsolete as most of the *centrales* had been built during the nineteenth century.[61] In order to combat costs, the length of the *zafra* was gradually reduced from about 300 days at the beginning of the twentieth century to an average of 210 days in the 1920s, 104 days in the 1930s, and 95 days in the postwar period. This revolution meant that there was a continuous extension of the *tiempo muerto* ("dead season"), which led to increasing levels of seasonal unemployment. Mesa-Lago has estimated that in 1956-1957, 16.4 percent of the labor force was openly unemployed and 13.8 percent was underemployed (meaning either working fewer than thirty hours per week or working for free).[62] Of those people who were employed, from 20 percent to 25 percent worked in the sugar sector, and the seasonal character of the *zafra* meant that these people had stable work for only three or four months of the year. Statistics from 1956-1957 show that open unemployment increased from 200,000 during the peak of the *zafra* to some 457,000 during the months of lowest activity.[63] Although strict comparisons are not possible, statistics on unemployment calculated in 1943,

1953, and 1956-1957 suggest that the situation was becoming increasingly worse.[64]

Cuba in the 1950s was also characterized by large differences in income and the standard of living. The standard of living of the *guajiro* ("rural worker") was extremely low. He lived in a *bohío*, a small house with an earthen floor and a roof made of palm thatch. For 90 percent of the *guajiros*, a kerosene lamp was the only form of lighting, and 44 percent of them had never attended school. Only 11 percent drank milk, only 4 percent ate meat, and only 2 percent ate eggs. The daily diet, which had a deficiency of 1,000 calories, was the main reason for a constant increase in the number of cases of tuberculosis, anemia, parasitic diseases, and other illnesses.[65]

Table 1.1. Per capita production of raw sugar and apparent per capita consumption of certain consumer and intermediate goods, 1905-1909, 1925-1929, and 1945-1949

	Annual Average for Period		
	1905-1909	1925-1929	1945-1949
Production			
Raw sugar (kg)	634	1,362	915
Apparent consumption			
Final products:			
Rice (kg)	50	58	47
Wheat flour (kg)	36	31	29
Potatoes (kg)	na	29*	20
Coffee (kg)	na	8	7
Beans (kg)	29	4	3
Beer (liter)	na	13	16
Cotton cloth (kg)	3.6	2.4	1.8
Passenger transport (passenger kilometers)	88	145	122
Intermediate products:			
Iron (kg)	24	23	18
Cement (kg)	30	85	59
Freight transport (ton kilometers)	0.15	0.36	0.24

* = imports only; na = not available

Sources: Production of raw sugar: Appendix 2, Table 2; Consumption: "El Desarrollo Económico de Cuba" (ECLA E/CN.12/218, 1951), quoted in Seers et al. (1964), p. 14.

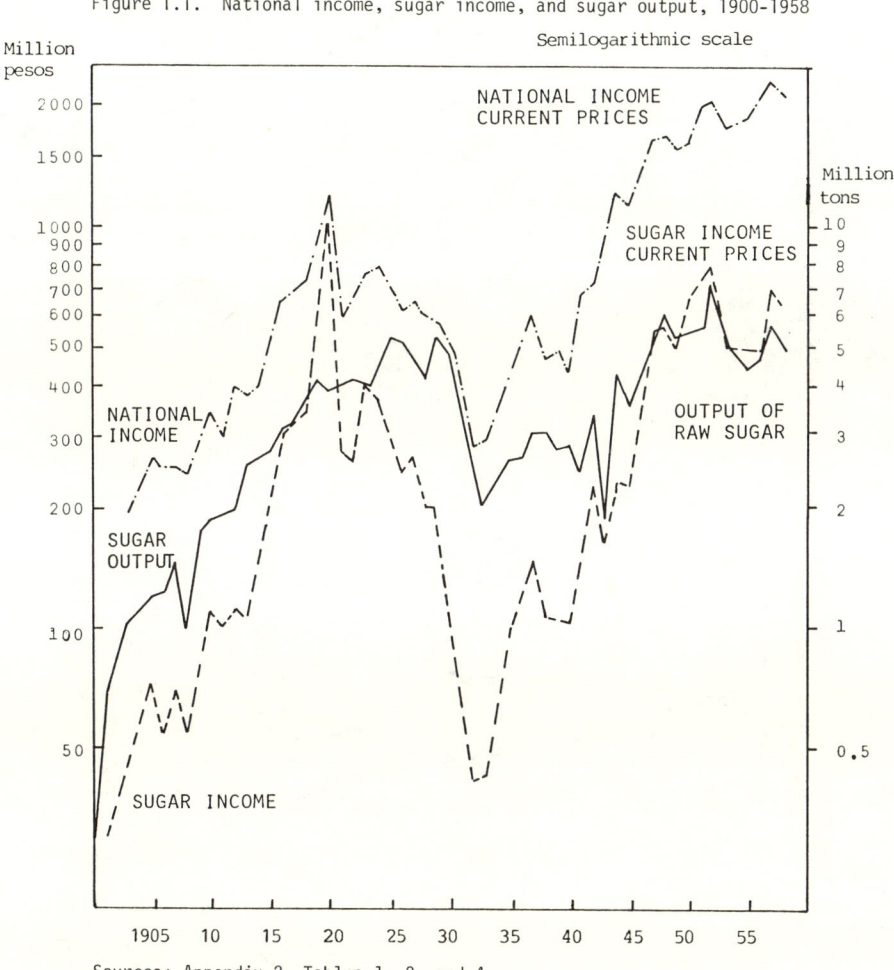

Figure 1.1. National income, sugar income, and sugar output, 1900-1958

Sources: Appendix 2, Tables 1, 2, and 4.

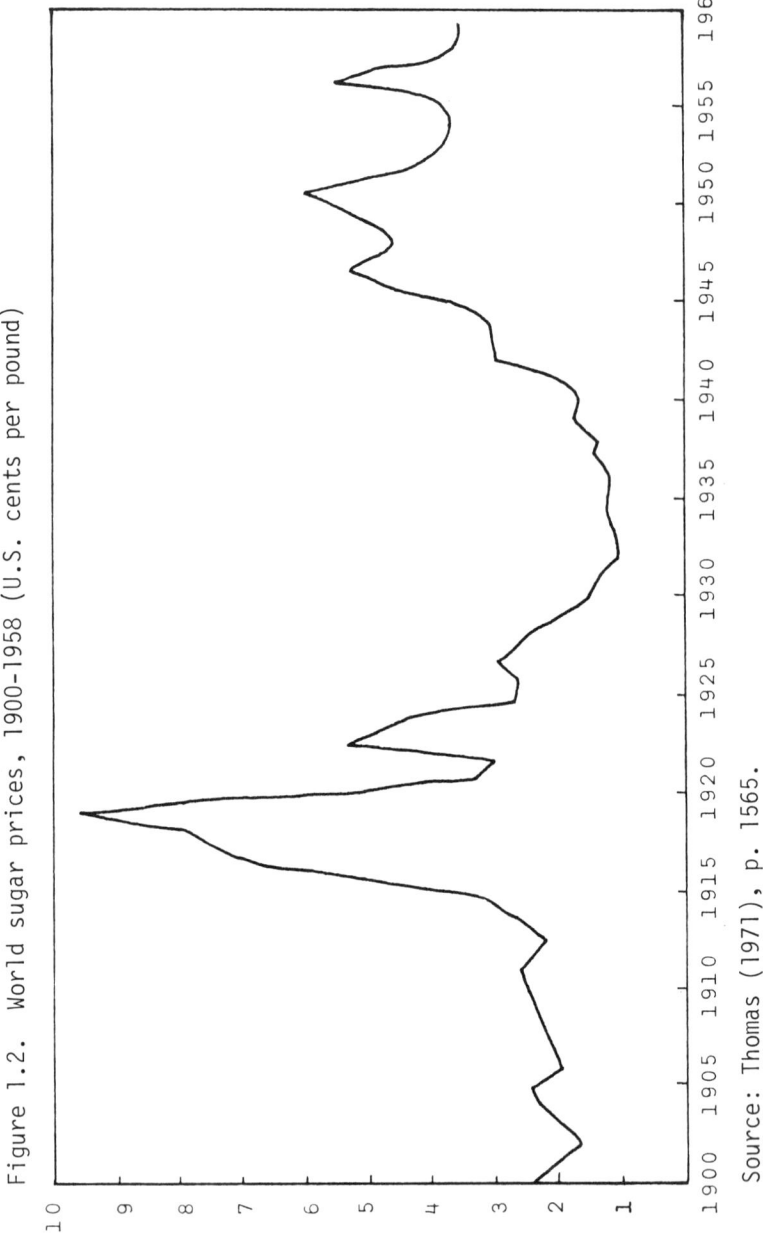

Figure 1.2. World sugar prices, 1900-1958 (U.S. cents per pound)

Source: Thomas (1971), p. 1565.

Table 1.2. U.S. direct investments in Cuba, 1929-1958 (million dollars)

	1929	1936	1940	1946	1950	1953	1958
Agriculture*	575	265	241	227	263	265	265
Petroleum	9	6	10	15	20	24	90
Mining	**	**	**	15	15	70	180
Manufacturing	45	27		40	54	58	80
Public utilities	215	315	233	251	271	297	344
Commerce	15	15		12	21	24	35
Other	60	38	76	8	13	18	7
Total	919	666	560	568	657	756	1,001

* = includes sugar mills; ** = included in "Other" category

Sources: Acosta (1973a), p. 60, and U.S. Department of Commerce (1956), p. 10.

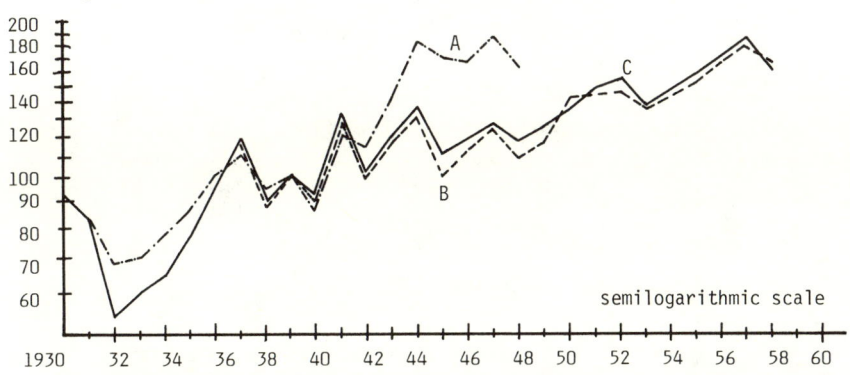

Figure 1.3. Growth estimates, 1930-1958 (1939=100)

A = Alienes's estimate of real national income
B = Domínguez's estimate of real national income
C = new estimate of real national income

Source: Appendix 2, Table 3.

Table 1.3. Growth indicators of the Cuban economy, 1946-1958

	Indexes for Selected Years in Period			Growth Rate Trend*	
	1946	1952	1958	1946-1952	1952-1958
Real national income	100	130	138	4.5	3.4
Per capita	100	112	105	2.4	1.4
Total material production	100	146	152	5.2	1.7
Per capita	100	122	119	3.1	-0.3
Sugarcane agriculture	100	188	144	6.3	-2.4
Per capita	100	158	113	4.2	-4.4
Nonsugar agriculture	100	95	111	1.5	2.8
Per capita	100	79	87	-0.6	0.8
Nonsugar manufacturing	100	138	185	5.9	5.4
Per capita	100	122	145	3.8	3.4
Construction	100	135	176	7.2	4.1
Per capita	100	119	138	5.1	2.1
Real nonagricultural wages	100	167	162	7.3	1.2
Sugar workers' real wages (United Fruit Co.)	100	125	120	3.4	-0.3

* = log trend, that is, $\log(y) = \log(a) + b^t$, where a is a constant and b the growth rate. The growth rate is based on all the years in the period 1946-1958, not only the years shown here. This explains the apparent contradiction between the indexes and the trend rates (for instance, in the case of Real national income).

Sources: Real national income: Appendix 2, Table 4; Total material production (and components): Appendix 2, Table 5; Real nonagricultural wages: Domínguez (1978), p. 74; Sugar workers' real wages: calculated from Zanetti and García (1976), pp. 441-442.

2
Measuring Economic Growth in Revolutionary Cuba

A Note on Statistics and National Accounting in Revolutionary Cuba

For any study on economic growth it is essential to have access to reasonably adequate, consistent, and reliable statistical information, which means one confronts a problem in studying revolutionary Cuba. But this problem is by no means unique to Cuba as similar difficulties have been encountered by scholars studying the economic performance of other socialist countries such as the Soviet Union, China, Poland, Czechoslovakia, and the German Democratic Republic.[1]

Fortunately, however, the situation in Cuba today is much better than during the early period of the revolution, and gone are the days when important macroeconomic variables, such as gross investments, had to be estimated, or even "guesstimated," from the speeches of Fidel Castro. Since 1972, the Comité Estatal de Estadísticas (CEE) has published regularly, and with gradually less delay,[2] statistical yearbooks that cover a wide area of topics from global indicators of the economy to detailed agricultural and industrial statistics, labor force data (although this section is admittedly poor),[3] and plenty of information on education, health, and foreign trade just to mention some areas. There is no doubt that many, if far from all, of the deficiencies in the adequacy, consistency, and reliability of Cuban statistics reported by Carmelo Mesa-Lago in his 1969 pioneering study[4] on the availability and reliability of Cuban statistics had been overcome by the end of the 1970s.

On the whole, statistical information today is much more available, adequate, and consistent than in the early 1960s, let alone during the first three years of the revolution. But this fact also presents a problem to economic historians. If we are interested not only in the Cuban performance during the last ten years but also in its relation to earlier periods—the 1960s and even the prerevolutionary era—how can we compare different periods if the data bases are different, the definitions have changed, and the coverage (of products) is no longer the same?

Another problem concerns the reliability of the data. In countries such as Cuba, which clearly wish to show the superiority of their economic and social systems, the temptation to hide or distort information might be overwhelming. But not to tell the whole truth is not the same as telling a lie. In an interesting essay on Soviet statistics,[5] Alex Nove has drawn three conclusions: First, Soviet index numbers are dangerous since they tend to inflate the levels of output.[6] Second, figures on units of output are much more reliable since the Soviet planners do not keep a double set of books and the raw data given are the same data the planners use and are as accurate as the statistical agencies can make them. Third, when the Soviet government wants to conceal something, it does not publish false figures; it just refrains from publishing anything on the matter.

Many of these tendencies would also hold for Cuban statistics, I am sure, which probably explains why much of the statistical information for 1969 and to some extent 1970 was withheld for a long time because of the disappointing performance of the Cuban economy in those years. But this reasoning certainly does not explain the serious lack of statistical data for the period 1959–1961. The reason for lack of data for those years is probably very simple: There were no intelligible data available to the planners—which would also help to explain the fantasies involved in the tentative, but abortive, Five-Year Plan for 1961–1965 discussed in Chapter 3.

The reasons for the lack of statistical data were many. First of all, statistical information was already deficient in prerevolutionary Cuba. There was no central statistical office, accounting practices in private business and government agencies were organized on an individual basis, and most of the statistics produced from the state sector were deduced from tax reports and the like.[7] The expropriation and confiscation process that started in 1959 did not improve the situation in spite of the fact that the state increasingly achieved control of the nation's means of production and services. At least in the short run, the flow of statistical data gradually diminished, partly because of institutional changes (for instance, when new agencies were created and responsibilities for statistical records changed) and partly because of serious mistakes committed by inexperienced militiamen when companies and haciendas were "intervened" that resulted in statistical records' being destroyed or lost. Another problem was that the statistical system, which was already primitive, deteriorated because most of the few trained statisticians (who had worked mainly for private businesses) emigrated after the revolution.[8]

In 1961, when work on the 1962 plan started, a new national accounting system was set up, and it was based on accounting practices in Czechoslovakia, the Soviet Union, and other socialist countries. Planning units were created in all parts of the administration, and thousands of forms had to be filled out by mostly inexperienced and not very qualified personnel. "The forms," says Edward Boorstein, who was an eyewitness to the economic transformation in Cuba at the time, "came out more adapted to Czechoslovakia than to Cuba; they [the Czech advisers] asked for accounting information from economic units in which accounting systems had not yet been installed, for statistics where none existed, for thousands of little estimates and projections which could not be made meaningful no matter how many telephone calls were made or meetings held, which could only tangle and confuse everything."[9]

Gradually, the statistical base started improving, although for quite some time the use of statistical information was restricted and an incommensurate amount of information was classified. One of the best sources of economic data for the 1959–1963 period is, as a matter of fact, a survey of the Cuban economy done by the UN Economic Commission for Latin America (ECLA).[10] In the commission's report, rudimentary national accounting for the period 1961–1963 (based on Soviet accounting principles) was presented abroad for the first time since the revolution. Macroeconomic variables, such as gross value of production by branches of the economy, were later introduced in the first *Boletín estadístico de Cuba* (1964), and the presentation was improved in successive issues. A careful study of this and other statistical publications makes it possible to more or less faithfully reconstruct the national accounting practices in Cuba since 1962. The result of such a reconstruction is shown in Figure 2.1.[11]

The concept of national income adopted in Cuba is that of material product,[12] gross or net (in the latter case, net of depreciation), and the methodology to determine that income falls generally into line with the Soviet practice.[13] The product for any one year is composed of the value added from agriculture, mining, manufacturing, electricity, construction, and those parts of the transport, communication, and trade sectors that serve the materially productive sectors. Omitted from consideration are finance and insurance, public administration, army and international security, education, health, private housing, and the independent professions. It follows from this definition that the method used is that which is generally known as the production approach instead of the income approach.[14]

A first step toward analyzing the economic growth of Cuba after the revolution would be to construct a time series for the aggregates shown in Figure 2.1, but in doing so, a problem arises—one that has both bothered and annoyed scholars studying the Cuban economy—which is that only parts of the national accounts appear in the statistical publications. In addition, some of the figures are given in constant (1965) prices, but others, and most of them after 1966, are given in current pesos. Since there are no price indexes available (simply for the reason that officially, there has been no inflation in Cuba since 1965), it is virtually impossible to deflate the current price figures. Also, the only macrolevel figure released by the CEE after 1970 is the global social product (GSP), broken down by economic sector. The CEE, however, does occasionally supply information to the United Nations on material product in current prices. This source also gives a percentage breakdown by use, which makes it possible to estimate aggregates such as personal consumption, social consumption, and capital accumulation (formation). Thus, I have tried to reconstruct the Cuban national accounts for the years 1962–1974 from various sources, and the result of this exercise is shown in Table 2.1

There was an intention in the 1960s to account only in constant prices, a task that supposedly would have been facilitated by the fact that monetary transactions between state enterprises in the industrial sector (*empresas consolidadas*) were being gradually abolished in a step toward the complete elimination of the market. This plan means that all macroeconomic aggregates are shown in constant prices, and only in constant prices, for the years 1962–1966.

The basic principle of this price policy was to use the prices quoted on 15 November 1961 in the so-called centralized budgetary system, pending the results of a new price policy.[15] In 1963, a general law of prices was formulated that laid down the principles for a new price system. The task of formulating the new system was, however, complicated by the fact that the importation of a series of new commodities, especially machinery, successively distorted the price system in use.[16] The situation was further aggravated by the disappearance of the Ministry of Finance in 1967—the agency that had been in charge of price revision. In view of this complex situation, the idea of formulating new prices was abandoned for the time being, and prices were frozen at their 1965 level.[17] However, a complication with this system arose in the trade sector because even if retail prices were frozen, there was still the problem of how to deal with foreign trade. The trade sector was therefore left as a residual (in current prices) in the national accounting until the economic reform of 1976, when the principle of "economic calculation," or a self-finance system (the Soviet concept of *khozrazchet*)[18] was gradually introduced into all sectors of the economy.[19]

Two problems arise in interpreting the data in Table 2.1. First, it is difficult to estimate growth rates when some of the figures are given in current prices and there is no reliable indicator of price changes. Second, it is hard to say how comparable any of the aggregates in Table 2.1 are with the estimates of prerevolutionary real national income discussed in Chapter 1.

A solution to this dilemma would be to consider only total material production (TMP), which embraces the sectors of agriculture (including fishing and forestry), mining (including smelting), manufacturing, electricity, and construction. One advantage of this approach is that the concept of total material production very closely corresponds to the Pérez-López concept of total industrial activities[20]—except for agriculture and construction—and thus a comparison of economic growth in revolutionary Cuba with economic growth in prerevolutionary Cuba is possible. Another advantage is that the TMP series are always shown in constant (1965) prices after 1965.[21] I have, therefore, opted for the calculation of gross value added of total material production (that is, at factor cost) for the following three periods: 1946–1961 (in 1952 prices), 1961–1968 (in 1965 prices), and 1968–1980 (in 1965 prices).

One of the problems, and perhaps the most critical, involved in the construction of output indexes is the selection of weights. In his study on economic growth in the People's Republic of China, Kang Chao says that "in a Soviet-type economy, where the market mechanism ceases to function and prices are arbitrarily determined by planners, there is no *a priori* reason why value weights, net or gross, are superior to nonvalue weights, since value weights in this case may not necessarily reflect the relative importance of the output components."[22] But the use of nonvalue weights also has disadvantages—which may more than offset the advantage of using them—because it is difficult to secure meaningful nonvalue weights for socialist countries.[23] The selection of weights in this study will be discussed for each of the three periods.[24]

Index of Total Material Production, 1946–1961

The starting point in the calculation of an index for this period is Pérez-López's estimate of Cuban industrial output from 1930–1958.[25] This study is an important contribution to the knowledge of the development of the industrial sectors in Cuba before the revolution since it is an independent estimate based on a revaluation of physical output data as opposed to the much criticized National Bank indexes of industrial production.[26]

One weakness of the Pérez-López study is that it is based on a rather limited number of products (forty to be precise), but Pérez-López claims that these products accounted for 62.8 percent of all sales in the nonsugar industrial sectors in 1953 (compared with 53 percent clearly dealt with in the National Bank index).[27] Pérez-López constructed a Laspeyre index based on 1952 year prices, which actually are a mixture of export prices, wholesale prices, and retail prices found in statistical publications and articles. In this way, he constructed production indexes for the following twelve branches of Cuban industrial production: beverages, tobacco, textiles, processed food, sugar, shoemaking, rubber products, paper and paperboard, construction materials, fishing, mining, and electricity and gas.[28]

The criterion used by Pérez-López in determining the relative importance of each of these branches was the percentage of gross value added created in each of them. Since there were no official Cuban value added data available, gross value added was estimated as the difference between the gross value of output (sales) and the purchase of materials and other services in each of the twelve branches. Such data for 1953 were derived from a report in the *Tribunal de cuentas*.[29] The estimates of gross value added in 1953 were thus used as weights in the calculation of an index of total industrial production for the period 1930–1958 (see Appendix 2, Table 3). In Table 2.2, I have added estimates for the years 1959–1961 in order to be able to link this index to estimates of TMP for the period 1961–1968 presented later.

Of the forty products considered in the Pérez-López index, it was possible to get physical output data for most of them for the years 1959–1961, and the "basket" is pretty much the same as the one used by Pérez-López. It should also be mentioned that the indexes in Table 2.2 start with 1946, not 1930, for two reasons: (1) because they will serve for the construction of indexes of TMP and estimates for the agricultural sector are not available for the years before 1946 and (2) because the estimates by Pérez-López are rather shaky for some of the years in the 1930–1945 period and are often interpolations or extrapolations in the absence of physical output data.[30]

The next step was to make estimates of TMP for the period 1946–1961. As shown in Figure 2.1, this concept is equal to the sum of agricultural activities (including fishing and forestry), industrial activities (including mining and electrical energy), and construction activities. The sum of the gross value of each of these sectors gives the gross value of TMP. But it also follows from Figure 2.1 that by subtracting the intermediate inputs from this gross value, we get what is equivalent to the gross value added of TMP, or TMP at factor cost. This latter concept is far better than the gross value of production since it avoids double counting.

In his study on the Cuban national income, Oshima also made estimates of net domestic income at factor cost by broad economic sectors (see Table 2.3). By using his net value added data (that is, net of depreciation) by sector as weights, it has been possible to construct an index of TMP at factor cost for the period 1946–1961, the details of which are shown in Appendix 2, Table 5. Oshima, unfortunately, did not distinguish between sugar and nonsugar agriculture, and values for these two subsectors have been estimated from the relative shares presented by Acosta.[31] The output indexes given in Table 2.2 have then been weighted by the net values added (as given by Oshima), but, as noted, the Pérez-López index does not include agriculture or construction. In the case of agriculture the solution was to use the Food and Agriculture Organization (FAO) index of agricultural output in Cuba for the period in question[32] and then subtract the value of sugar production (which is already known) to arrive at an estimate of the value of nonsugar agricultural production. In the case of the construction industry, the National Bank index of construction for the period 1946–1958 has been applied.[33] Since there are no estimates available for the development of the construction industry in the period 1959–1961, I have simply used official figures for cement production as crude indicators for those years.

One advantage of extending the 1946–1958 index to 1961 is that the result allows for an appraisal of the first three crucial years after the revolution, a period for which growth claims have varied widely in the past. Both O'Connor and Noyola maintain that industrial production grew by 17 percent in 1959 and by no less than 29 percent in 1960 (by 25 percent according to Noyola),[34] and a Cuban source claimed in 1968 that industrial production increased by 13 percent in 1960 and by 6.2 percent in 1961.[35] Although there are no longer any official references to growth during this so-called transitional phase (toward socialism) of the Cuban economy, the 1960 growth rate of 13 percent was repeated by the Cuban economist José-Luis Rodríguez in an article that appeared in 1979.[36]

The figures in Table 2.4 suggest much more moderate growth rates during the first three years after the revolution, with manufacturing production (excluding sugar) increasing by 8.8 percent in 1959, increasing a mere 0.1 percent in 1960, and declining by 8.0 percent in 1961. Including sugar, the corresponding percentages would be +7.0 percent (in 1959), −0.5 percent (in 1960), and −1.2 percent (in 1961). These estimates do not, of course, necessarily mean that the higher growth rates mentioned above are not correct.[37] What they do mean is that these are the growth rates of the basket of goods used by Pérez-López for the period 1946–1958, valued in 1952 prices and weighted by gross value added in 1953. However, Mesa-Lago, using a composite index of agriculture and industry weighted by 1957 prices, also suggests that the early growth estimates were probably inflated.[38]

Index of Total Material Production, 1961-1968

Fortunately, much more information is readily available for the period after 1961. There are rather complete sets of national accounts for 1962–1968, and the definitions of categories are reasonably homogeneous for that period. Since Cuban production series are given in 1965 prices, the logical starting point would be to estimate the value added of total material production for that year. Unfortunately, however, there are no published official value added estimates for 1965, so, I have had to resort to the year 1962 as the point of departure for the estimates of value added in 1965.

In the absence of data for value added (gross, or net of depreciation), the total wage funds by sectors are sometimes used as crude weights instead. Hodgman employed wage bill weights in 1954 in order to construct an index of Soviet industrial production for the period 1928–1951,[39] and Kang Chao used the same method in his estimates of the rate of growth of industrial production in China during the years 1949–1957.[40] Although wage bills no doubt are better as weights than nonvalue weights (such as labor inputs), one of the shortcomings in using such weights is that they implicitly overrepresent primary activities since the share of wages and salaries in that area (in relation to value added) is generally much higher than in industrial production. For this reason, these weights are only used as a complementary tool here.

The method has been the following. Official Cuban statistics give the gross value of production of the global social product (and thus also for TMP) in constant (1965) prices for 1962. These figures are reproduced in the first column of Table 2.5. The ECLA study referred to earlier also gives an estimate of gross value added of TMP for the years 1961–1963 in 1961 prices (the 1962 figures are shown in column 2 of Table 2.5). The problem, however, is not only that the prices are those of 1961, but also, and more seriously, that there are some errors in the ECLA estimates. For instance, the gross value added from forestry turns out to be more than three times larger than the gross value of production from forestry, which is, of course, impossible, and the wage bill in the construction materials sector turns out to be larger than the gross value added from that category.

I have therefore chosen to use the wage bill in the various sectors as a check. The problem then arises that official Cuban statistics record wages and salaries only for the state sector (column 3), which means that a large share of all income is excluded, primarily in the agricultural sector, which accounted for 79 percent of total private employment in 1962.[41] Fortunately, there are estimates of private employment in 1962, both for agriculture (by subsector) and for manufacturing (although not broken down),[42] and there are also average monthly income estimates for the same categories.[43] Therefore, it has been possible to make an estimate of the total wage bill by sector (column 4).

In the case of the agricultural subsectors, an adjusted gross value added has been derived (column 5), on the assumption that the total wage bill of those sectors amounts to 85 percent of the gross value added.[44] In the case of the manufacturing areas, the procedure has been slightly different because there are value added estimates for other years. Juceplan, in a 1966 study, reports that the state wage bill accounted for 41 percent of gross value added in the manufacturing sector in 1964.[45] If that percentage is applied to 1962, and since we know the total wage bill referred to (464.2 million pesos), we can derive the gross value added in manufacturing (1,129.3 million pesos). The Juceplan report also gives value added figures by industrial branches for 1963. Since the growth rates of industrial production by subsectors are known,[46] it is easy to estimate, by applying these weights, the value added figures not only for 1962 and 1963 but also for the whole period 1962-1968. The estimates of TMP at factor cost (or gross value added) and the annual growth rates for those years are shown in Appendix 2, Tables 7 and 8. An estimate for 1961 has been added since it was considered important to have an estimate for that year of TMP in 1965 prices to serve as a link with the earlier estimates for the period 1946-1961, which were based on 1952 prices. The 1961 figures were estimated on the basis of the ECLA study published in 1965, which gives gross value added for both 1961 and 1962 (in 1961 prices). The 1962 estimate is based on a selection of physical output data, the quality of which is unknown, but it has nevertheless been suggested that these data are the best available for this period.[47] By applying the weights in 1962 to the growth indicators by sectors between 1961 and 1962, I have arrived at the 1961 estimate shown.

Finally, a consistency check, Table 2.6 shows total material production and gross material product (GMP) at factor cost, by branches, for the year 1965, as well as the official global social product figures for the same year. The total GMP figure of 4,137.5 million pesos is the same as the official GMP figure referred to in Table 2.1.

Index of Total Material Production, 1968-1980

There is a serious breach in the homogeneity of the statistical series after 1966 (and especially after 1968), which makes global indicators like those presented in Table 2.1 difficult to evaluate for later years. In some cases there are not even figures after 1974 (for instance, GMP, net material product [NMP], disposable product, and consumption). For-

28   *Measuring Economic Growth in Revolutionary Cuba*

tunately, however, the statistical series of physical output data are quite detailed after 1968, and for this reason I have opted for a revaluation of physical output using constant prices as weights.

The next problem was which prices to use. As indicated earlier, the CEE and Juceplan still use 1965 prices, but that statement must be modified since all new products in Cuba have the price of the year they were first produced in or introduced into the country. The prices of these new products present a serious problem since it is commonly believed—in Western countries at least—that the fixing of these prices is responsible for the upward bias in the production indexes of centrally planned economies.[48] When industrial output increases at a rapid rate, and from a low level, it is difficult for the planners to establish "fixed prices" for products, particularly those in the mechanical industry, that did not exist in the base period when fixed prices were established.[49] There have been a great variety of new products introduced in the Cuban economy since 1965, but the Cubans still insisted on accounting with "1965 prices" until 1981. This policy should not be construed as meaning that there was a deliberate attempt by the Cubans to exaggerate growth, rather, it was a result of a frustrating search for an alternative and better price system.

The Cuban State Committee on Prices has facilitated the task for me by publishing a complete listing of retail prices applied in Cuba in 1978.[50] Officially, these are "1965 prices," but they are a mixture of prices for the reason mentioned above. As a matter of fact, one could say that they are "1978 prices" since they were the prices paid by the Cuban consumer in 1978. Ideally, it would be better to use factory prices, or wholesale prices, but retail prices are better than no prices at all. Physical output data were thus revaluated with the familiar Laspeyre measure $\Sigma p_i^o q_i^t$, with 1965 retail prices as weights (p_i^o). Unfortunately, retail prices are generally limited to final consumer goods, and in the cases of the basic and intermediate industries I have had to use the official sector indexes of output, with the exception of the mining industry for which the 1965 export prices have been used as weights. The production indexes by sectors were then weighted by the 1968 value added weights, thus linking the series to the 1961–1968 series, and the results are shown in Appendix 2, Table 9. Some of the physical output data for the period 1958–1980 are shown in Appendix 2, Tables 11–16.

An Estimate of Cuban Gross Domestic Product, 1958–1981

On the basis of the information collected and the estimates of value added of total material production in constant prices in the preceding sections, it is now tempting to make at least a rough estimate of gross domestic product at factor cost since GDP is a much handier concept if we want to compare the Cuban performance with other countries. It should, however, be noted that this exercise is based on a much shakier foundation than the earlier estimates of TMP. GDP estimates for the period 1958–1981 are found in Table 2.7, and the estimates are based on the following assumptions.

The points of departure were the TMP figures in constant prices (1965 pesos) that have already been given. The next step was to calculate the gross material product, which, in accordance with Figure 2.1, is equivalent to global social product minus the intermediate inputs, or value added of TMP plus transport, communication, and trade. Real GMP in 1965 prices is already given for the years 1962–1966 (Table 2.1), and since prices underwent only slight modifications before 1970, it is assumed that the GMP in current prices (as shown in that table) did not change between 1967 and 1970. After 1970, however, important price movements were reflected in an inflated commercial sector, but since no official price deflator exists, it has simply been assumed that the GMP has increased at the same rate as the TMP between 1970 and 1981.

The remaining share of GDP to account for is the so-called nonmaterial services (NMS), which, as a rule, are excluded in national accounting in centrally planned economies. The lion's share of these services in Cuba is no doubt accounted for by education and health services. As a proxy for NMS and its growth, the combined index of education and health services (explained in Chapter 4) is used, taking total government expenditures on social services in 1965 as the point of departure. Adding the resulting estimate of NMS in constant 1965 prices to the GMP figures already given, we arrive at a rough estimate of GDP at factor cost in 1965 prices. The procedure could be summarized as follows.

Value added of:
  Agriculture, forestry, and fishing
  Mining
  Manufacturing   = TMP
  Electricity
  Construction

+ Value added of:
  Transport
  Communication   = GMP
  Commerce

+ NMS   = GDP

Finally, the GDP figures have been converted into 1980 U.S. dollars using a conversion ratio of US$1 (1980) equals 0.71 pesos, which was the official rate in Cuba in 1980.[51] The dollar GDP has then been divided by official midyear estimates of population to obtain the GDP per capita.

The question then arises, To what extent is this estimate of Cuban GDP in constant U.S. dollars reliable? Mesa-Lago and Pérez-López have meticulously gone through all the various types of official and unofficial estimates of economic growth in Cuba after 1959 in connection with a World Bank project on converting Cuba's material product system (MPS), used in centrally planned economies, into system of national accounts (SNA) categories used in market economies.[52] The result of their work is rather disenchanting as the growth rate alternatives vary from negative to highly positive for the same year depending on the sources used. Unfortunately, Mesa-Lago and his associate make no attempt to evaluate the quality of the different sources used—their seriousness, reliability, and consistency with other sources. Thus, they give considerable attention to the various and highly conflicting growth figures given in the World Bank *Atlas* in spite of the fact that "the World Bank was unable to provide information on how these estimates were made."[53]

It is interesting to note, however, that Mesa-Lago and Pérez-López, using the socalled univariate physical indicators approach, estimate that Cuban GDP per capita was $1,355 in 1977,[54] a figure that comes very close to my own estimate in Table 2.7. Mesa-Lago and Pérez-López also estimate that the share of NMS in the estimated GDP for 1978 was 30.0 percent,[55] which is again close to my own estimate (28.7 percent). It can thus be assumed that the estimates of the level of Cuban GDP and its main components by the end of the 1970s are reasonably reliable. Table 2.8 shows the growth rate—or decline—of the GDP and its major components after the revolution.

Figure 2.1. The Cuban national accounting system

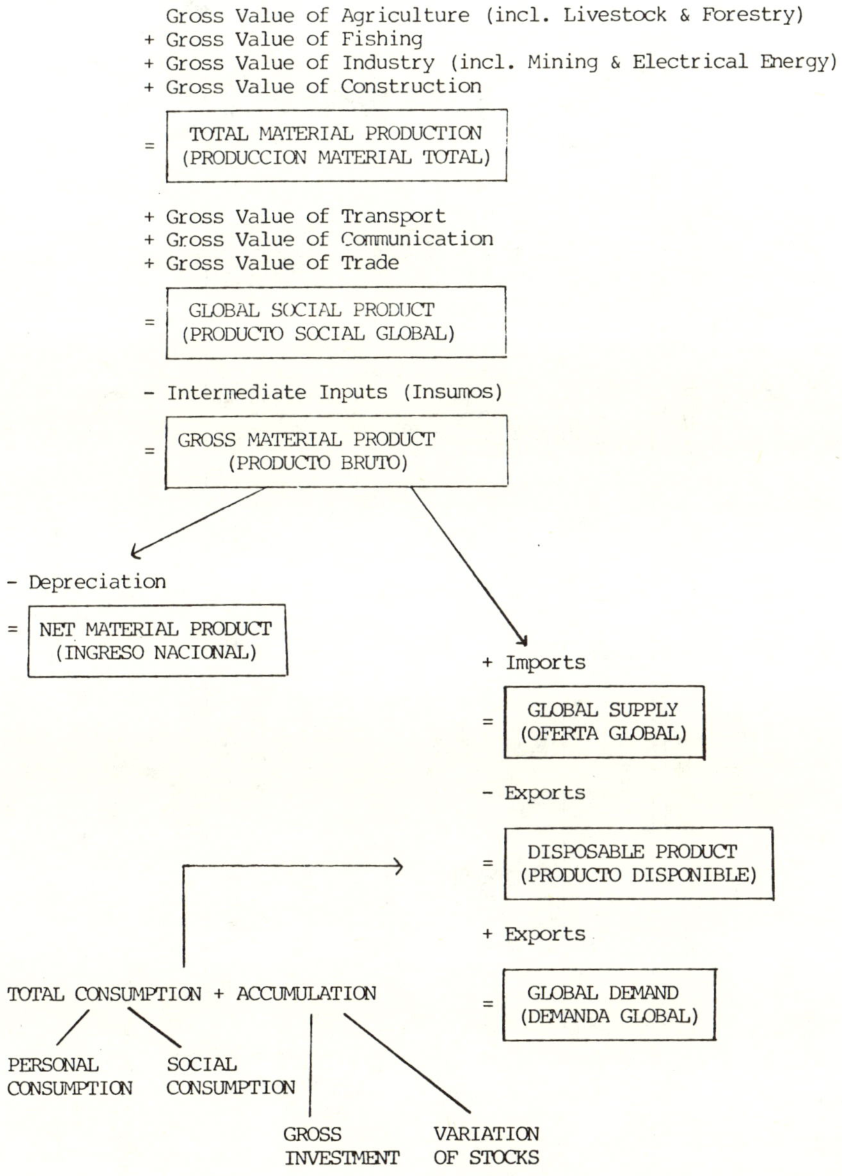

```
      Gross Value of Agriculture (incl. Livestock & Forestry)
    + Gross Value of Fishing
    + Gross Value of Industry (incl. Mining & Electrical Energy)
    + Gross Value of Construction

    = | TOTAL MATERIAL PRODUCTION   |
      | (PRODUCCION MATERIAL TOTAL) |

    + Gross Value of Transport
    + Gross Value of Communication
    + Gross Value of Trade

    = | GLOBAL SOCIAL PRODUCT    |
      | (PRODUCTO SOCIAL GLOBAL) |

    - Intermediate Inputs (Insumos)

    = | GROSS MATERIAL PRODUCT |
      | (PRODUCTO BRUTO)       |
```

- Depreciation

= | NET MATERIAL PRODUCT |
  | (INGRESO NACIONAL) |

    + Imports

    = | GLOBAL SUPPLY |
      | (OFERTA GLOBAL) |

    - Exports

    = | DISPOSABLE PRODUCT |
      | (PRODUCTO DISPONIBLE) |

    + Exports

TOTAL CONSUMPTION + ACCUMULATION = | GLOBAL DEMAND |
                                    | (DEMANDA GLOBAL) |

PERSONAL   SOCIAL
CONSUMPTION   CONSUMPTION

              GROSS   VARIATION
              INVESTMENT   OF STOCKS

Table 2.1. Global indicators of the Cuban economy, 1962-1974 (million current pesos)

	Global Social Product	Inter-mediate Inputs	Gross Material Product	Depreci-ation	Net Material Product	Imports	Global Supply	Exports
1962*	6,082	2,384	3,698	188	3,510	783	4,482	689
1963*	6,013	2,277	3,737	193	3,544	769	4,507	475
1964*	6,455	2,380	4,075	218	3,857	991	5,066	568
1965*	6,771	2,633	4,138	250	3,888	886	5,022	713
1966*	6,709	2,724	3,986	259	3,727	894	4,880	596
1967	7,212	3,129	4,083	267	3,816	999	5,082	705
1968	7,331	2,954	4,377	285	4,092	1,102	5,479	651
1969	7,236	3,055	4,181	272	3,909	1,222	5,403	671
1970	8,356	4,152	4,204	281	3,923	1,311	5,515	1,046
1971	8,936	4,114	4,822	na	na	1,387	6,209	861
1972	10,349	4,308	5,041	na	na	1,190	7,231	771
1973	11,910	5,198	6,712	560	6,152	1,463	8,175	1,153
1974	13,424	6,010	7,414	461	6,953	2,226	9,640	2,237

* = constant (1965) prices

na = not available

Table 2.1 (continued)

	Disposable Product	Consumption			Gross Investment	Accumulation		
		Personal	Social	Total		Variation of Stocks	Total	
1962*	3,793	2,491	417	2,908	626	259	885
1963*	4,032	2,653	397	3,050	733	249	982
1964*	4,498	2,781	489	3,269	810	419	1,229
1965*	4,309	2,888	474	3,362	842	105	947
1966*	4,294	2,772	474	3,246	935	113	1,048
1967	4,330	2,678	517	3,195	1,032	103	1,135
1968	4,781	3,298	490	3,788	918	75	993
1969	4,732	na	na	na	817	na	na
1970	4,746	3,615	168	3,783	800	163	963
1971	6,460	na	na	na	964	na	na
1972	na	na	na	na	1,094	na	na
1973	7,582	5,503	134	5,637	1,475	470	1,945
1974	7,864	5,486	148	5,634	1,712	518	2,230

Sources: Figures for 1962–1966: BEC (1968); for 1967–1968: BEC (1970) and (1971); for 1969: AEC (1972); for 1970–1974: United Nations (1979), Table 187. Investment data after 1970 are all from Juceplan (1980a), p. 33. Some data are derived in accordance with Figure 2.1.

Table 2.2. Indexes of Cuban industrial production, 1946-1961
(1953=100)

	1946	1947	1948	1949	1950	1951	1952	1953
Beverages	78.0	76.0	78.4	80.3	87.8	99.6	112.1	100.0
Tobacco	90.9	95.9	99.1	95.8	93.4	96.5	103.7	100.0
Textiles	70.0	66.5	54.8	66.5	136.3	98.9	110.4	100.0
Processed food	49.4	49.4	49.4	54.9	58.5	56.1	77.3	100.0
Sugar	78.0	111.8	107.0	101.0	106.8	110.8	139.4	100.0
Shoemaking	86.4	124.9	96.0	81.0	88.7	89.8	89.3	100.0
Rubber products	70.7	76.8	71.9	66.6	103.8	129.5	112.3	100.0
Paper & paperboard	121.3	50.0	65.0	55.4	85.9	90.0	87.2	100.0
Construction materials	59.1	68.0	70.1	76.8	77.8	94.2	103.3	100.0
Total manufacturing	73.8	84.0	82.3	82.0	93.0	95.7	112.7	100.0
Excluding sugar	71.7	70.0	69.9	72.4	86.0	88.1	99.3	100.0
Electricity & gas	52.9	56.8	63.5	68.6	75.4	83.1	91.3	100.0
Mining	62.6	42.4	37.9	40.1	44.5	55.2	80.2	100.0
Total industrial production	71.6	84.8	87.3	81.9	90.6	94.7	114.2	100.0
Excluding sugar	66.6	63.7	64.2	67.1	78.0	82.1	94.7	100.0

* = interpolation

Table 2.2 (continued)

	1954	1955	1956	1957	1958	1959	1960	1961
Beverages	100.1	100.7	104.8	107.5	102.8	121.0	114.8*	108.5
Tobacco	93.5	97.2	104.1	113.0	106.4	108.5	93.7*	79.0
Textiles	126.2	116.6	130.5	141.2	144.7	184.1	152.6	113.5
Processed food	100.4	107.4	120.5	130.9	128.7	136.9	152.8	122.7
Sugar	106.6	108.8	101.6	108.7	117.2	120.8	118.8	137.1
Shoemaking	107.3	114.6	126.4	139.1	145.5	151.8	128.1	64.6
Rubber products	119.2	119.0	151.1	177.7	290.9	290.0*	289.4	305.5
Paper & paperboard	103.8	109.1	122.5	126.9	128.5	162.5	160.0	217.8
Construction materials	103.3	112.0	145.4	158.4	175.9	160.8	194.5	208.3
Total manufacturing	104.6	107.3	113.6	121.9	124.3	131.6	130.6	135.2
Excluding sugar	103.6	106.5	119.6	128.5	132.9	144.5	144.6	133.0
Electricity & gas	108.1	119.2	131.4	134.4	145.2	144.1	149.4	149.7
Mining	87.7	98.5	88.8	92.3	93.2	76.1	53.0	47.9
Total industrial production	104.0	108.1	110.5	117.8	124.4	128.4	126.3	129.6
Excluding sugar	102.1	107.6	117.5	124.9	130.0	134.4	132.1	123.7

Sources: 1946-1958: Pérez-López (1974), pp. 70, 75, and 140-141; 1959-1961: based on physical output data given in ECLA (1965), p. 278; Mesa-Lago (Summer 1969), p. 62, and ECLA (1969), pp. 79-87.

Table 2.3. Net domestic income at factor cost in 1953 (million current pesos)

Agriculture, forestry, and fishing	533.4	22.7%
Mining and quarrying	28.4	1.2%
Manufacturing	517.0	22.0%
Construction	81.2	3.5%
Electricity, gas, water, sanitary services	32.2	1.4%
Transportation and communication	120.7	5.1%
Wholesale and retail trade	347.9	14.8%
Banking, insurance, and real estate	56.9	2.4%
Ownership of dwellings	102.1	4.3%
Public administration and defense	140.1	6.0%
Services, unspecified	389.4	16.6%
Total	2,349.3	100.0%

Source: Oshima (1961), p. 215.

Table 2.4. Growth estimates, 1959-1961 (annual percentage rate)

	1959	1960	1961
Estimates in this study			
Total material production	4.3	1.5	2.8
Sugarcane production	5.1	-1.1	14.3
Nonsugar manufacturing	8.8	0.1	-8.0
Mesa-Lago			
Combined index of agriculture and industry	5.6	-1.5	7.1
Noyola			
Industrial production	17.0	25.0	
PEL			
Industrial production		13.0	6.2

Sources: Appendix 2, Table 5; Mesa-Lago (1971c), p. 329; Noyola (1961), p. 416; PEL (1968), p. 16.

Table 2.5. Estimate of total material production at factor cost in 1962 (million pesos)

	Gross Value of Production (1965 prices)		Gross Value Added (1961 prices)		Wages & Salaries (State Sector)		Estimate of Total Wages & Salaries (Incl. Private Sector)		Adjusted Gross Value Added (1965 prices)	
	m. pesos	%	m. pesos	%	m. pesos	%	m. pesos	%	m. pesos	%
Agriculture,* forestry, & fishing	924.5	22.9	700.8	36.7	276.0	28.4	631.0	45.5	742.3	33.0
Sugarcane	(267.6)	(6.6)	(204.8)	(10.7)	(117.3)	(12.1)	(208.3)	(15.0)	(245.0)	(10.9)
Nonsugar agriculture	(316.3)	(7.8)	(266.4)	(13.9)	(97.6)	(10.1)	(225.0)	(16.2)	(264.7)	(11.8)
Livestock	(310.2)	(7.7)	(175.9)	(9.2)	(57.1)	(5.9)	(174.5)	(12.6)	(205.3)	(9.1)
Forestry	(12.2)	(0.3)	(38.3)	(2.0)	(3.2)	(0.3)	(9.3)	(0.7)	(10.9)	(0.5)
Fishing	(18.2)	(0.5)	(15.4)	(0.8)	(0.8)	(0.1)	(13.9)	(1.0)	(16.4)	(0.7)
Mining	66.8	1.7	43.7	2.3	26.1	2.7	26.1	1.9	56.6	2.5
Manufacturing	2,600.3	64.3	900.1	47.1	464.2	47.8	524.7	37.8	1,129.3	50.2
Metallurgy & mechanical industry	(127.7)	(3.2)	(64.4)	(3.4)	(40.3)	(4.1)	na	na	(75.4)	(3.4)
Construction materials	(152.1)	(3.8)	(36.5)	(1.9)	(57.0)	(5.9)	na	na	(76.1)	(3.4)
Petroleum	(279.8)	(6.9)	(94.3)	(4.9)	(14.1)	(1.5)	na	na	(136.5)	(6.1)
Chemicals	(231.1)	(5.7)	(106.5)	(5.6)	(31.4)	(3.2)	na	na	(153.0)	(6.8)
Textiles & leather	(273.7)	(6.8)	(126.5)	(6.6)	(64.7)	(6.7)	na	na	(139.9)	(6.2)
Sugar	(425.7)	(10.5)	(99.9)	(5.2)	(119.8)	(12.3)	na	na	(153.7)	(6.8)
Food	(626.5)	(15.5)	(155.9)	(8.2)	(51.1)	(5.3)	na	na	(208.6)	(9.3)
Beverages & tobacco	(279.8)	(6.9)	(149.4)	(7.8)	(46.9)	(4.8)	na	na	(108.3)	(4.8)
Other industry	(203.9)	(5.0)	(66.7)	(3.5)	(38.9)	(4.0)	na	na	(77.8)	(3.5)
Electricity	79.1	2.0	58.6	3.1	28.0	2.9	28.0	2.0	66.6	3.0
Construction	369.9	9.1	207.2	10.8	176.8	18.2	176.8	12.8	253.1	11.3
Total material production	4,040.6	100.0	1,910.4	100.0	971.1	100.0	1,386.6	100.0	2,247.9	100.0

* = excluding "agricultural services"; some percentage totals do not add because of rounding

Sources: Gross Value of Production: BEC (1968), pp. 18 and 20; Gross Value Added: ECLA (1965), pp. 275, 286, and 290; Wages and Salaries: BEC (1968), p. 23; Total Wages and Salaries: calculated from Minrex (1966), p. 58, and O'Connor (1970), p. 210; Adjusted Gross Value Added: author's estimates.

Table 2.6. Reconstruction of total material production, global social product, and gross material product, 1965 (1965 prices)

TMP	Gross Value of Production million pesos	%	Gross Value Added (factor cost) million pesos	%
Agriculture, forestry, & fishing	1,074.0*	15.9*	829.8	20.1
Sugarcane	(365.6)	(5.4)	(334.7)	(8.1)
Nonsugar agriculture	(257.3)	(3.8)	(215.4)	(5.2)
Livestock	(385.9)	(5.7)	(255.3)	(6.2)
Forestry	(6.8)	(0.1)	(6.1)	(0.1)
Fishing	(20.3)	(0.3)	(18.3)	(0.4)
Mining	74.5	1.1	63.1	1.5
Manufacturing	2,743.7	40.5	1,190.4	28.8
Metallurgy	(115.1)	(1.7)	(68.0)	(1.6)
Construction materials	(149.0)	(2.2)	(74.5)	(1.8)
Petroleum	(291.1)	(4.3)	(142.0)	(3.4)
Chemicals	(237.0)	(3.5)	(156.9)	(3.8)
Textiles & leather	(291.1)	(4.3)	(148.8)	(3.6)
Sugar	(555.2)	(8.2)	(200.4)	(4.8)
Food processing	(602.6)	(8.9)	(200.6)	(4.8)
Beverages & tobacco	(291.1)	(4.3)	(112.7)	(2.7)
Other industry	(211.5)	(3.1)	(86.5)	(2.1)
Electricity	94.8	1.4	79.9	1.9
Construction	521.8	7.7	357.0	8.6
Total material production	4,508.8*	66.6*	2,520.2	60.9
GSP and GMP				
Transport	348.1	5.1		
Communications	51.5	0.8		
Trade	1,838.7	27.2		
Other	23.8	0.3	1,617.3	39.1
Global social product	6,770.9*	100.0*		
Gross material product			4,137.5	100.0

* = including "agricultural services"; some percentage totals do not add because of rounding

Sources: Appendix 2, Table 7, and BEC (1968).

Table 2.7. Estimate of Cuban gross domestic product at factor cost, 1958-1981 (constant prices)[1]

	Population (000s)	TMP (factor cost) (m. pesos)	GMP (m. pesos)	NMS (m. pesos)	GDP (m. pesos)	GDP (m. US$)[2]	GDP per capita (US$)[2]
1958	6,763	2,116	3,480[3]	678	4,158	5,856	866
1959	6,901	2,207	3,628[3]	737	4,365	6,148	891
1960	7,027	2,240	3,685[3]	742	4,427	6,235	887
1961	7,134	2,303	3,787[3]	819	4,606	6,487	909
1962	7,254	2,248	3,698	843	4,541	6,396	882
1963	7,415	2,173	3,737	880	4,617	6,503	877
1964	7,612	2,397	4,075	982	5,057	7,123	936
1965	7,810	2,520	4,138	967	5,105	7,190	921
1966	7,985	2,451	3,986	1,020	5,006	7,051	883
1967	8,139	2,711	4,083	1,032	5,115	7,204	885
1968	8,284	2,648	4,377	1,058	5,435	7,655	924
1969	8,421	2,554	4,181	1,107	5,288	7,448	884
1970	8,551	2,976	4,204	1,060	5,264	7,414	867
1971	8,691	3,066	4,127	1,099	5,226	7,361	847
1972	8,859	3,344	4,405	1,261	5,666	7,980	901
1973	9,035	3,792	4,902	1,490	6,392	9,003	996
1974	9,192	4,097	5,241	1,708	6,949	9,787	1,065
1975	9,335	4,576	5,708	1,967	7,675	10,810	1,158
1976	9,471	4,783	5,959	2,355	8,314	11,710	1,236
1977	9,593	4,983	6,409	2,644	9,053	12,751	1,329
1978	9,694	5,362	6,844	2,760	9,604	13,527	1,395
1979	9,766	5,450	6,988	2,834	9,822	13,834	1,417
1980	9,732	5,580	7,179	2,874	10,053	14,159	1,455
1981	9,804	6,525	8,040[4]	2,949	10,989	15,477	1,579

[1]Cuban pesos 1965
[2]Equivalent to US$ 1980 (US$1 = 0.71 pesos)
[3]Between 1958 and 1962 GMP is assumed to have increased at the same rate as TMP
[4]Based on a 12.0% growth rate of GSP in 1981 as reported by CEE (AEC [1981])

Sources: AEC (various issues); Tables 2.1, 2.4, 2.6, 4.9; and Appendix 2, Tables 7 and 9.

Table 2.8. Growth rates of Cuban GDP and main components, 1959-1981 (constant prices)

	TMP	GMP	NMS	GDP	GDP per capita
1959	4.3	4.3	8.7	5.0	2.9
1960	1.5	1.6	0.7	1.4	-0.4
1961	2.8	2.8	10.4	4.0	2.5
1962	-2.4	-2.4	2.9	-1.4	-3.0
1963	-3.3	1.1	4.4	1.7	-0.6
1964	10.3	9.0	11.6	9.5	6.7
1965	5.1	1.5	-1.5	0.9	-1.6
1966	-2.7	-3.7	5.5	-1.9	-4.1
1967	10.6	2.4	1.2	2.2	0.2
1968	-2.3	7.2	2.5	6.3	4.4
1969	-3.5	-4.5	4.6	-2.7	-4.3
1970	16.5	0.6	-4.2	-0.5	-1.9
1971	3.0	-1.8	3.7	-0.7	-2.3
1972	9.1	6.7	14.7	8.4	6.4
1973	13.4	11.3	18.2	12.8	10.5
1974	8.0	6.9	14.6	8.7	6.9
1975	11.7	8.9	15.2	10.5	8.7
1976	4.5	4.4	19.7	8.3	6.7
1977	4.2	7.6	12.3	8.9	7.5
1978	7.6	6.8	4.4	6.1	5.0
1979	1.6	2.1	2.7	2.3	1.6
1980	2.4	2.7	1.4	2.3	2.7
1981	16.9	12.0	2.6	9.3	8.5

Source: Table 2.7.

3
The Economic Performance of Revolutionary Cuba

The Unfolding of a Revolution

Although there were no concrete actions proposed in the first program of the revolutionary government—the so-called Program Manifesto of the 26th of July Movement[1]—the economic goals of the government could be summarized as increase the rate of growth, reduce the dependence on sugar, diversify agriculture, develop the industrial sector, diversify trade relations, and increase the standard of living of the population through the expansion of health, education, and welfare programs. The only problem was that no priorities were given—it was just taken for granted that everything could be carried out at the same time, since it was tacitly assumed that the revolution would bring about such a qualitative change in the relations of production (principally through a profound agrarian reform) that the productive forces would expand by themselves.

The main themes of the Program Manifesto had been the questions of national sovereignty and social justice, and implicit in the early actions by the leaders of the revolution was the redistribution of income, from the rich to the poor and from the towns to the rural areas. At the beginning of 1959, however, the propertied classes and the bourgeois opposition to Batista, which had supported the 26th of July Movement, still had reasons to be rather optimistic about the future. Castro even announced that all debts of the past regime would be honored in order to strengthen the credit system and to maintain investor confidence.[2]

Nevertheless, almost immediately after taking over the premiership in January 1959, Fidel Castro revealed his adamant determination and seriousness by seizing the U.S. owned Cuban Electric Company, which had been the target of many accusations of inefficient operations and monopoly profits.[3] At the same time, Castro announced important measures to benefit the poorest sector of the population, especially those in the rural areas. In January 1959, electrical rates for rural areas were reduced by half, and in March, a Rent Law was announced, which called for reductions of 50 percent in the rents of all people who paid less than 100 pesos per month and between 40 percent and 30 percent for the tenants in higher brackets.[4] This action came as a shock for the wealthy who had money invested in real estate and was Castro's first "betrayal" of those people. In the Rent Law, the revolutionary government gave the first clear indication of its indifference to the vested property interests, and this was the first time there was a clash between Castro's promises to the poor of a better future and his assurance to the capitalist class that they had nothing to fear. From that moment on, Castro became implacable in carrying through his reforms, yielding nothing to his opponents.

The real estate interests were soon hit by another decree, the Vacant Lot Law, which wiped out any appreciation in the market value of urban real estate in excess of 15 percent.[5] The reaction was not long in coming, and the conservative daily *Diario de la marina* warned that the Rent Law would virtually paralyze investment, which would cause stagnation and increased unemployment in the construction industry. Indeed, private construction in 1959 decreased 56.5 percent in relation to the previous year.[6] Soon after the announcement of the Vacant Lot Law, Fidel Castro laid the cornerstone of a people's housing project in East Havana for the construction of 2,000 units for low-income families, a project to be financed by the national lottery. In this way, Castro showed that there were ways of getting houses built without counting on the cooperation of the capitalists.[7]

Socialist Upsurge in the Countryside

By far the most important reform during the first year was the Agrarian Reform Law of 17 May 1959. This reform has been extensively discussed by many authors and just the main features will be summarized here.[8]

The Agrarian Reform Law had been drafted by the 26th of July Movement in Sierra Maestra in October 1958, three months before the fall of Batista. The basic purpose of the reform was a radical transformation of ownership as a means of accelerating economic growth and raising the level of living of the peasants and the rural workers. The plantation system in Cuba had established a form of farming that was based on very primitive techniques coupled with the abundant use of cheap labor. The agrarian reform was designed to convert the land into the property of the people working it and to take over unproductive farms, particularly the cattle estates, and organize them into people's farms. The expropriated sugar plantations would be converted into cane cooperatives as an intermediate and provisional solution.[9]

The reform furthermore set a maximum limit of 402 hectares (30 *caballerías*) for land ownership, which could sometimes be raised for cattle farming to 1,340 hectares (100 *caballerías*). Appropriated land was to be compensated for by Agrarian Reform Bonds, which were redeemable within a period of twenty years with an annual interest of 4.5 percent.[10] A good-sized plot of 27 hectares (2 *caballerías*) was fixed as the "vital minimum" for a family of five people; this amount of land was distributed free, and the farmer had the right to buy another 40 hectares (3 *caballerías*). It has been estimated that some 100,000 "poor peasants" benefited from this provision of the reform.[11]

The expropriation and distribution of land started at a slow pace, and ten months after the proclamation of the reform only 850,000 hectares (or just some 10 percent of the expropriable area—see Table 3.1) had been expropriated, and only 40,200 hectares had been distributed to 6,000 beneficiaries. At this rate, it would have taken twenty years to satisfy the needs of some 150,000 potential beneficiaries,[12] but at the beginning of 1960, the rhythm of expropriation and confiscation of property falling under a special decree on Recuperation of Ill-Gained Wealth[13] accelerated, and in one week in January, more than 600,000 hectares were confiscated.[14]

The sugar farmers (including the *colonos*) had owned or administered 2.5 million hectares of land in 1959, but only 1.3 million hectares had been actually cultivated with sugar; the rest had been kept in reserve or used for extensive cattle farming.[15] No less than 70 percent of the sugar land, and 20 percent of the total farmland, had been controlled by twenty-two *latifundios*, of which thirteen were U.S. owned and nine more owned by Cubans or nationalized Cubans.

The real upsurge in the countryside came in the summer and autumn of 1960, and no doubt the growing dispute with the United States was one of the major driving forces behind it. The definitive clash started with oil, however, not sugar. The Americans, British, and Dutch had built refineries in Cuba in order to process crude oil from their properties in Venezuela, paying what the Cubans considered to be inflated prices as Soviet oil could be obtained at lower world market prices. The petroleum companies were about to agree to refine Soviet oil, although under protest, but the Eisenhower government told them to reject the plan—against U.S. ambassador Philip Bonsal's desire and without his knowledge.[16] Cuba cannot exist without importing virtually all its oil, and the blackmail tactics of the oil companies were a direct challenge to the authority of the revolutionary government. Fidel Castro and Che Guevara, at that time president of the National Bank and perhaps the most implacable adversary of the oil companies, did not yield one inch from their position, and on 29 June, the refineries were "intervened" (provisionally taken over by the government), and in one stroke, Cuba became totally dependent on Soviet oil and gasoline. The U.S. reaction was quick as on 6 July 1960, President Eisenhower retaliated by reducing Cuba's remaining sugar quota imports for 1960.

The dispute over the Soviet oil was no doubt a turning point in the relations between Cuba and its powerful neighbor, but it would be futile to speculate whether the Cuban revolution would have taken another course had the U.S. policy been more flexible and wiser. One fact is, however, clear: At that time the revolution was not yet of a socialist character, at least not openly, although the rules of the game with the bourgeois opposition had been clearly spelled out. Che Guevara told a U.S. newsreporter as late as November 1960 that

> what lies ahead depends greatly on the United States. With the exception of our Agrarian Reform, which the people of Cuba desired and initiated themselves, all of our radical measures have been a direct response to direct aggressions by powerful monopolists, of which your country is the chief exponent. U.S. pressure on Cuba has made necessary the "radicalization" of the Revolution. To know how much further Cuba will go, it will be easier to ask the U.S. government how far it plans to go.[17]

The retaliation by the United States in response to Cuba's action in regard to oil did lead to a wave of nationalizations, starting with law 851 of 6 August whereby the lion's share of the U.S. investments in Cuba was seized, including all sugar mills and the oil refineries.[18] Through a decree of 17 September, the U.S.-owned banks were nationalized, and finally, on 13 October, a new law (890) was proclaimed whereby 287 larger companies, foreign as well as national, were expropriated or confiscated, of which 105 were sugar mills; 18, distilleries; 16, rice mills; and 61, textile and garment plants.[19]

Washington's answer to the Cuban "October revolution"[20] came just a week later when a trade embargo was placed on everything except nonsubsidized foodstuffs and medical supplies. Within a few months even those exceptions were banned,[21] and in retaliation the Cubans also nationalized the remaining U.S. properties including the Havana Hilton, the Nicaro nickel plant, a Coca Cola plant, and Sears, Woolworth, and many other companies. Although the surge of nationalization began as a retaliation against the United States, other foreign- and Cuban-owned properties were also affected. By early 1961, 75 percent of Cuban industry and 30 percent of the country's land had been collectivized.[22] The embargo was still in force at the beginning of the 1980s, even though there were some frustrated attempts at U.S.-Cuban rapprochement while President Carter was in office.[23]

After the "October revolution" of 1960, it was quite clear that the revolution had entered into a socialist phase, and on 15 April 1961, just two days before the Central Intelligence Agency–sponsored Bay of Pigs invasion, Fidel Castro referred to the Cuban revolution for the first time as a "socialist revolution carried out under the noses of the Yankees."[24] After the aborted invasion—the first defeat of U.S. imperialism in the Americas, as the Cubans call it—large areas of land owned by "counterrevolutionaries" were confiscated in accordance with the amendment to Article 24 of the Constitution, which permitted the confiscation of property of people who left the country or who carried out activities judged to be counterrevolutionary.[25]

The situation in Cuba was no longer so much an agrarian reform as an agrarian revolution. The situation as of May 1961 is summed up in Table 3.2. If "voluntary sales" and donations to INRA (Instituto nacional de reforma agraria; the Agrarian Reform Institute) are added to the various decrees of confiscation, we find that only 1.2 million hectars of the 4.4 million hectares of expropriated land, or less than one-third, were affected as a result of the Agrarian Reform Law of 1959.

Mounting Pressures Against Resources

During the first half of 1961, the revolutionary spirit was high in Cuba, and the optimism about sustained economic growth was unaffected. The revolutionaries had just delivered a mortal blow to the enemy abroad and the counterrevolution on the island, and a vigorous literacy campaign was in full swing. In the spring, the country celebrated the ending of the first people's *zafra* with a harvest of 6.2 million tons of raw sugar, the largest since the record harvest of 1952. The wave of nationalizations in the autumn of 1960 had created the base for a planned and rational industrialization of the country, and the industrial department of INRA was transformed into the new Ministry of Industries with Che Guevara as the first minister.

One reason for the optimism was the relatively good economic results during the first two years of the new government. In contrast to other revolutions, such as those in Russia and China, there was an increase in the output of most branches of the economy just after the revolution, but the increases were probably more modest than the government first thought. The Mexican economist Juan Noyola, adviser to the revolutionary government, claimed, among other things, in an enthusiastic article about the impact of the revolution on economic growth that Cuba had launched an agrarian reform that was unique in the world since it was the first time such a reform had led, not to decreasing production, but to an increase in agricultural output.[26] Appendix 2, Table 6, at first glance also gives some credit to Noyola's claim, as it shows that sugar agriculture increased 5.1 percent and nonsugar agriculture increased 4.2 percent in 1959. But Felipe Pazos retorted that Noyola's optimism was based only on the output figures for 1959, by which time the effects of the agrarian reform could hardly have made themselves felt.[27]

On this issue at least Pazos proved to be right. The confiscation of the cattle farms in early 1960 no doubt had some very serious effects as too many cattle were slaughtered. The Chilean adviser to INRA, Jacques Chonchol, has estimated that some 800,000 cattle were slaughtered in 1958 (out of an estimated stock of 6 million). During 1959, this figure increased to some 950,000, and during 1960, to about 1.1 million head.[28] These figures mean that slaughtering increased by 19 percent in 1959 and by another 16 percent in 1960, which seriously affected the reserves of cattle. There were two reasons for this trend.

First, there was a rapidly increasing demand for beef as a result of the redistribution of income in favor of the poor that took place during those years (see Chapter 5), and second, no limits were set for meeting this demand. Thus, in May 1960, INRA claimed that it was regularly satisfying the demand for beef in Havana "in spite of the fact that consumption has increased up to 60 percent with respect to 1958,"[29] and Pazos observed that "the rise in the real income of the working class should have brought an increase in the consumption of beef of not less than 50 percent."[30]

For some time the government did not worry too much about the situation since it was thought that there were immense, underutilized reserves in agriculture. For instance, Noyola claimed that "there has [in the case of Cuba] not been a reduction but an *increase* in the cattle stock and a still more considerable increase in the production of beef and milk as *a result of a better utilization* of the cattle herds" (italics mine).[31] Not even such sober observers as Huberman and Sweezy had any doubts about the brilliant future of Cuban agriculture as they wrote in 1960 "that there could be no better evidence than this [the currently maturing supply of beef cattle] that (1) the Revolution has already transformed the standard of living of the Cuban masses and, (2) this new and higher standard of living has come to stay."[32]

Those statements are not quoted in order to embarrass early observers of the Cuban revolution for having been mistaken, and it is important to stress that the Cuban leaders were not alone in their optimistic projections during the early 1960s. For instance, the French agronomist René Dumont, one of the first advisers to the revolutionary government and later one of the most bitter critics of the regime, exclaimed in September 1960 that *underproduction was such, before the Revolution,* that Cuban agriculture cannot but advance, even if errors are still committed. One can now say that the Cuban Revolution is in the process of catching up on the economic plane with the very high level it had already attained on the political plane.³³

If land in Cuba were cultivated with the same intensity as land in South China, the island would be able to feed a population of 50 million, according to Dumont.³⁴ No less optimistic was Charles Bettelheim, who wrote in a memorandum to the government after finishing a mission there in September 1960:

> Cuba is a country with absolutely exceptional agricultural possibilities. Studies made by specialists in agriculture and livestock show that within a relatively few years (generally from 10 to 12), it will be possible to multiply the production of many commodities by a factor of 3.4.5 or even more, *without any great investment effort* [italics mine]. This is an unprecedented situation. All the other countries that have entered the road of planning have had to make great efforts to raise their agricultural output to a much more modest degree—whether because this increase could not be realized without prior important investments (as in the Soviet Union) or whether because it demanded much labour and a tremendous organizational effort (as in China). In Cuba, on the other hand, the system of large rural property and the domination of foreign capital have produced an immense underutilization of the relevant means of production. The latter could therefore be brought into operation immediately, or almost immediately by essentially political and technical means.³⁵

It is no wonder that this euphoria spread to the Cuban leadership! The Polish economist Michal Kalecki sketched a Five-Year Plan for the period 1961–1965 in December 1960 in the wake of the October nationalizations.³⁶ He made a series of optimistic projections that were based on the expected growth of the internal market as a result of population growth and anticipated increases in per capita income, and the plan was based on demand conditions exclusively, disregarding realistic supply conditions. Kalecki projected an annual growth rate of the gross material product of 13 percent, and per capita consumption was expected to increase by 7.5 percent a year. Kalecki's estimates were based on the prerequisite that sugar exports should reach 9.4 million tons by 1965—which, incidentally, was the same as the projected figure for 1965 set by the U.S. Department of Commerce in 1956.³⁷

But the mounting pressure against resources soon began to be felt—and not only with respect to beef production. In the spring of 1961, people began to notice that some goods such as toothpaste, soft drinks, and beer were sometimes not available, but it was thought that the shortages were limited and temporary.[38] In the early summer, shortages of basic foodstuffs suddenly arose, and this first eruption of serious economic difficulty came as a shock.[39] But the shock apparently did not perturb the basic optimism of the revolutionary leaders. In August 1961 Che Guevara told an Organization of American States (OAS) meeting in Punta del Este, Uruguay, that Cuba was counting on a per capita growth of 10 percent per year, thus challenging the representatives from the other American states. Guevara's confidence in the bright future for Cuba seemed to know no limits:

> What does Cuba expect in 1980? Well, a net income per capita of some $3,000, or more than the actual per capita income of the United States. And if you do not believe me, all right. We are here to challenge you, gentlemen. If you just leave us in peace, if you let us develop and in twenty years let us come back, we shall see if the chant of the siren was that of revolutionary Cuba or not. But we announce, responsibly, this annual growth rate.[40]

This general optimism also permeated the debates at the National Production Conference—organized jointly by the government and the ORI (Organizaciones revolucionarias integradas; Integrated Revolutionary Organization, the embryo of Cuba's Communist Party)—which took place at the end of August just weeks after Che Guevara's return from Punta del Este. Regino Boti, head of the newly created planning office, Juceplan, and one of the first speakers, presented a 1962–1965 plan with growth projections of total material production "at a rate of not less than 10 percent (per year) and probably not more than 15.5 percent."[41]

These growth targets are perhaps even more surprising when one considers that the conference was actually convened in order to discuss the shortages that had arisen during the spring and summer and what should be done about them. It is true that most of the speakers seemed to be aware of the shortages, and Fidel Castro admitted that "we have problems of supply... [but] they were fundamentally due to the fact that the purchasing power of our people is 500 million pesos higher than before the triumph of the revolution.... The problem to resolve is how, with the resources at our disposal, to satisfy the fundamental demands of the people."[42] But although everybody seemed to be aware of the limits of resources available, nobody questioned the growth rates. There was a basic assumption that rapid socialization of the means of production coupled with sophisticated planning techniques would be a sufficient panacea for the problems. Probably there was also the widespread idea that there were almost endless untapped reserves in both agriculture and industry. But even if it were true that idle capacity in some branches of industry was as large as 60 percent as claimed,[43] it should have been obvious that sooner or later (and probably sooner), there would be bottlenecks ahead.

As a matter of fact, and as demonstrated in Figure 3.1, simple extrapolations of total material production based on the 1946–1958 trend projection yield figures that are surprisingly close to the actual volume of output reached during 1959–1961. This figure would tend to refute the argument that there was a great deal of unused or underutilized capacity in the Cuban economy on the eve of the revolution. What probably happened was that there were large stocks in the stores waiting for new consumers with freshly acquired purchasing power and this blossoming market for consumer goods lulled the government into false expectations about the future. The problem that was arising was what to do when there were no longer any stocks on the shelves and unused capacity had been tapped in most areas.

The Goods Famine of 1962–1963 and the Great Debate

The Four-Year Plan (1962–1965) presented by Regino Boti was an outline of what has later been denominated the "first growth strategy" after the revolution.[44] At the center of this strategy was a rapid industrialization through a wide range of import-substituting industries including metallurgy, chemical products, machinery, and even an automobile assembly plant. Most of the equipment for these new plants—investments totaling 620 million pesos—was to be supplied by the Soviet Union, the German Democratic Republic, and Czechoslovakia.[45] Nowhere in the plan was it envisaged that there might be any curtailment of consumption via rationing as a consequence of this high investment rate, because there was a basic underlying prerequisite that was more or less taken for granted: The rapid expansion of nonsugar agriculture would lead to self-sufficiency in food production and would eliminate queuing and problems of food supply by the end of 1962.[46]

The year 1962, officially baptized the "year of planning," was the first year of this optimistic plan, and the start could hardly have been worse. There was a severe drought in the spring of 1962, and much of the sugar harvest was lost. At the same time, the supply of food steadily dwindled, and by March 1962, it was necessary to introduce general food rationing. However, rationing was probably the only sensible solution unless the whole process of redistribution were to have been reversed, and food rationing did not necessarily mean that the people at large were worse fed than before. The Cuban agricultural worker no doubt had a better diet in 1962 than before the revolution, and large sectors of the urban population were also eating better. All children below seven were getting a liter of milk per day, and several million people who had seldom eaten meat or eggs were now getting a regular ration. But for the middle and upper classes and the better-paid workers in the towns, rationing undoubtedly meant less food than they had been used to.[47]

The years 1962 and 1963 turned out to be the worst economic years since the revolution. Total material production decreased by 2.4 percent in 1962 and by another 3.3 percent in 1963 (see Appendix 2, Table 8). The situation in the agricultural sector was disastrous with output falling by 11.3 percent in 1962 and by another 5.8 percent in 1963. But even the industrial sector, which was expected to be the spearhead in the Four-Year Plan, showed a disappointing 0.4 percent growth in 1962 and a decline of 1.5 percent in 1963. It became more and more obvious that the road ahead would be much more difficult than had been thought at the outset, but the problem was not only the result of the misjudgment of available resources. The embargo policy by the United States was being seriously felt in those years, especially when it was discovered that the deliveries of complete plants from the socialist countries would be delayed for at least some years.[48] In October 1962, at the height of the political tension that resulted from the missile crisis, which led the world to the brink of disaster, the embargo was extended to an outright naval blockade of the island.[49]

The final blow to Cuba's bold plans came in the fall of 1962 when the preliminary balance of payments figures for 1962 indicated a severe deficit. There had been a trade surplus of $38 million in 1960, the surplus had turned into a small deficit of $14 million in 1961, and in 1962, the trade deficit was expected to be $170 million.[50] The deficit mercilessly revealed the limitation of the plan. Edward Boorstein says that "the balance of payments deficit culminated the process by which the Cuban economy began to press against the limits of its resources."[51] It became clear that choices would have to be made, and a pressing need for deciding priorities began to be felt.

When Che Guevara spoke at a seminar on planning organized in Algeria in July 1963, he was much less optimistic than he had been at the OAS meeting two years earlier. He blamed much of the frustrating economic performance on the dependency inherited from the past, on the low level of skills, and on the lack of technological advance, but he also delivered some honest self-criticism.

> We did not base our arguments on statistical facts, nor on historical experience. We dealt with nature in a subjective manner, as if by talking

to it we could persuade it, and we discarded other experiences. When, for instance, we were told that there is no country in the world which could develop its agriculture at an annual rate of growth of 20 percent, we said: We shall do it. But we did not. When we considered the question of annual growth of our country we did not first check what we had to start with, what we could spend and what would be left to us, but we said: Calculate a 15 percent rate of growth and then we shall see what we have to do. To make global growth rate calculations is easy, and the task even seems easy when we consider what we have to do in order to grow by 15 percent, but for a monocultivating country, with all the problems I have told you, to grow by 15 percent was simply ridiculous.[52]

This was the atmosphere when the so-called great debate started in Cuba. Although the debate as such came to center around moral versus material incentives, centralization versus decentralization, and the functioning of the law of value in a transition economy, implicit in the discussions were the commodity shortages that had arisen in 1961 and intensified in the following two years. The debate took place from 1963 to 1965 in the form of articles, replies, and rebuttals in periodicals such as *Cuba socialista, Nuestra industria,* and *Comercio exterior.*

All people participating in the debate agreed that the road to industrialization was much more complicated than had been envisaged by the 1962–1965 plan, which resembled more the famous Feldman models of the late 1920s in the Soviet Union[53] than an operational medium-term plan. The participants also agreed that agriculture would have to be the pillar upon which to build the future industrialization of the island—or, as the Chinese said about the same time, "agriculture is the base and industry the leading sector of the economy."[54] The issue that emerged from the debate was, How can one determine value when there is a disturbing discrepancy between available resources and needs? In a market economy, the relative scarcity of commodities determines their prices, but this method would be inexcusable in a socialist society which is why there was complete consensus on the correctness of rationing basic consumer goods.

But if prices are administered—through the plan—does the law of value cease to function? Comandante Alberto Mora, at the time minister of foreign trade, unleashed this issue in June 1963 by criticizing "some comrades" for suggesting that the law of value does not function in the state sector. That Mora was addressing himself to the minister of industry, Che Guevara, among others, was no secret. Mora said that the law of value does, indeed, continue to function in a socialist economy: "It is precisely in the conscious decision of the planning authority (Juceplan) where value appears more clearly as an economic criterion, as a regulator of production."[55] And the law of value continues to function even in the state sector, which in Cuba in no way constitutes "a single large enterprise" as claimed by Che Guevara. "Value as a category will cease to operate (have a meaning) only when the development of the productive forces is such that enough resources are produced to satisfy socially recognized needs."[56]

The most profound criticism of Che's theses came from Charles Bettelheim, who believed that the role of the law of value in the commodity categories within the socialist sector is due to the insufficient level of development of the productive forces. This point raised by Bettelheim was of great importance because in a commodity shortage situation, a situation in which Cuba found itself, there seemed to be only two roads: either a tactical retreat by giving more stimulation to the private sector (and hence profits and material incentives) or continue socializing the remaining parts of the economy in an attempt to rapidly increase the level of the forces of production. Bettelheim seemed to reverse the argument by saying that the forms of property, or relations of production, cannot assume a higher level than that allowed by the level of the productive forces. Implicit in Bettelheim's argument were the facts that state enterprises should maintain a certain freedom of action (through self-finance, for instance) and that the system of material incentives could not be arbitrarily abolished on moral grounds.[57]

Surprisingly, none of the participants in the debate made any reference to the rich experience of the Soviet Union in discussing just such a problem in the 1920s.[58] The so-called industrialization debate had raged in the Soviet Union after the "goods famine" of 1925. There, as in Cuba forty years later, the root of the problem was accumulation in a transition economy. The goods famine had been preceded by the so-called scissors crisis,[59] when the terms of trade between the town and the village were turning increasingly against the latter in 1923.[60] In 1924, the Soviet government decided to rectify the situation, and the scissors also began to "close" in that year. But then came the shortages of commodities, or the goods famine of 1925. The discussion that followed centered around the nature of the shortages (just as the discussions in Cuba at the National Production Conference in August 1961 did). During the new economic policy (NEP) period,[61] output had expanded, thanks to large unused or underutilized resources, but by the mid-1920s, it was clear to everyone that the capacity reserves were exhausted and that any further increase in the level of output had to be predicated on a still greater increase in fixed capital investment.

In the Soviet Union, two groups evolved during the debate. One, led by Leon Trotsky, Eugeni Preobrazhenskii, and others, advocated a rapid industrialization at the expense of the *kulak* peasantry (implying a forced collectivization drive in agriculture—a policy later effectuated by Stalin). The other group argued that raising agricultural output and light industry should be given priority in the short run. Lev Shanin, an exponent for this group, said that "we must definitely realize that the heavy industries can be developed only on the basis of extensive preliminary development of light industry" and that "our economic strategy should involve, first, export of agricultural commodities, and second, investment of capital in the branches which serve the export."[62]

Shanin's ideas concerning export-led growth are surprisingly similar to the new growth strategy hammered out in Cuba during 1962 and 1963. Nobody seemed to question any longer that a renewed reliance on sugar to provide the necessary foreign exchange for the importation of capital goods would be the best road toward accumulation. The focus of the debate in Cuba was on the implications of this strategy rather than on the strategy itself. Could accumulation take place without a heavy renewed reliance on material incentives?[63] and what should be the role of the state in this accumulation? The position of Che Guevara was clear. First of all, he stood up in defense of the budgetary system of financing state enterprises, used within the Ministry of Industry, in contrast to the self-finance, or self-management, system practiced by the INRA (headed by Carlos Rafael Rodríguez) and by the Ministry of Foreign Trade (headed by Alberto Mora), which followed the practices of the Soviet Union and Eastern European countries. Second, and even more important, he made it clear that "while not denying the objective need for material incentives, we maintain that the development of consciousness does more for development of production in a relatively short time than material incentives do."[64]

The outcome of this debate was the adoption of what Mesa-Lago and others call the "Sino-Guevara line of thinking."[65] The allusion that Guevara was inspired by the Chinese no doubt stems from the fact that there was a debate going on in China at the time about the consequences of the economic crisis that had emerged in the wake of the Great Leap Forward (1958–1959).[66] There, as in Cuba, the debate centered on the role of profits and on moral versus material incentives. But the Chinese debate differed from the one in Cuba in that it also attacked the "revisionists" within the party, notably Liu Shao-chi, and, indirectly, the "revisionist clique" in Moscow and the Liberman followers in the Soviet Union.[67] Although neither Guevara nor Castro, who later unconditionally supported Che's stand, could hardly have been aware of the discussions in China, there is no evidence that they were actually influenced by the Chinese. Many of the participants in the debate did mention the Liberman school of thought, but only en passant.

The Revolutionary Offensive and the 10-Million-Ton *Zafra*

The system implemented between 1966 and 1970 was a radical extension of Che's system of central budgeting, and Cuba moved steadily away from being a market economy. Free services were extended, for instance, for local telephone calls, and in 1966, Fidel Castro announced that "starting in 1970, rent for housing will be practically nonexistent."[68] By gradually offering more free services, the government thought that money wages would progressively lose their importance and thus the reliance on moral incentives and voluntary labor would be easier to accept. The priority of moral over material incentives was officially proclaimed at the Twelfth Workers' Congress in August 1966.[69]

In 1967, there was again an atmosphere of cautious optimism in Cuba because there was reason to believe that the new orientation of the economic policy was yielding fruit. There had been a recovery, although nothing more than that, in a number of sectors (see Figure 3.2 and Appendix 2, Table 7). Rightly or wrongly, it was believed that the major obstacles for the development of the productive forces were the remaining bourgeois or petty bourgeois classes that still had some economic power. In October 1963, there had been a second agrarian reform that had virtually eliminated the remnants of the rural bourgeoisie—or, as it was declared in the preamble of the reform, "the existence of a rural bourgeoisie is incompatible with the interests and objectives of the Socialist Revolution."[70] Through this reform all farmland between 5 and 30 *caballerías* (67 and 402 hectares) was taken over by the state, which affected about 19 percent of the land and about 24 percent of the owners. The small farmers (those who owned fewer than 5 *caballerías*) had already organized the ANAP (Asociacion nacional de agricultores pequeños; Small Farmers' Association) in 1961, which represented about 150,000 farmers, of whom about two-thirds had been allotted land after the first agrarian reform of 1959.[71] The second agrarian reform gave explicit guarantees that the land of the small farmers would not be expropriated.[72]

There had been a vigorous campaign to diversify agriculture in the early 1960s, but the immediate economic results of the accelerated collectivization of land were not so good. The output of nonsugar agriculture continued to decrease in both 1964 and 1965 (see Appendix 2, Table 7), and the situation for rice production was especially disastrous. In 1966, the supply of rice, a basic ingredient in the Cuban diet, became critical when the deliveries promised by China failed to materialize in an apparent attempt by the Chinese to put pressure on the Cuban government to break its links with the Soviet Union. Production of hulled rice declined by more than half between 1963 and 1966 and started to recuperate only in the 1970s.[73] But another reason for the decline in agricultural production was the reorientation toward sugar after 1964. The area planted with sugar more than doubled between 1963 and 1968, and in the case of the state farms, the increase was more than three times.[74]

In late 1963, the Cuban government fixed a target of 10 million tons of raw sugar for the 1969-1970 *zafra*, a 150 percent increase over 1963. In 1965, a plan was set for the gradual increase of sugar production to be facilitated by an agreement with the Soviet Union in 1964, which arranged for a gradual enlargement of Soviet purchases at a fixed price of 6.11 cents per pound, substantially above the world market price at the time.[75] The plan also envisaged an amplification of installed capacity, the replacement of obsolete equipment, the introduction of new sowing techniques, and a gradual mechanization of the harvest.[76]

As already mentioned, there was an atmosphere of optimism in Cuba in 1967. The economy showed signs of recovery in most fields, and sugar production reached its highest level since the postrevolutionary record of 1961, although the figure was 17 percent below the planned target for the year.[77] There were, however, still signs of commodity shortages, and the black market was flourishing. In an attempt to eliminate this market, the government launched a "revolutionary offensive" in March 1968, whereby the state nationalized 55,600 small private businesses, which accounted for approximately one-third of retail trade sales.[78] In defense of the nationalizations, Fidel Castro said that "we did not make a revolution in order to establish the right to trade," and on May Day 1968, Raúl Castro explained the offensive in these terms: "To say that the small merchants lived better because they were influenced by material incentives is true. And for that very reason we reject material incentives. We do not want a small merchant mentality for our people."[79]

By using this drastic measure, the state, in fewer than ten years, collectivized almost the whole economy except for about one-third of the agricultural sector. The figures in Table 3.3 indicate that this rapid process also continued in the 1970s, and this trend continued at least until 1980 when private services such as hairdressing, laundry, and repair services were again allowed, although on a very restricted basis.[80]

Cuba's rapid collectivization of the means of production has, however, a parallel in history. During the forced collectivization campaign in the Soviet Union between 1924 and 1936, the private sector's share of production fell from 97.8 to 2.3 percent in agriculture, from 20 to 0.2 percent in industry, and from 50 to zero percent in trade.[81]

That the revolutionary offensive in Cuba was a political as well as an economic mistake is admitted today by the leaders of the revolution.[82] The measure of expropriating the relatively small private sector did not eliminate the black market; on the contrary, it gained in importance at the same time that people with excess purchasing power were incriminated for buying illegal goods and services.

One of the most serious bottlenecks for achieving the 10-million-ton *zafra* goal was thought to be the acute shortage of manpower. The Cuban sugar industry had been technically backward before the revolution with yields per hectare among the lowest in the Western Hemisphere[83] and mechanization of planting as well as of harvesting and loading virtually nonexistent.[84] The Prospective Sugar Plan was elaborated without a previous technical study of feasibility and opportunity costs. Knowing all the limitations, it is easy to see in retrospect that the plan could not but fail. Accumulated output in the 1965–1975 period was 25 percent below the target,[85] and although it is true that the 1970 figure of 8.5 million tons represented a record high in the sugar history of Cuba, it was produced at too high a cost and with a waste of resources.

Most of the prerequisites for the fulfillment of the plan, explicitly pronounced or implicitly assumed, never materialized. Of the projected investment of 1 billion pesos for modernizing the sugar industry, only 40 percent was actually invested; of the area planned for irrigation, only one-third was completed; and the application of fertilizers also fell short of the target set.[86] Most serious, however, was the failure to mechanize the harvest. The mechanizing of the lifting/loading phase of the harvest was remarkably successful (increasing from 20 percent in 1964 to 85 percent in 1970),[87] but the goal of rapidly mechanizing the most labor-intensive phase, cane cutting, failed, although there were frustrating attempts to introduce Soviet-imported harvesters in the mid-1960s.[88]

The failure to mechanize was crucial. The number of professional cane cutters had drastically decreased after the revolution (from 370,000 in 1958 to some 80,000 in 1970),[89] and to make matters even worse, the productivity of those remaining was estimated to have fallen by at least 20 percent. In order to make up for the deficit of harvesters and skilled cane cutters, several hundred thousand often unexperienced volunteers had to be mobilized to achieve the sacred goal of 10 million tons. No fewer than 350,000 cane cutters participated in the *zafra*, and sufficient cane was cut in order to produce the 10 million tons.[90] The problem was that the sugar content of the cane was too low—because it had not ripened, because it had been cut too high, or because it had been left too long on the ground before being collected (the last was usually the result of a breakdown of the transportation system).

The Second Decade: Sustained Economic Growth

Following the disappointing growth performance of the 1960s and the frustrating "great leap forward" policy of the 1969-1970 *zafra*, there was a vigorous recuperation of the economy in the first half of the new decade, with an annual growth rate of 10.0 percent in the years 1971–1975 (see Figure 3.2). According to Mesa-Lago,[91] this growth was the result of more efficient organization, previous investments, and a better allocation of capital. Also important were the steady outflow of trained personnel (managers, engineers, skilled workers) and the booming sugar prices (see Table 3.4). The postponement of Cuba's debt to the Soviet Union in 1972, the provision of new Soviet credit lines, and the relaxation of the U.S. embargo combined with substantial credits from many Western countries were other important factors.

Cuba's success story in terms of economic growth during the first half of the 1970s was primarily the result of accelerated industrialization and, notably, the growth of heavy industry as the share of nonconsumer goods in total industrial output increased from 47 percent in 1970 to 54 percent in 1975.[92] An important aspect of the expansion of capital goods is that it was the result of a planning effort to build up a domestic resource base around agriculture along the lines discussed earlier. For instance, Cuba today has a modest but relatively important sector producing combine harvesters, fertilizers, pesticides, and other inputs for agriculture (see Appendix 2, Tables 11–16). At the same time, efforts were made to increase the number of by-products from sugarcane, like bagasse for the paper industry and methanol for the chemical industry.[93] There have, however, been no plans to use pure alcohol from sugar (ethanol) as a substitute for gasoline, which is the current trend in Brazil.[94]

But the expansion of the capital goods sector is not only related to agriculture. Another Cuban success has been the rapid growth of the fishing industry, from some 22,000 metric tons of catch before the revolution to about 150,000 in the mid-1970s. Since the late 1960s, Cuba has generally produced a large number of vessels for this increasingly important sector. By 1975, Cuban shipyards had built some 6,000 small and medium wood vessels, 400 medium ferroconcrete vessels, and 90 large steel vessels.[95] There have also been important expansions of fishmeal processing and cold storage and freezing facilities. Cuba has changed from having been a net importer of fish in 1958 to being a net exporter and the seventh largest fishing nation in Latin America.[96]

Other important investments that will be of great importance in the 1980s are those that have gone into expanding the nickel production industry—the export product with the greatest potential for Cuba's economic diversification. Soviet aid for the modernization and expansion of the two existing plants was agreed upon in 1972 when Cuba's outstanding debt with the Soviet Union was renegotiated and new credit lines awarded. These plants today produce about twice the levels reached prior to the revolution. The goal had originally been to reach a level of 47,000 tons by 1980, but this objective was postponed until 1983. There have been plans to build two, perhaps even three, more plants in the Moa Bay area with Soviet assistance, and output is scheduled to increase to 69,000 tons by 1985 and to 100,000 tons by 1990.[97] Apparently, however, there have been problems with the technology supplied by the Soviets since the Cuban deposits are laterite ores with a low nickel content and are much more costly to process because of high energy costs than the more common sulfide ores are.[98]

The industrial growth during the first half of the 1970s was highly correlated with the price of sugar and with the Cuban terms of trade position and import capacity in general (see Table 3.4). The change in relation to the gloomy 1960s is conspicuous, but unfortunately for the Cubans, the favorable trend did not continue after 1975. Juceplan prepared three variants of the first officially approved Five-Year Plan (1976–1980) to allow for possible reverses in the price of sugar. Since prices fell more than expected, twenty-two major investment projects had to be cancelled, most of which were to be financed with credit lines from the West.[99] As had happened so many times before, the Soviet Union had to come to the rescue of the Cubans, and thanks to Cuba's steadily improving terms of trade with the Russians, the trade balance with the Soviet Union was favorable in 1976 for the first time since the early 1960s. However, more than the fall in Cuba's terms of trade with the West—25 percent lower during 1976–1979 than during 1971–1975 (see Figure 3.3)—was responsible for the declining growth rates during the first Five-Year Plan. There were also important difficulties in agricultural and livestock production at the end of the period because of plagues and pests, such as sugar rust, tobacco blue mold, and African swine fever.[100]

The Fight Against Unemployment

One of the fundamental changes in the employment policy of the 1970s was that for the first time, productivity took priority over employment creation.[101] In the 1960s, open unemployment had fallen from 11.8 percent in 1960 (the figure was the same in 1958) to 1.3 percent in 1970, but the full employment policy had created new problems. Thus, quite a lot of people were employed in low-productivity work places, the labor force tended to be rigidly immobile, and investment tended to go more and more into capital-intensive projects. All these factors were natural since the problem envisaged in the 1960s was one of labor shortage rather than one of labor surplus.

Because of the concern about such a shortage, there was a drive to induce women to enter the work force. Women have always constituted a large labor reserve in Cuba, as in most other parts of Latin America, but they had not been motivated to work outside the home—partly because of traditional attitudes and partly because of already high unemployment and underemployment rates. No doubt another important reason for the slow integration of women into the work force in the 1960s was the lack of material incentives to do so since there were simply no consumer goods to satisfy this potential increase in purchasing power.

In the mid-1970s, the situation radically changed. First of all, the supply of labor gained momentum as a result of two phenomena: one, the rapid increase in the number of young women who entered the labor force after completing primary or secondary education and, two, the effects of the baby boom of the early 1960s.[102] The growth of the female labor force between 1972 and 1976 is quite outstanding (see Table 3.5), and in fact, the female labor force more than doubled in the period 1970–1979. Ironically, this explosion took place when the government was pleading for increased productivity in all fields and making commitments to link wages to productivity, so it should have been easy to predict that a growing and serious discrepancy between the supply of and the demand for labor would be the inevitable outcome. From this fact alone, it is also easy to predict that unemployment probably increased after the record low level of 1970 (1.3 percent). Nevertheless, Mesa-Lago has estimated that there was a slight increase in unemployment between 1970 and 1974, but he has also estimated that unemployment was almost as low in 1978 as in 1970.[103] For various reasons, however, I think Mesa-Lago's estimates are erroneous. It is certainly true that the baby boom of the early years of the revolution resulted in an accelerated rate of growth of working-age people during the 1970s, but this fact explains only a part, and perhaps only a minor part, of the increased supply of labor. The other, and more important, factor is the impressive increase in the number of women in the labor force.

Table 3.5 shows some characteristics of the Cuban labor force in the 1970s. The estimates are based as far as possible on official data, and I have drawn especially on the results from the 1970 census and a 1979 demographic survey (a detailed explanation of the estimates is found in Appendix 1). As the figures clearly indicate, there was a growing rather than a diminishing unemployment rate from 1970 until at least

1979. (It is possible, however, that the exodus of some 146,000 people in 1980 alleviated the unemployment pressure to some extent after 1979.)[104] As Table 3.5 indicates, unemployment was as high as 188,000, or 5.4 percent of the labor force, in 1979. What is more remarkable, however, is that 129,000, or 69 percent, of the unemployed were women. In other words, while male unemployment only increased from 1.3 percent of the male labor force in 1970 to 2.5 percent in 1979, female unemployment increased from 1.2 percent to 12 percent. From this fact, one should not draw the conclusion that the number of economically *inactive* women was growing in relation to the female working-age population. As a matter of fact, as shown in Appendix 1, Table 5, the number of employed women as a percentage of the number of working-age females (minus students) increased from 24.9 percent in 1970 to no less than 44.5 percent in 1979. The major factor behind the growing unemployment rate was thus the increase in the female labor force rather than the baby boom of the early 1960s. Female employment accounted for 70 percent of the new jobs created between 1970 and 1979, but apparently the job creation for women was still not sufficient to meet the demand for work on the part of women.

Mechanization of Sugar Production and Return to Material Incentives

The increase in the supply of labor coincided with the drive to increase productivity in all fields, especially agriculture. Sugar continued to be the mainstay of the economy, but a more efficient policy was implemented.[105] There was an attempt to introduce the Australian technique of burning the cane, but the results were disappointing.[106] On the other hand, there has been a real breakthrough in the mechanization of cane cutting (see Table 3.6), and it was estimated that almost half of the cutting would be mechanized in the 1980 *zafra*. At the beginning of the 1970s, most of the mechanized cutting was done by imported Massey-Ferguson harvesters, but by the end of the decade, the Cuban-Soviet designed KTP-1 did most of the job.[107] In addition to the changes in cutting, both plowing and lifting were completely mechanized in 1980.[108] The technical transformation taking place in the sugar sector has led one expert in the field to state that by the end of the 1970s Cuba had assumed characteristics that are more commonly associated with industrial activity—expressed in terms of equipment, labor-skills, and productivity trends.[109]

The policies pursued in the 1970s meant, however, that a new conflict was arising between maintaining full employment and raising productivity. The Cuban leaders seem to have been well aware of the possibility that the specter of unemployment would reappear in the near future, and as early as 1973, Fidel Castro warned that "the time might come when we will have a headache finding jobs for all those who want to work."[110] There is officially no unemployment in Cuba, but the increase in the number of *disponibles* (temporarily laid off workers who receive 70 percent of their most recent wage while waiting for a new job assignment) is a symptom of the mounting difficulties of providing enough jobs.[111]

Another important aspect of change is the renewed reliance on material incentives and the revitalization and democratization of the labor movement. Both issues were discussed at the Thirteenth Workers' Congress in November 1973. There was a redefinition of the role of the trade union, which, in the words of the minister of labor, Jorge Risquet, had been more "the bureau of the vanguard workers" than a genuine workers' movement.[112] At the congress, the unions were reaffirmed as independent organizations of the working class, and the workers forced the adoption of a resolution that would allow them to have more direct participation in the planning process.[113] The work quota system was also changed to allow for variation in remuneration according to productivity, that is, rewards would be given to workers who produced beyond their quota.

Linked to the principle of reward according to work was the question of the supply of consumer goods. As long as there were no material incentives, there was no need to increase the output of consumer commodities. If people were to be materially incited to produce more (and in the case of women to enter the labor force), it was argued that there would also have to be consumer goods available to absorb this purchasing power. As a result, not only was there an increase in the supply of such goods, but a so-called parallel market was also introduced in which products outside the rationed quota could be bought at prices that reflect supply and demand.

External Dependency and Structural Economic Changes

The question of whether Cuba is more or less "dependent" now than before the revolution has been subject to debate ever since the first commercial agreement was signed between Cuba and the Soviet Union in 1960. The debate on dependency has dealt not only with Cuba's commercial and financial dependency on the Soviet Union but also on the supposedly negative consequence of this dependency on the structural economic changes—or rather the lack of such changes—inside Cuba. I shall here deal with some of these issues and try to show that at least some of the arguments that have been presented are fallacious.

First of all, let us turn to the question of revolutionary Cuba's continuing—and some claim increasing—dependency on foreign trade. The customary measure of estimating such a dependency is simply to relate exports and/or imports to the gross national product or the gross domestic product. Studies of prerevolutionary Cuba have shown that Cuban exports averaged 30.6 percent of GNP in the period 1946–1958, with a slightly decreasing trend (32.0 percent in 1946 compared to 27.9 percent in 1958).[114] Both Leo Grande and Mesa-Lago have analyzed Revolutionary Cuba's trade dependency, but each has drawn different conclusions.[115] Thus, Mesa-Lago claims that there was a deepening of Cuba's trade dependency in the 1970s, and Leo Grande stresses that "the decline in the exports indicator [after the revolution] shows that Cuba has begun to escape the export economy pattern."[116] How is it possible, one might ask, to arrive at such diametrically opposed views from seemingly identical data? The explanation appears to be that although Leo Grande prefers to compare averages for the prerevolutionary and the postrevolutionary periods, Mesa-Lago finds it more illuminating to compare the decline of the exports indicator in the 1960s with the apparent increase in the 1970s.

There is an important flaw in the arguments of both authors, however, which is that the series are not comparable. First of all, the prerevolutionary series relates exports to GNP, and the postrevolutionary series relates exports to the gross material product, which is undoubtedly smaller than both GNP and GDP. Leo Grande recognizes that this difference leads to a systematically biased underestimate of the reduction of trade dependency after the revolution. There is, in addition, another more serious flaw, which has to do with the weights (prices) used. In contrast to Mesa-Lago, Leo Grande at least seems to be aware of this dilemma as he says that the sharp rise in the dependency indicators in 1974–1975 resulted, not from any sudden structural change in the Cuban economy in those years, but "from an extraordinary increase in the world market price of sugar during the period."[117] But although this statement is no doubt true, it is not the whole truth because even if the world market price of sugar is important for Cuba's export performance, the subsidized price paid by the USSR is even more important. Neither Leo Grande nor Mesa-Lago seem to be aware of the important effect of this price on the dependency indicators they use. Leo Grande's series ends in 1975, and up to that point, the subsidized price effect was perhaps not so evident, but Mesa-Lago's more recent analysis includes trade data for the period 1976–1978, and they demonstrate a steadily increasing trade dependency (exports over GMP).[118]

The problem is that Mesa-Lago is relating exports in current prices (that is, including price subsidies) to GMP and the latter is basically given in constant prices in Cuba (see Chapter 2). Thus, there is, by definition, a bias in this method of calculating trade dependency since export prices tend to rise over time. In the Cuban case, it can easily be demonstrated that while the value of exports in current prices increased threefold between 1970 and 1980—from 1 billion pesos to 3.7 billion pesos—the increase in the volume of exports (in constant prices) was only 5.6 percent. This important distinction between value and volume of exports—and the difference it makes in estimating trade dependency in the case of Cuba—is shown in Table 3.7.

The table shows that my estimates of Cuba's trade dependency—relating exports in constant 1965 prices to GMP and to rough estimates of GDP—do not agree with the conclusions of Mesa-Lago and that Cuba's dependency on trade has decreased since 1970. Although Mesa-Lago's estimates indicate that there was a drastic reduction in export dependency between 1958 and 1965 (a reduction that was more a result of declining exports than of a rise in GMP), his figures also indicate that there was a continuous and rapid rise in export dependency after 1970—the year of the bumper sugar harvest. In contrast, my own estimates in constant prices suggest that although there was a definite rise in trade dependency between 1965 and 1970, there was a definite reduction in the trade dependency after 1970—and the reduction was probably significant in relation to 1958.

But the volume concept is important not only for the calculation of trade dependency, but also for making estimates of export diversification. Both Leo Grande and Mesa-Lago make a point of stressing that sugar accounts for as much, or even more, of Cuba's total export earnings today as it did in the prerevolutionary period, but this continuing supremacy of sugar in export earnings does not necessarily mean that the Cubans have not had any success in diversifying exports. During the 1970s, Cuba expanded exports of a range of new products, such as seafood and citrus fruits, at a much more rapid rate than it expanded the volume of sugar exports, and Cuba would have diversified exports even more had it not been for delays in nickel development plans. Even so, the estimate of the structure of the volume of exports in constant prices in Table 3.8 shows that sugar exports fell from 83.1 percent of total exports in 1970 to 70 percent in 1980—to be compared with an average of 84.5 percent for the period 1946-1958. The main reason for this apparent contradiction between the different methods used is found in the highly subsidized sugar prices paid by the Soviet Union in the 1970s, especially after 1975, which caused a significant rise in current earnings of sugar exports that was not accompanied by a corresponding increase in export volume.

Likewise, it could be argued that the high estimates of regional concentration of exports in Leo Grande's and Mesa-Lago's studies are biased. Since the Soviet Union pays a price for Cuban sugar that is substantially higher than the world market prices, especially since 1975, the result will obviously be an increasing partner concentration (see Table 3.9). The only way to reverse this trend would be to divert export volumes to other countries, and this is exactly what the Cubans have been trying to do, with varying success. In years when the International Sugar Agreement (ISA) prices have been exceptionally high, such as 1974 and 1980, the USSR has apparently abstained from using all of its agreed allotment, which has resulted in a lesser degree of partner concentration.

In summary, measuring exports in constant prices indicates that Cuba is not more dependent on trade today than it was in the 1960s—or the 1950s for that matter—at least not in the sense that exports are more important as a share of the GDP or the GNP. Nor does it seem to be true that sugar exports have increased in relation to total exports. Cuban exports today are more diversified even if sugar still makes up an excessive portion of export volumes. The same situation exists in regard to partner concentration. The Soviet Union is by far Cuba's most important trading partner, even if the partner concentration is not quite as great as it was between Cuba and the United States in the 1950s (62.7 percent). On this latter point, however, it should be stressed that there are indications that the Cubans would more than welcome a break in this seemingly perpetual trade dependence on the Soviet Union. In 1976, when a thaw in U.S.-Cuban relations was in sight, a high Cuban official in the Ministry of Foreign Trade told a U.S. business group that a desirable distribution of future Cuban trade would be 40 percent with socialist countries, 30 percent with the United States, and 30 percent with other market economies.[119] However, as long as the terms of trade with the West continue to be as dismal as in the past, it would be extremely disadvantageous for Cuba to shift its trade to non-socialist countries.

One weakness inherent in estimating trade dependency in constant prices is that such a relationship (e.g., between exports and the GDP) does not reveal the actual financial dependency that might be the result of deteriorating terms of trade. In the case of Cuba, terms of trade with the West deteriorated rapidly in the latter half of the 1960s, and this fact led to a reorientation of trade toward the socialist countries, especially the USSR, the only country willing and capable of extending long-term credit on easy terms. In the 1960s, the difference between the price paid for sugar by the Soviet Union and the world market price was not very significant (see Table 3.9), and because Cuba needed to import not only food and other basic consumer goods but also investment goods for the industrialization of the country, the balance of trade deficit grew, and the outstanding debt to the Soviet Union increased. In December 1972, the debt with the USSR was renegotiated on very favorable terms for Cuba.[120] The exact amount of the debt has never been revealed, but it has been estimated that the accumulated repayable debt was equivalent to about $3.7 billion by the time it was renegotiated.[121]

According to the 1972 agreement, payments on debts contracted by Cuba as a result of accumulated trade deficits with the USSR were postponed until 1 January 1986, and repayment was to be spread over a period of twenty-five years without interest. Since Cuba has increased its trade deficit with the Soviet Union still further since 1973—in spite of favorable terms of trade—because of massive imports of machinery and other capital goods, it could be assumed that these new credits will also have to be repaid beginning in January 1986, which will coincide with the beginning of the third Five-Year Plan (1986–1990). It has been estimated that outstanding debt to the Soviet Union would reach $7 billion by the end of 1982.[122] Repayment in twenty-five equal installments would mean that Cuba would have to pay $280 million annually, which would amount to less than 10 percent of current exports to the USSR. This is a burden that would not be too heavy to bear were it not for the growing deterioration of Cuba's debt situation with the West.

During the boom years of the first half of the 1970s, Cuba's creditworthiness in international banking circles was apparently increasing and Cuba had relatively easy access to credit in the West on favorable terms. However, since the price of sugar has begun to fall (with the exception of 1980), it has become increasingly difficult for Cuba to meet its repayment obligations in spite of stabilized levels of sugar exports. In this respect, the case of Cuba is, of course, not unique as it seems that renegotiation of external debt has been the rule in the Third World for several years, especially since the worldwide recession that affected most countries in 1981 and 1982. It is thus not strange that Cuba decided to seek renegotiation of its financial obligations with the West in August 1982.

The government explained that external circumstances had made this decision necessary, and Cuba argued that its problems were minor compared to those facing other countries in the hemisphere. A report by the Cuban National Bank in 1982 revealed that Cuba had an outstanding debt of 2.9 billion pesos (U.S. $3.5 billion), of which 1.1 billion pesos, or about one-third of the total, were short-term obligations.[123] The major reasons Cuba found it difficult to meet its obligations, the report stated, were drastically falling sugar prices (from 28 cents per pound in 1980 to 7 cents per pound in August 1982) and soaring interest rates (between 14 and 16 percent in 1982). Because of the latter reason, interest payments alone amounted to $537 million in 1982 compared to $119 million in 1980, but even so, Cuba's debt service ratio compares favorably to that of most Latin American countries. Cuba's debt service in 1980 amounted to 18.7 percent of exports, but the corresponding figure for the rest of Latin America was 24.0 percent,[124] and in 1981, the figure had increased to 28.2 percent in Cuba and to 36.6 percent in the rest of Latin America.[125]

In its plea for renegotiation, Cuba sought to reschedule $1.2 billion that were to fall due before 1985 and requested postponement of repayments for ten years with a three-year grace period. In October 1982, it was reported that Cuba had made substantial progress in renegotiating its debt in spite of U.S. pressure on international banks to stop credit lines to Cuba.[126] In March 1983, news emerged that representatives of thirteen creditor countries had agreed in Paris to reschedule $413 million of Cuba's debt that matured between September 1982 and the end of 1983.[127] The debt is to be repaid by the end of 1990—somewhat tighter terms than the ten-year deadline with a three-year grace period originally requested by the Cubans. A similar agreement was simultaneously reached with respect to a $468 million debt owed by Cuba to commercial banks in the West. As late as December 1983, however, U.S. regulatory authorities tried to block a rescheduling agreement between Cuba and a consortium of 150 Western banks. The pretext used was that the American Express Company had in March 1983 acquired majority control of the Swiss-based Trade Development Bank, and the loan (5 million West German marks) extended by the bank to Cuba in 1978 was thus subject to a U.S. ban on loans to Cuba. In January 1984, however, an agreement was finally signed after notification by the American Express Company that it had sold its Cuban loan to an unidentified, non-U.S. bank on December 30, 1983.[128]

As mentioned earlier, Cuba has been financially more tied to the Soviet Union than to the West. In a certain way, this situation is fortunate for Cuba since the credit terms have been much easier and the USSR has given substantial subsidies to sugar and nickel imported from Cuba as well as to petroleum supplied to the island. Although there are no official figures on the total amounts of these subsidies, one report by the U.S. Congress made an estimate of Soviet economic assistance to Cuba between 1961 and 1979. According to this estimate, the total accumulated Soviet assistance as of 1979 amounted to U.S. $16.7 billion, of which no less than $11.0 billion was in the form of subsidies on commodities traded with the USSR (exports of sugar and nickel and imports of petroleum).[129] According to the report, Cuba had an outstanding repayable debt of $5.7 billion to the Soviet Union in 1979.

The heavy dependence of Cuba on the Soviet Union for economic and financial support of development projects has, however, not necessarily had negative side effects on the economic transformation of the country. Some observers of the Cuban economy have insisted that Cuba's dependence on sugar and trade with the USSR has retarded industrialization in Cuba. As evidence, Mesa-Lago, for instance, takes the apparently increasing share of sugar production in the global social product and the apparently falling share of industry as an indicator of the hegemony of sugar production.[130] The problem again is that Mesa-Lago is mixing two concepts since sugar exports are recorded in current values and industrial output—and thus a large part of GSP—is recorded in constant (1965) prices. If Mesa-Lago's calculations were to be taken at their face value, they would actually mean that commerce has been the most dynamic sector in postrevolutionary Cuba—a rather breathtaking discovery for a frequent visitor to the island. The truth is rather that commerce is the only sector in Cuba's national accounting in which current prices are used. If we relate the value added of the industrial activities to the estimates of the gross domestic product instead, we find that the picture is quite the reverse of Mesa-Lago's conclusion.

The figures in Table 3.10 strongly indicate that there have indeed been profound economic changes in Cuba since the revolution—the changes were rather modest during the first decade, but they then took place at an accelerated pace in the 1970s. Thus, in spite of a stabilized sugar output by the end of the second decade of about 8 million tons of crude sugar, the share of sugar (both agricultural and industrial activities) fell from 14 to 7.9 percent of GDP between 1970 and 1981, and the agricultural contribution to GDP fell from 18.1 to 12.9 percent during the same period. The simple explanation is that there was a vigorous growth of virtually all industrial activities in the 1970s, with the manufacturing industry as a whole growing at a rate of 7 percent per year and the capital goods industry growing at 15.5 percent per year. Most spectacular was the growth of the construction industry, which increased at a rate of 14.2 percent per year during the period.

The rapid growth of the construction and capital goods industries is also reflected in the accelerated rate of capital accumulation. Gross investments increased from an average of 839 million pesos in the 1960s to an average of almost 2,000 million pesos in the 1970s (see Table 3.11), and gross investment as a percentage of GDP increased from an average of 17 percent to an average of 26 percent in the same period. Investment allocated to industrial projects increased from 480 million pesos during 1971–1975 to 1,350 million pesos during the first Five-Year Plan (1976–1980).[131] A number of new industrial plants were built such as cement factories, textile plants, and an integrated plant for the supply of agricultural equipment, including combines for the sugar harvest. Work began on twenty-seven large dams and numerous small ones. Irrigation systems were built for almost 300,000 hectares of land, and more than 1,000 agricultural projects were completed. In addition, millions of pesos were invested to expand roads and to construct 970 new schools and several large hospitals.

Table 3.1. Land tenure in Cuba at the beginning of 1959*

	Area		Farms		Owners	
	Hectares	%	Hectares	%	Hectares	%
Up to 5 caballerías (67 ha)	628,673	7.4	28,735	68.3	20,229	66.1
Between 5 and 30 caballerías (67 and 402 ha)	1,641,440	19.3	9,752	23.2	7,485	24.5
More than 30 caballerías (402 ha)	6,252,163	73.3	3,602	8.5	2,873	9.4
Total	8,522,276	100.0	42,089	100.0	30,587	100.0

* = in accordance with declarations given by the owners

Source: Chonchol (1963), p. 75.

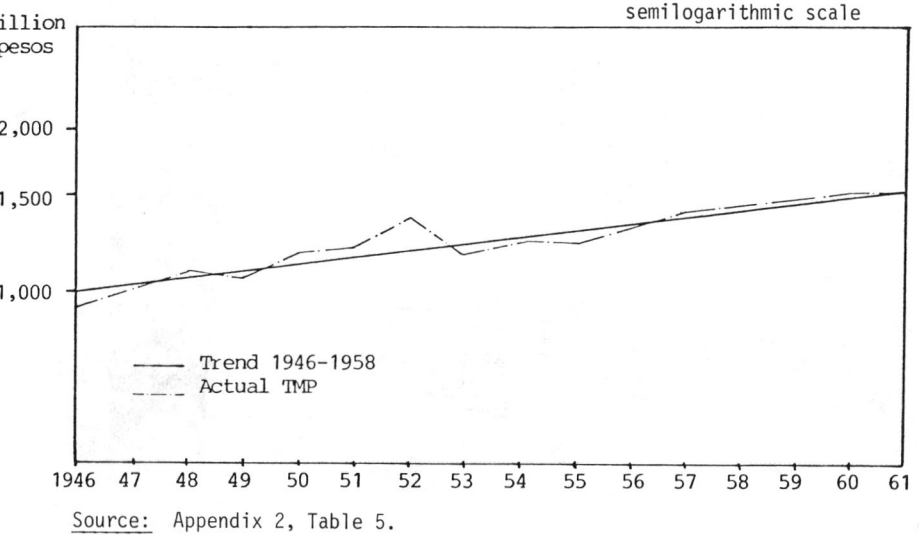

Figure 3.1. Total material production 1946-1961, actual and trend projection (based on 1946-1958 trend)

Source: Appendix 2, Table 5.

Table 3.2. Land expropriations, as of May 1961

	Area in Hectares	%
Agrarian Reform Law	1,199,184	27.0
Recuperation of Ill-Gained Wealth Law	163,214	3.7
Donations to INRA	322,590	7.3
Voluntary sales and Article 24	581,757	13.1
Nationalization Law (No. 851)	1,261,587	28.4
Nationalization Law (No. 890)	910,547	20.5
Total	4,438,879	100.0

Source: Gutelman (1967), p. 57.

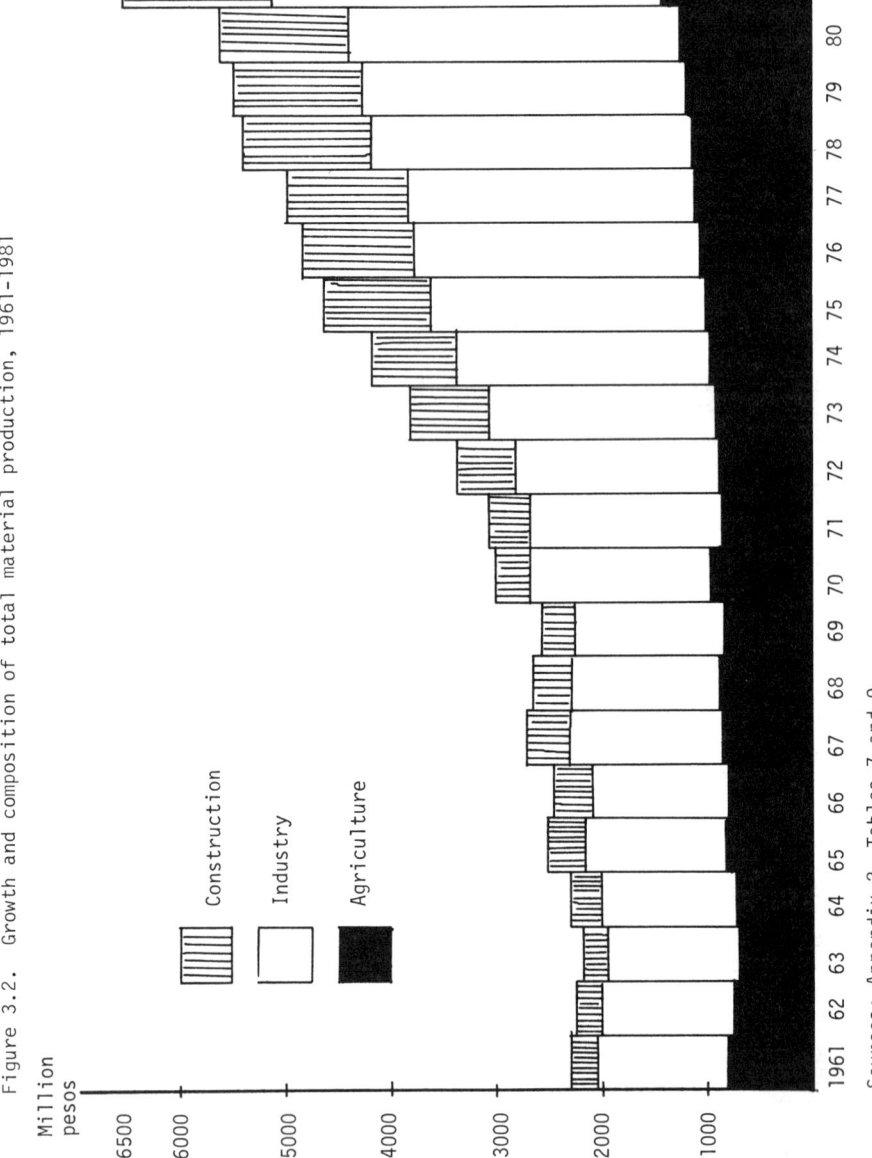

Figure 3.2. Growth and composition of total material production, 1961–1981

Sources: Appendix 2, Tables 7 and 9.

Table 3.3. Collectivization of ownership of means of production and services in Cuba, 1961-1977 (percent)

Sector	1961	1963	1968	1977
Agriculture	37	70	70	79
Industry	85	95	100	100
Construction	80	98	100	100
Transportation	92	95	98	98
Retail trade	52	75	100	100
Wholesale & foreign trade	100	100	100	100
Banking	100	100	100	100
Education	100	100	100	100

Source: Mesa-Lago (1981), Table 1, p. 15.

Table 3.4. Economic performance indicators, 1961-1980

	1961-1965	1966-1970	1971-1975	1976-1980
Annual Growth Rates				
TMP	2.1	3.3	10.0	3.7
Agriculture	-0.2	3.7	3.9	4.3
Construction	9.2	-6.3	21.8	3.8
Industry[1]	1.9	5.2	9.5	3.0
Capital goods[2]	3.7	6.1	11.2	3.6
Consumer goods[2]	0.7	4.4	7.1	2.4
Population	2.3	1.7	1.8	0.7
Civ. employed Labor force	2.4	4.6	2.3	4.3
Productivity TMP[3]	1.4	-1.3	8.2	1.1
Agriculture	2.3	na	3.8	6.3
Industry	-2.8	na	7.5	-2.9
Gross investments	17.2[4]	-1.4	21.0	6.0
Material production	26.8[4]	-1.3	16.9	5.7
Nonmaterial production & services	-5.1[4]	-2.3	38.4	6.8
Average Sugar Prices (US cents/pound)				
Agreement with USSR	5.30	6.11	14.86	39.09
World market	4.35	2.50	14.25	13.15
Cuban Term's of Trade (1970=100)				
With USSR	98.2	98.3	147.5	223.3
With Western countries	170.3	73.1	197.6	148.1

[1] Includes mining and electricity
[2] Definitions explained in note 92
[3] Value added divided by number employed
[4] 1962-1965

Sources: Growth of output based on Appendix 2, Tables 7 and 9; Population and Labor force: Appendix 2, Table 17; Investments: SEV (1979); Sugar prices: Torres (1981), Table 4, and ECLA/CEPAL (1982a), Table 7; Terms of trade: Torres (1981), Table 3, and ECLA/CEPAL (1982a), Table 11.

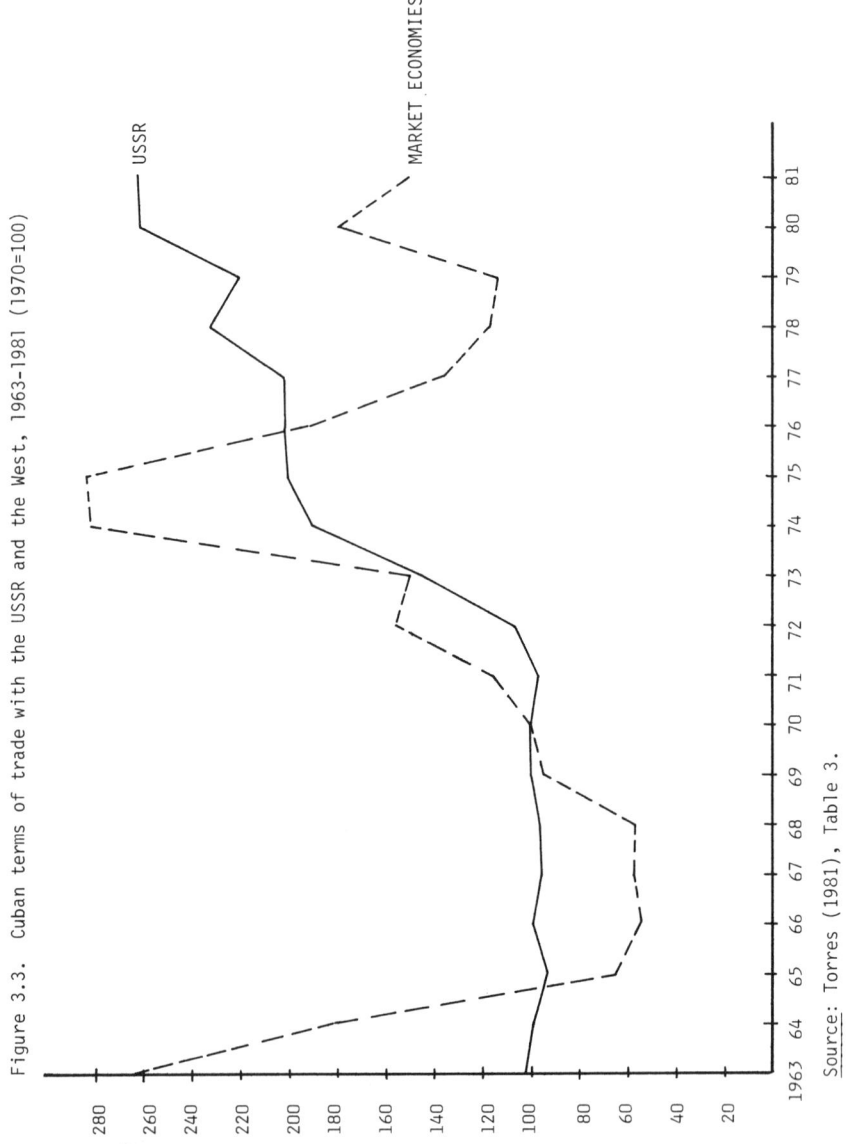

Figure 3.3. Cuban terms of trade with the USSR and the West, 1963-1981 (1970=100)

Source: Torres (1981), Table 3.

Table 3.5. Some characteristics of the Cuban labor force, 1960-1980

	Total Labor Force (000s)	Female Labor Force (000s)	Female Share of Labor Force (%)	Unemployment Rates (%)		
				Total	Male	Female
1960	2,276	300	13.2	11.8	8.8	31.7
1970	2,633	482	18.3	1.3	1.3	1.2
1972	2,787	576	20.7	2.8	2.0	5.7
1974	2,947	688	23.3	3.9	2.2	9.7
1976	3,117	823	26.4	4.8	1.7	13.6
1978	3,339	983	29.4	5.3	2.3	12.5
1980	3,527	1,108	31.4	4.1	2.5	7.8

Sources: Appendix 1, Tables 3, 4, and 5.

Table 3.6. Employment and mechanization in the sugar sector, 1957/1958–1980/1981

Zafra[1]	Total Sugar-Cane Harvest (million tons)	Production of Raw Sugar (96°) (million tons)	Number of Cane Cutters at Peak of Zafra (000s)	Number of Combine Harvesters	Degree of Mechanization (%) Cutting	Degree of Mechanization (%) Loading/Lifting
1957/1958	45.7	5.9	370.0	0	0	0
1963/1964	37.2	4.5	na	+	0	20
1969/1970	79.8	8.5	350.0	172[3]	1	85
1974/1975	50.8	6.3	175.6	1,007	25	94
1975/1976	52.0	6.2	153.3	1,284	32	96
1976/1977	56.1	6.5	139.1	1,577	36	98
1977/1978	67.0	7.4	153.9	2,006	38	99
1978/1979	73.1	8.0	126.4	2,298	42	100
1979/1980	61.6	6.7	110.0	2,450[2]	45	100
1980/1981	66.4	7.4	100.0[2]	2,700[2]	50[2]	100

+ = negligible; na = not available

[1] Zafra usually starts in November or December and ends in April or May
[2] Author's estimate based Latin American Commodities Report cited in sources
[3] Zafra 1970/1971

Sources: AEC (1974) and (1981); Pollitt (1981), pp. 8 and 10; CEE (1981b), Table 67; Latin American Commodities Report, 24 December 1982, p. 3.

Table 3.7. Cuba's trade dependency, 1946-1980

	Exports as % of GNP (current prices)	Exports (current prices) as % of GMP (constant prices)	Exports as % of GMP (constant prices)	Exports as % of GDP (constant prices)
1946	32.0			
1952	28.2			
1958	27.9			
1965		16.7	16.7	13.5
1970		24.9	19.4	15.5
1974		30.0	12.7	9.8
1978		33.8	12.4	9.0
1980			11.1	8.1

Sources: Column 1: Leo Grande (1979); column 2: Leo Grande (1979) and Mesa-Lago (1981); columns 3 and 4: author's calculations.

Table 3.8. Commodity and partner concentration in Cuban exports, 1965-1980 (current and constant prices)

	Sugar Exports as % of Total Exports		Exports to Soviet Union as % of Total Exports	
	Current Pr.	Constant Pr.	Current Pr.	Constant Pr.
1965	88.3	88.3	48.2	35.1
1970	77.3	83.1	50.2	40.4
1974	87.2	73.7	36.4	36.4
1978	88.2	73.5	73.8	48.3
1980	89.2	70.0	57.8	38.8

Sources: BEC (1968) and AEC (1974-1981).

Table 3.9. Sugar exports, sugar prices, and commodity and partner concentration in Cuba's foreign trade, 1959-1982

	Total Exports (m. pesos)	Sugar Exports (%)	Soviet Share of Sugar Exp. Volume	Soviet Share of Sugar Exp. Value	Sugar Price* Paid by USSR	Sugar Price* World Market	Total Imports (m. pesos)	From USSR (%)	Imports Food %	Imports Fuel %	Imports Cap. Goods %
1959	636	77	2	2	2.97	2.97	675	—	27	9	19
1960	608	80	17	17	3.14	3.14	580	14	na	na	na
1961	626	85	40	49	4.09	2.75	639	41	na	na	na
1962	522	83	33	42	4.09	2.83	759	54	na	na	na
1963-1972 average	725	81	35	42	6.11	4.05	1,089	54	23	9	21
1973	1,153	75	35	42	12.02	9.45	1,463	55	24	11	21
1974	2,237	87	36	37	19.64	29.66	2,226	46	25	9	21
1975	2,947	90	56	58	30.40	20.37	3,113	40	19	10	21
1976	2,692	88	53	65	30.95	11.51	3,180	47	17	11	32
1977	2,918	83	61	77	35.73	8.10	3,462	54	16	14	33
1978	3,440	88	54	80	40.78	7.82	3,574	65	17	18	27
1979	3,550	88	53	76	44.00	9.65	3,687	68	15	20	25
1980	3,967	88	44	62	44.00	28.66	4,545	62	15	20	26
1981	na	na	53	76	47.17	16.83	na	na	na	na	na
1982	na	na	63	89	47.17	10.39	na	na	na	na	na

* = U.S. cents per pound; na = not available

Sources: BEC (1968-1971), AEC (1972-1981), Torres (1981), and Banco Nacional de Cuba (1982).

Table 3.10. Structural changes in the Cuban economy, 1961-1981

	Sector Contribution to GDP (%)			Average Annual Rate of Growth		
	1961	1970	1981	1961-1970	1970-1981	1961-1981
Agriculture[1]	18.2	18.1	12.9	1.5	3.6	2.7
Sugarcane	(7.9)	(9.2)	(4.9)	3.2	1.0	2.0
Other	(10.3)	(8.9)	(8.0)	0.0	5.8	3.1
Industry	31.8	38.4	46.4	3.6	8.4	6.2
Manufacturing	(24.4)	(29.7)	(30.7)	3.6	7.0	5.5
Capital goods	(1.6)	(2.5)	(6.6)	6.5	15.5	11.5
Sugar & deriv.	(4.7)	(4.8)	(3.0)	1.8	2.2	2.0
Construction	(5.2)	(5.7)	(13.0)	2.4	14.2	8.9
Total sugar[2]	12.6	14.0	7.9	2.7	1.4	2.0
TMP	50.0	56.5	59.4	2.8	7.1	5.2
GMP	82.2	79.9	73.2	0.2	5.9	3.3
NMS	17.8	20.1	26.8	2.9	9.3	6.4
GDP	100.0	100.0	100.0	1.5	6.7	4.3

[1] Including forestry and fishing
[2] Sugarcane and sugar refining
Sources: Table 2.7 and Appendix 2, Tables 7 and 9.

Table 3.11. Gross investment by economic sector, 1962-1981 (current prices)

	1962 m. pesos	1962 %	1966 m. pesos	1966 %	1970 m. pesos	1970 %	1975 m. pesos	1975 %	1981 m. pesos	1981 %
Productive Sphere										
Agriculture	184	29.4	378	40.4	254	31.7	560	24.3	871	27.2
Forestry					7	0.9	18	0.8	27	0.8
Industry	145	23.1	156	16.7	163	20.4	630	27.3	1,118	34.9
Construction	27	4.3	21	2.2	84	10.5	141	6.1	130	4.0
Transport	59	9.5	134	14.3	142	17.8	357	15.5	422	13.2
Communication					11	1.4	31	1.3	40	1.3
Commerce	28	4.4	30	3.2	25	3.1	42	1.8	84	2.6
Other productive activities							4	0.2	15	0.5
Total	443	70.7	719	76.8	686	85.8	1,783	77.4	2,707	84.4
Nonproductive Sphere										
Communal and personal sectors	84	13.5	90	9.6	61	7.6	170	7.4	252	7.9
Science and technology					5	0.6	18	0.8	17	0.5
Education	51	8.1	41	4.4	20	2.4	238	10.3	101	3.2
Cultural activities					4	0.4	7	0.3	12	0.4
Public health and social activities	13	2.0	11	1.2	13	1.6	47	2.0	68	2.1
Finance, insurance, and administration	35	5.7	74	8.0	3	0.4	40	1.7	44	1.4
Other nonproductive activities					8	1.0	2	0.1	5	0.1
Total	183	29.3	216	23.2	114	14.2	522	22.6	499	15.6
Total gross investments	626	100.0	935	100.0	800	100.0	2,305	100.0	3,206	100.0

Sources: 1962 and 1966: Mesa-Lago (1981), Table 8; 1970, 1975, and 1981: CEE (1982e), Table 48.

4
Basic Needs and Economic Growth

A Yardstick of Basic Needs

It is widely recognized that immediately after the revolution, Cuba strongly emphasized the elimination of poverty through radical measures of income redistribution coupled with impressive efforts to raise the educational and health levels of the population, especially in the rural areas.[1] In the 1960s, it was often assumed that these drastic measures would hamper economic growth because of declining investment ratios at least in the short run.[2] As shown in the preceding chapter and elsewhere, economic growth was rather sluggish during the whole period of the 1960s, but is has also been shown that the growth record during the 1970s was quite impressive. It should then be of interest to compare the Cuban growth performance with its basic needs performance since the revolution.

To make such a comparison, we need some kind of measure, or yardstick, of basic needs. For a rather long time, there have been numerous attempts to define basic needs as well as attempts to measure both the efforts involved in and the results of satisfying such needs. It is argued that some kind of yardstick would facilitate the comparison of basic needs achievements, or nonachievements, in developing countries.[3]

The basic needs approach to development has been summarized in the resolution of the World Employment Conference held in 1976:

> Strategies and national development plans and policies should include explicitly as a priority objective the promotion of employment and the satisfaction of the basic needs of each country's population.... Basic needs include two elements. First, they include certain minimum requirements of a family for private consumption: adequate food, shelter and clothing, as well as certain household equipment and furniture. Second, they include essential services provided by and for the community at large, such as safe drinking water, sanitation, public transport and health, educational and cultural facilities.[4]

Determining how well these basic human needs are being met requires an indicator, or a set of indicators, that can measure both deprivation and advances in the satisfaction of such needs. Norman Hicks and Paul Streeten have identified and reviewed four different approaches to the measurement problem:[5]

adjustments to GNP
social indicators
social accounting system
composite indexes

The work on various adjustments of GNP estimates to incorporate various welfare aspects of development has received well-merited attention ever since the debate on growth versus development started some decades ago. However, the many pitfalls of using GNP measures in intercountry comparisons are widely recognized.[6] Colin Clark was one of the pioneers in attempting to make national accounts comparable, measuring output in international prices, and Beckerman, Gilbert and Kravis, and Kravis et al. have made more recent attempts to compare gross products and purchasing power.[7]

In international agencies—like the United Nations, the Organization for Economic Cooperation and Development (OECD), and the United Nations Educational, Scientific, and Cultural Organization (UNESCO)—a considerable amount of work has been done to collect sets of social indicators in an attempt to define social progress through a series of nonmonetary variables such as expectation of life at birth, calorie consumption, school enrollments, number of hospital beds, and density of physicians. Such indicators can make intercountry comparisons more meaningful since they avoid the valuation problem, but a disadvantage of this approach is the absence of a single, comprehensive indicator that can measure a country's relative success or failure over time and the relation of its performance to that of other countries.

As a sequel to the search for adequate and meaningful social indicators, Hicks and Streeten also mention the incipient research devoted to developing a system of social accounts. For instance, both Stone[8] and Seers[9] have proposed the use of a lifetime activity sequency in which total life expectancy is divided into segments showing the average time various categories of people can be expected to spend in different activities such as school, work, leisure, and retirement. Such a system, however, goes far beyond the data available in most developing countries, and, in the case of revolutionary Cuba, any attempt to apply such a system would no doubt be a frustrating exercise.

Another much discussed effort is Morris D. Morris's physical quality of life index (PQLI),[10] which consists of three simple indicators with equal weights: life expectancy (at age one), infant mortality, and literacy. Two advantages (and perhaps the only two) of selecting only three indicators is that the PQLI can be calculated for a wide range of countries and the comparison of changes over time is facilitated. However, the disadvantages of this index appear to heavily outweigh the advantages, and the method has been criticized for being both oversimplistic and useless.[11]

The PQLI converts the raw data on the three component variables into a scale of 1 to 100, and a simple linear combination is then achieved by simply dividing by three, thus giving equal weight to each component. The result that has been obtained is a handy table of indexes of "life quality" for 150 countries according to which Cuba gets a score of 84; Brazil, 68; Peru, 62; and the United States is indexed at 94 (the optimal index, by definition, is 100).[12]

The question is, How meaningful is such an index? Larson and Wilford go as far as to say that the three input variables are so closely associated and correlated with each other that "accordingly, in order to avoid the weighting problems associated with a composite index, it would be preferable, in the interest of parsimony, to use only one component."[13] Hicks and Streeten also point to the fact that even if the components move in different directions, the meaningfulness of the composite index would be highly doubtful since

> to have the same index for a situation in which mortality is high and literacy low, as for one in which literacy is high and mortality low, implies evaluating the "trade off" between literacy and life expectancy. Unless the basis for such an evaluation can be established, all weighting remains arbitrary and misleading and composition is impossible.[14]

A Composite Basic Needs Index for Cuba

The dilemma with respect to the search for a basic needs yardstick thus seems to be that either the index is based on so many complex components that it turns out to be both unreliable and difficult to interpret or the index is so simplistic (like the PQLI) that one might just as well use any one of the social indicators. In the light of this dismal conclusion, it might seem bold to suggest an alternative basic needs index for Cuba, especially since Hicks and Streeten no doubt are right when they say that "there is no obvious way to combine different social indicators."[15] Nevertheless, I shall here develop a composite index that I shall then use to assess the basic needs performance in Cuba from 1958 to 1980.

As a starting point, I have taken Hicks and Streeten's own recommendation for future work: to define the best indicator(s) for the essential basic needs, which are considered to cover six areas—nutrition, education, health, sanitation, water supply, and housing. With respect to most of these fields, there would not be any insurmountable problem in finding adequate time-series data for Cuba. The problem is to find an acceptable system of weights that will make it possible to combine the core indicators into a composite basic needs index. Hicks and Streeten pessimistically say that "the chances of an acceptable system of weights being developed are extremely small."[16]

In spite of this gloomy prophecy, I have decided to develop a basic needs index based on the revaluation of quantity data in the same way real consumption is sometimes measured as an alternative to the more common practice of deflating nominal consumption expenditures.[17] The main advantage of this approach is that it does not depend on price indicators over time, which, as a general rule, are not easily accessible for developing countries. In this respect, Cuba is no exception. Although price information is extremely hard to find, information in regard to quantity has gradually become more readily available, although there still remain quite a few problems and doubts in the construction of a longer time series (see Chapter 2).

The first steps in developing a basic needs index for Cuba are to find corresponding quantity data for the consumption of basic needs and then to find some adequate relative prices to use as weights. The revaluation of basic needs consumption is approximated simply by using the conventional Laspeyre measure, which is then converted into the index by dividing by the value of the measure in the base year.

In applying this method to Cuba, two problems arise: one, finding an adequate and reasonably reliable time series of quantity data for the basic needs categories and two, finding adequate and meaningful weights, or relative prices. In the following sections, the quantity data for Cuba will be presented and discussed for the following basic needs categories: food and beverages, clothing, housing, education, and health.

Food and Beverages

Meeting the nutritional needs of the population is no doubt one of the most urgent tasks confronting a government that wants to change the state of the poor in the country. As discussed in the preceding chapter, Cuba's leaders had illusions in the early 1960s about the possibilities of solving this problem in the short run. Instead, the situation got gradually worse in the 1960s, partly as a result of limited domestic resources, partly because of obvious errors in the strategy followed, and partly because of the increased isolation of the island. In order to guarantee a minimum ration to all citizens, a rigorous rationing system was introduced in March 1962.

In estimating the availability of food and beverages to the Cubans between 1959 and 1980, I have used quantity data that are mainly based on official data on the distribution of consumer goods to the population in the years 1963–1980.[18] These figures have then been divided by official mid-year population estimates for the respective years. Appendix 2, Table 18, shows per capita consumption of forty basic food products as well as of soft drinks and beer for 1963–1980. These per capita estimates might be somewhat underestimated since, presumably, they do not include the consumption of independent farmers and their families.[19] Another problem is that there are no consistent series for 1958–1962 so as a crude estimate for those years, I have simply applied the production indexes for food and beverages presented in Table 2.2.

In order to arrive at an index of the availability of food and beverages in Cuba, it is necessary to use some kind of relative prices as weights. Since most indexes in Cuba are calculated in 1965 prices, the best method would seem to be to use the official retail prices of that year. I have also been able to consult the official list of retail prices, which although dated 1977, are usually the same as those of 1965.[20] But a problem arises because even if it is true that prices on the rationed quota have not changed, this fact does not mean that the real per capita expenditures on food and beverages are necessarily reflected by these prices. In a market economy, where prices, at least in principle, reflect the relative scarcity of goods, the use of market prices as weights makes sense, but in a system with administered prices, the question is much more complicated. What is the true price of beef or black beans, for instance, if an unknown, but probably substantial, share of the supply of each is sold outside the rationed market at prices that may be five to ten times the official price?[21] And this possibility does not necessarily mean that the goods are being sold on an illegal, or black, market. The policy of Cuba's government since the early 1970s has been to sanction a legal "parallel market" on which excess supplies of goods are sold at prices that better reflect supply and demand. It could be argued that the true price should be a weighted average of the price on the rationed market and the price in the parallel market, but to obtain this weighted average would require detailed information about the relative weights of those markets that is impossible to incorporate in this study, so I have therefore had to use the official prices as weights.

However, there could be a bias when one uses official Cuban prices as weights, so I have also used shadow prices in an alternative index estimate as a check. As shadow prices, I have used Dan Usher's 1961 Canadian prices, which he used for a similar exercise and for more or less the same products. The results of both estimates are detailed in Appendix 2, Tables 20 and 21, and a complete listing of the prices applied is shown in Appendix 2, Table 19. The indexes yield surprisingly similar trends as shown in Figure 4.1.

A closer look at the two indexes, however, reveals some interesting differences between the weights used. Table 4.1 shows the indexes for selected product groups and years, and there are some striking discrepancies, particularly in 1968. These differences occur when products that have relatively high prices also have relatively high growth rates and/or when products with relatively low prices also have relatively slow growth rates. In the long run, however, it seems that these differences tend to diminish.

Both indexes indicate that the per capita availability of food and beverages increased by about 50 percent between 1963 and 1980. (It should then be recalled that 1963 was a very bad year; if a comparison is made with 1958, the increase is 33 percent and 39 percent in Cuban and Canadian prices, respectively.) But increase in consumption is only part of the story. Cuba before the revolution depended heavily on importing many food products. For instance, in the 1940s, 95 percent of the rice consumption was met by imports, and although there was a rapid expansion of domestic rice production in the 1950s, the import share was still 45 percent in 1956.[22] There was a drastic reduction in rice production between 1963 and 1969, and in 1966, almost 80 percent of the consumption had to be covered by imports.[23] Since 1970, there has been a gradual increase in the domestic supply of rice, and the amount of imported rice consumed had declined to 42 percent by the end of the 1970s.[24] Even this figure was a disappointment though, because the target for the first Five-Year Plan (1976–1980) was self-sufficiency in rice by the end of the period.[25]

Clothing

The calculation of an index of clothing follows the same lines as the index of food and beverages; that is, I have used the official retail prices as weights for the most common textiles, apparel, and footwear used in Cuba such as cotton and rayon cloth, shirts, dresses, pants, underwear, and leather shoes. Detailed statistics on the availability of these consumer items for the period 1963–1980 are shown in Appendix 2, Table 24. As in the case of food and beverages, I have also calculated an alternative index based on Usher's Canadian prices—both indexes are depicted in Figure 4.2. The index for 1958 to 1963 is based on the output index for textiles and shoemaking industries presented in Table 2.2 and is thus identical for both estimates. The estimated total per capita expenditures on clothing in both Cuban and Canadian prices are shown in Appendix 2, Tables 22 and 23.

The expenditures measured in Canadian prices are much lower than when they are measured in Cuban prices, which is partly the result of the fact that the consumption of textiles is not included in the estimate using Canadian weights for the simple reason that Usher had no price information on textiles. Since the Cubans, like people in many other developing countries, often make their own clothes, I felt it important to include purchased textiles. However, even if textiles are excluded, per capita expenditures weighted by Cuban prices are much higher than when weighted by Canadian prices, which reflect the much lower relative prices of clothing in Canada (for a price comparison see Appendix 2, Table 19).

The Cuban textile industry was one of the most adversely affected industries after the revolution, as the textile mills had been heavily dependent on imported machinery and raw materials from the United States.[26] In the late 1960s, the Soviet Union agreed to help modernize the textile industry, but the first effects became noticeable only in the mid-1970s. Also in the 1960s, there was a drive to replace synthetic fibers with cotton fibers. Cotton had been produced in Cuba in the nineteenth century but not for most of the current century,[27] and attempts to cultivate cotton since 1959 have apparently not met with any great success.[28]

Housing

Adequate shelter is an essential part of basic needs, but at the same time, it is perhaps the most difficult area to measure in a meaningful and reliable way. First of all, information is often rudimentary, and trustworthy data of the standard of housing are usually available only through censuses held at ten-year intervals or more.

In order to construct a housing index, one needs above all some measure of the housing space per inhabitant—ideally, the number of square meters per capita and average rents per square meter. This information is not available for Cuba, at least to my knowledge, and apparently it was not available to Usher for Canada because he used the number of dwellings per thousand inhabitants subdivided according to the number of rooms, which were "evaluated according to the purchase price of dwellings in 1961 on the assumption that house rents are proportional to house prices."[29]

In order to construct a housing index for Cuba for the period 1958–1978, I have used three sources: *Censo de población y viviendas 1970*, *Censo de población, viviendas y electoral 1953*, and scattered information about annual housing construction between 1958 and 1980. In order to get an estimate of the annual stock of dwellings by number of rooms, I started with the 1970 census, which gives the stock of dwellings in Cuba in September 1970 by number of rooms, and made the following assumptions. First, it was assumed that no houses were demolished, at least not completely, during the period 1958–1980,[30] and second, it was assumed that the distribution of rooms has been the same in each new phase of housing construction. In this way, I was able to draw up the stock estimate shown in Table 4.2.[31]

Of all basic needs, housing is the sector that has had the poorest showing since the revolution, but this fact does not mean that the situation was better before 1959. The 1953 housing census showed that only 43 percent of the population lived in more or less acceptable conditions,[32] and in the five-year period preceding the revolution, construction of dwellings averaged only about 5,000 units annually. Of that construction, between 71 and 83 percent was concentrated in Havana province, and of that percentage, between 60 and 88 percent represented construction of large residences and luxury apartment houses.[33]

The revolutionary government was determined from the outset to ameliorate the housing situation, not only by stepping up construction, but also by decreasing the burden of rent for the population. Rents were cut in half for most people in March 1959, and an Urban Reform Law in October 1960 enabled tenants to become owners of their homes within a five-to-ten-year period.[34] By 1972, three-fourths of all householders in Cuba had become owners of their homes for life.[35]

The government also made a serious effort to rapidly increase housing construction, and an average of 17,000 new dwelling units were built annually during the first five years after the revolution—35 percent of them in the rural areas. But this increase was too slow to keep up with population growth and remedy the accumulated deficits of the past. In 1964, Fidel Castro estimated that there was a housing deficit of 655,000 units, and he later raised the figure to 1 million.[36] This harsh reality was in marked contrast to the gradual slowdown in housing construction, which reached a trough in 1970 when only 4,000 units were built, probably a consequence of the acute shortage of labor that resulted from the *zafra* campaign. In the 1970s, housing construction again increased, but it was still far short of the goal of 100,000 dwellings originally set for 1980.[37] In the second Five-Year Plan, for 1981–1985, the target was lowered to an average of 40,000 dwelling units to be built annually, but even this goal will be hard to reach.[38]

During the first half of the 1970s, the lack of construction workers was considered to be one major bottleneck, and therefore a system of microbrigades was created. The concept of the microbrigade was simple. Workers in any center of production could ask to form a brigade to construct houses in order to meet their own work center's current needs. As a rule, a brigade would consist of thirty persons, on paid leave from their normal jobs, supervised by two or three qualified building workers. In the meantime, it was assumed that production levels would be maintained by those people who remained in the work centers by their doing extra work in the evenings or on weekends. At their peak in 1973, these microbrigades accounted for about 65 percent of all houses built in Cuba,[39] but the idea of relying on microbrigades to solve the housing deficit was later abandoned as being too costly in terms of both material and labor.[40]

In order to construct an index that reflects the per capita availability of shelter in Cuba, and conforms with the expenditure concept used in the preceding sections, we need to arrive at some price per dwelling following the Usher methodology referred to earlier. It would be meaningless to use actual rents paid in Cuba as weights since the large majority of Cubans pay rents that are related to their income or pay no rents at all. Instead, I have used an arbitrary rent per number of rooms based on information from 1958 on construction costs per square meter.[41] The 1970 census gives the distribution of dwellings by number of rooms, and in this way I have estimated the total expenditures on housing in 1970 (see Table 4.3). The total stock of dwellings has been estimated for the period 1958–1980 (see Appendix 2, Table 25), and known per capita housing expenditures in constant Cuban prices have been estimated for the same period (see Appendix 2, Table 26). As an alternative estimate, I have also used Usher's Canadian prices, which not surprisingly are substantially higher than Cuban prices. The index of per capita expenditures on housing is depicted in Figure 4.3.

To understand the housing situation, however, it is important to look at not only the dwelling space per capita, but also to look at the houses' quality and basic facilities. In the housing section of his study on consumption in Canada, Dan Usher has adjusted original quantity data on dwelling expenditures per capita by what might be called quality change.[42] For this purpose, he constructed a quality index based on the percentage of dwellings with running water, flush toilets, and baths or showers. The quality index for Cuba is a somewhat modified version of Usher's index. Instead of access to bath or shower, which is hardly a top priority for basic needs, I have considered the quality factor of electricity.

Quality data do not exist, of course, for each of the years in the 1950–1980 period, but the 1953 and 1970 censuses each have information on housing conditions in both urban and rural areas, and a summary of this information is shown in Table 4.4. We can see that there have been improvements in housing conditions between 1953 and 1970, especially in the rural areas. During the first years after the revolution, the government installed sanitary facilities and cement flooring in more than 100,000 dwellings in the countryside and furnished thousands of dwellings in the poorer urban districts with running water and other facilities.[43]

The quality index is simply the unweighted average (divided by 100) of the three basic facilities considered. In order to get a quality index for each of the years, it has been assumed that all new housing has been equipped with electricity, flush toilets, and running water—a reasonable assumption. An alternative housing index has then been calculated by adjusting the original estimates of housing expenditure per capita for quality change by multiplying these values by the quality index. This alternative index is also shown in Figure 4.3—for full details see Appendix 2, Table 26. The adjustment for quality gives a slightly better picture of housing conditions in Cuba since the revolution. Although the unadjusted index shows a steady deterioration since 1958, the index adjusted for quality change shows a rather stationary trend.

Education

Literacy rates, enrollment ratios, and other educational data are standard factors in evaluations of a particular country's basic needs performance, partly because education is a very important aspect of basic needs, but also because such statistics are usually readily available for developing countries. Cuba is no exception as educational data are considered to be among the most reliable of Cuban statistics.[44]

As educational achievement indicators, I have (in conformity with Usher) chosen enrollment ratios per capita by level of education. I have, however, also considered adult education, partly because of its great importance in general in developing countries, but also because it is a measure of the eradication of illiteracy, which is difficult to evaluate in monetary terms. Enrollment statistics for the period 1958–1980 are shown in Table 4.5.

The next step is to translate these enrollment ratios into expenditure per capita. Usher used costs per student (valued in 1961 dollars and including the amount of earnings lost) as weights, but it is difficult to find similar cost estimates for Cuba. However, a study prepared by the Cuban Ministry of Education in the 1960s reveals there were strikingly similar relative costs by levels of education in Cuba and Canada. A comparison of the two estimates is shown in Table 4.6. In the index using Cuban weights, I have distinguished between basic rural and basic urban secondary education because of the much higher costs involved in building and operating schools in the countryside.

The educational upsurge in the rural areas is perhaps the most spectacular accomplishment in Cuba since the revolution (see Appendix 2, Table 27). Before 1959, there were no secondary schools at all in the countryside, and as late as 1971, secondary rural enrollment amounted to only some 3,000 students. Since the 1970s, however, a continuous effort has gone into the construction of boarding schools in the countryside, which are based on the principle of half-time work and half-time study. By the end of the 1970s, there were 368 such *escuelas en el campo* with more than 200,000 students, accounting for 25 percent of total secondary enrollments.

Although the emphasis during the 1970s was on expanding secondary and higher education, the priority in the 1960s had understandably been to increase primary education and at the same time, to make adults, especially in the rural areas, literate. It has been estimated that the illiteracy rate on the eve of the revolution was about 21 percent.[45] An intensive, and world-famous, literacy campaign was launched in 1961 when some 200,000 Cubans were mobilized under the slogan, Let those who know more teach those who know less,[46] and the Cuban government claimed that the illiteracy rate dropped to 3.9 percent in less than one year—a claim that was later investigated by UNESCO and described as probably unequaled in the world.[47] This figure is probably exaggerated, and it was even questioned at the time by Richard Jolly, an expert in the field.[48] Although the official 1970 census has no tables on educational attainment, it has been reported that that census registered an illiteracy rate of no less than 12.9 percent.[49] One reason for this contradiction could of course be that a new definition of literacy was used; another reason could be that hidden, undiscovered illiteracy was much higher than thought in 1961. At any rate, a national survey in April 1979 showed that the adult illiteracy rate had fallen to 4.0 percent.[50]

An important aspect of the literacy campaign, and perhaps the most important one, is that when the campaign ended, an ambitious program to elevate the educational levels of the people at large was launched and primary and secondary schooling was offered in farms, factories, offices, and night schools.[51] Courses leading toward a third-grade education were made available to more than half a million adults in the mid-1960s, culminating in 848,000 enrolled in 1964. The next phase was the "battle for the sixth grade," the target being that all workers and farmers should attain an educational level corresponding to a completed elementary education (see Figure 4.4). This target was reportedly reached in 1980,[52] and a new battle, the battle for the ninth grade, was launched at the Second Congress of the Communist Party in December 1980.

Figure 4.5 shows the two alternative estimates of per capita expenditures on education, and there is a clear agreement between the two indexes. Both indicate a rapid growth during most of the whole postrevolutionary period but accelerated growth in the 1970s because of the expansion of secondary and higher education, which has resulted in much higher relative weights for each in both indexes.

Health

As indicators of the efforts going into health services, I have, like Usher, used four variables: physicians, dentists, nurses, and hospital beds, all expressed as number per 1,000 inhabitants (see Table 4.7). Translating these indicators into value terms, I have again followed Usher's method of measuring the services of physicians and dentists by their (1961) average gross incomes. Graduate nurses and hospital beds were considered to be "surrogates for all other aspects of medicine including drugs and services of medical equipment."[53] Unfortunately, it is not clear exactly how these surrogates were evaluated as Usher only says that "nurses' services are evaluated . . . at a price substantially higher than the nurse's wage, and the value of the services of hospital beds is measured as the difference between total expenditure on medicine and estimated expenditure on doctors, dentists and nurses."[54] The Canadian prices used by Usher are shown in Table 4.8, together with corresponding weights used when measuring with Cuban prices, which are based on the average annual salary level for physicians, dentists, and nurses in 1968.[55] The price per hospital bed is an attributed value corresponding to the same price ratio between physician/hospital bed applied by Usher.

The two indexes of health expenditures per capita in Figure 4.6 both show similar trends, which is not surprising since the relative weights used are almost identical. The indexes show that Cuba's overall advances in health care are not as spectacular as those in education. It especially seems that there was a very slow advance in the 1960s, which is corroborated by other indicators. For instance, the infant mortality rate, which was 33.4 per 1,000 children below one year of age in 1958, increased to 46.7 per 1,000 by the end of the 1960s, but the rate then fell rapidly to 19.3 per 1,000 in 1979, a record low in Latin America.[56]

During the 1970s, many diseases were completely eradicated in Cuba, including malaria and poliomyelitis, and mortality rates as a result of diseases such as tuberculosis, diphtheria, and intestinal parasitism were sharply reduced.[57] These improvements no doubt were the result of the rapid expansion of medical facilities in the 1970s. (The increase in the number of physicians is particularly remarkable when one considers the fact that it has been estimated that more than half of the active physicians in 1958 have left the country.[58] The success in health services is particularly noticeable in the rural areas. Medical treatment is totally free, and newly graduated doctors have to serve at least two years in a rural area. The administration of health has been centralized, but at the same time, its execution has been very much decentralized. In addition to free medical care, there have been active mobilizations of the population to obtain immunizations, donate blood, clear garbage dumps, and other similar activities—in most cases organized by the numerous Committees for the Defense of the Revolution.[59]

A Composite Index of Basic Needs Performance

The indexes calculated for the five different basic needs categories can be summarized in a composite index of Cuba's basic needs performance. In the case of both indexes, measured in Cuban and Canadian prices, respectively, the composite index is simply the result of the sum of the expenditures in the five categories (see Appendix 2, Table 28). The results of these calculations are shown in Tables 4.9 and 4.10 and are also illustrated in Figure 4.7.

A comparison of the two composite indexes shows that per capita expenditures on basic needs were 60 percent higher in 1980 than in 1958 if measured in Cuban prices, 88 percent higher if Canadian prices are used. The reason for this difference is mainly that food expenditures (which have relatively low weights in Canada) have increased at a lower rate than education and health expenditures (which have relatively higher weights in Canada). This is not a surprising result as the same findings have been drawn in international comparisons of real products and purchasing power. One such report, for instance, states that "the income of one country relative to another will usually appear higher when its quantities are valued in the other country's prices than when valued in its own prices."[60]

The composite indexes clearly show that Cuba's basic needs performance, as measured by per capita expenditures, rapidly improved during the first two or three years after the revolution. After 1962, however, there was a period of relative stagnation and even decline until 1970; then there was a period of sustained growth during the 1970s. This

92   *Basic Needs and Economic Growth*

description also fits the growth trend of total material production (TMP) discussed in Chapters 2 and 3—which one might argue, is logical because food and clothing expenditures are included in both aggregates. However, even if food and clothing are excluded in the composite indexes, there is still a striking resemblance among the growth trends as shown in Table 4.11, especially in the 1970s as the growth rates for that period are almost identical. The interesting deviation from this pattern is the very first period after the revolution when basic needs expenditures increased at a faster rate than TMP, especially if measured in Canadian prices.

The fourth column of Table 4.11 shows a weighted average of the growth trends of the TMP and basic needs indexes. In a way, this average could be used as a substitute for an index of gross domestic product since the former includes both production and services (except for transport, communication, trade, and some of public administration). Such a weighted "total performance index" indicates that per capita growth was sluggish during most of the first decade after the revolution, there was an exceptionally high level of growth during the first half of the second decade, and the growth rate fell to about 3 percent during the latter half of that decade.

Figure 4.1. Index of per capita expenditures on food and beverages, 1958-1980 (1963=100)

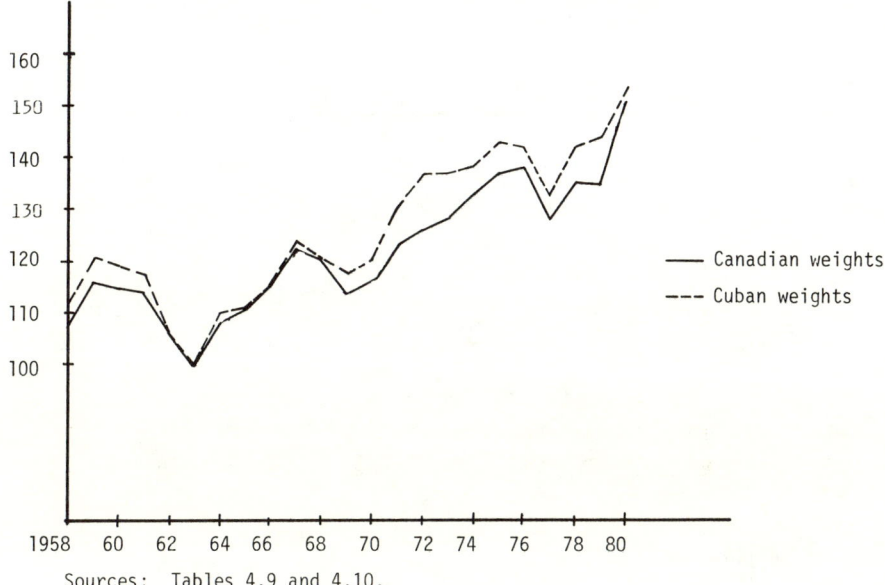

Sources: Tables 4.9 and 4.10.

Table 4.1. Indexes of consumption of food and beverages, Cuban and Canadian weights (1963=100)

	1968	1975	1980
Meat products			
Cuban weights	120.1	113.6	138.9
Canadian weights	106.0	115.8	141.3
Oils & fats			
Cuban weights	102.4	123.6	141.9
Canadian weights	117.9	125.5	133.4
Cereals			
Cuban weights	144.3	174.3	177.2
Canadian weights	147.9	179.6	179.6
Milk products			
Cuban weights	178.7	263.4	293.3
Canadian weights	165.1	246.4	273.8
Beverages			
Cuban weights	98.1	132.5	131.4
Canadian weights	88.2	99.8	104.3
Total food & beverages			
Cuban weights	120.4	142.5	154.1
Canadian weights	120.2	137.2	150.7

Sources: Appendix 2, Tables 20 and 21.

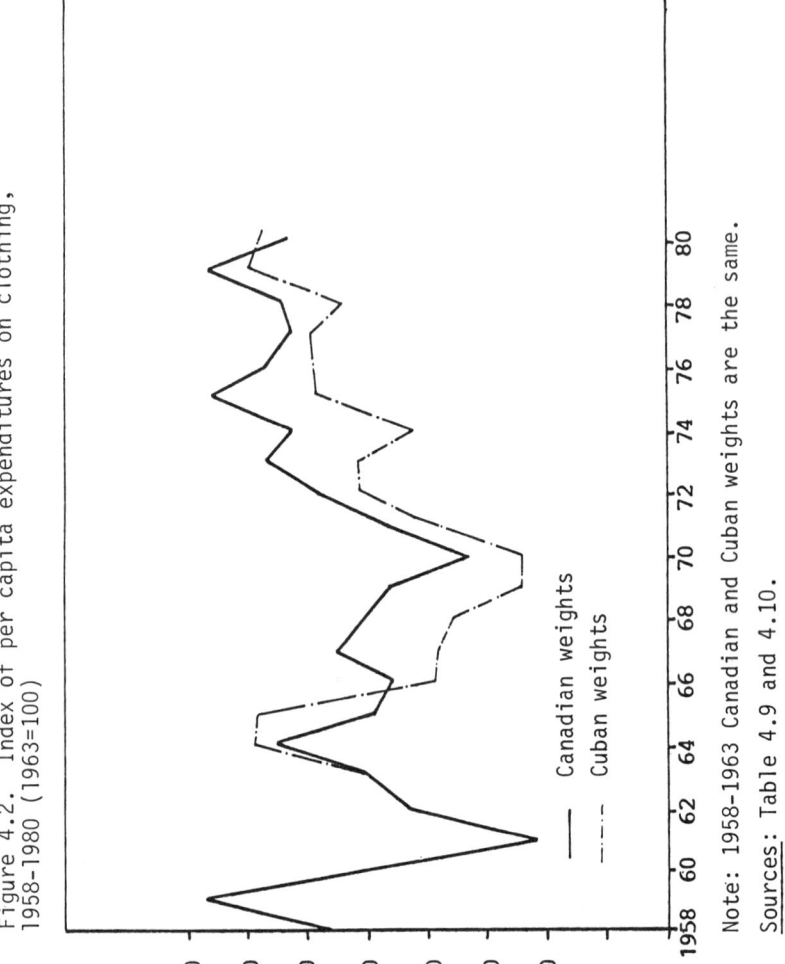

Figure 4.2. Index of per capita expenditures on clothing, 1958-1980 (1963=100)

Note: 1958-1963 Canadian and Cuban weights are the same.

Sources: Table 4.9 and 4.10.

Table 4.2. Annual construction and estimated stock of dwellings, 1958-1980

	Annual Construction (units)	Estimated Stock (000 units)
1958	4,961	1,763.7
1959		1,771.7
1960		1,799.9
1961	85,447	1,821.3
1962		1,837.6
1963		1,849.1
1964	7,129	1,856.2
1965	5,065	1,861.3
1966	6,271	1,867.6
1967	10,257	1,877.8
1968	6,458	1,884.3
1969	4,817	1,889.1
1970	4,004	1,893.1
1971	5,014	1,898.1
1972	16,807	1,914.9
1973	20,710	1,935.6
1974	18,552	1,954.2
1975	18,602	1,972.8
1976	15,342	1,988.1
1977	20,024	2,008.1
1978	17,012	2,025.2
1979	14,201	2,039.4
1980	14,800	2,054.2

Sources: CERP (1965), p. 435; BEC (1968, 1970, 1971); AEC (1974, 1979); BEM (March 1981).

Table 4.3. Number of dwellings and shadow rents paid by number of rooms, 1970

Number of rooms	Number of Dwellings		Total Shadow Rents	
	Units	%	Cuban Prices (000 pesos)	Canadian Prices (000 dollars)
1	185,784	9.8	30,097	40,501
2	280,160	14.8	75,643	145,683
3	395,415	20.9	149,467	326,217
4	447,511	23.6	211,490	514,817
5	353,285	18.7	209,851	524,664
6	146,842	7.8	103,083	258,692
7	51,897	2.7	42,037	96,970
8	19,507	1.0	17,907	41,062
9	7,117	0.4	7,302	14,981
10 or more	5,570	0.3	6,316	14,811
Total	1,893,088	100.0	853,193	1,978,398
Expenditure/capita			100.48	231.81

Sources: Censo de población y viviendas 1970 (1975), Table 26; Cuban Prices: CERP (1965), p. 433; Canadian Prices: Usher (1980), Table 10.2(c).

Figure 4.3. Index of per capita expenditures on housing, 1958-1980 (1963=100)

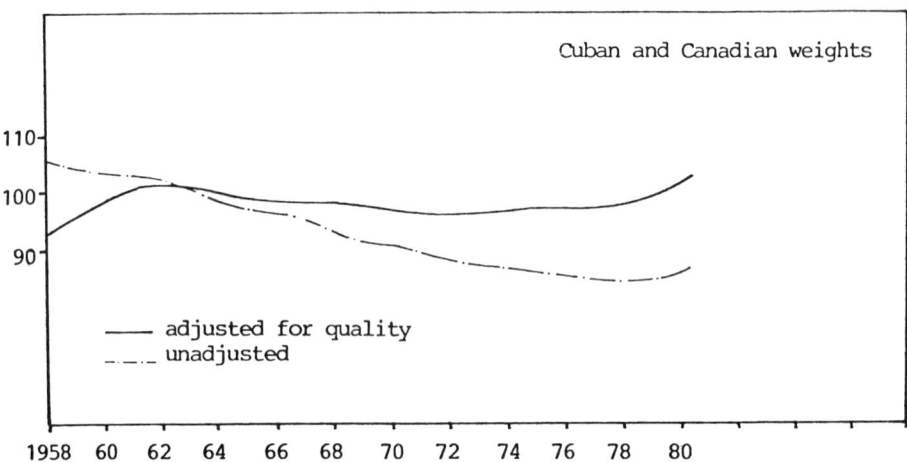

Source: Appendix 2, Table 26.

Table 4.4. Dwellings with basic facilities, urban and rural, 1953 and 1970 (percent)

	Electricity		Flush Toilet		Piped Water	
	1953	1970	1953	1970	1953	1970
Urban areas	87.0	98.1	42.8	53.4	54.6	64.2
Rural areas	9.1	19.6	3.1	5.6	2.3	11.0
Cuba average	58.2	70.7	28.0	36.7	35.2	45.7

Sources: Censo de población, viviendas y electoral, 1953 (1953), quoted in Seers et al. (1964), p. 96; Censo de población y viviendas 1970 (1975), Tables 28, 30, and 32.

Table 4.5. Basic needs indicators, education, 1958-1980 (students as % of population)

	Primary	Secondary	Higher	Adult	Total
1958	10.61	1.30	0.38	0.10	12.39
1959	15.83	1.31	0.28	1.06	18.48
1960	16.17	1.75	0.28	0.95	19.15
1961	16.36	2.12	0.25	6.12	24.84
1962	16.78	2.30	0.24	6.84	26.16
1963	17.75	2.72	0.28	6.52	27.26
1964	18.01	2.58	0.35	11.14	32.07
1965	17.06	2.60	0.34	7.45	27.44
1966	17.12	2.94	0.35	5.65	26.07
1967	17.17	2.88	0.36	6.14	26.55
1968	17.70	3.03	0.39	5.04	26.16
1969	18.50	3.04	0.41	4.28	26.23
1970	19.47	2.78	0.41	4.27	26.93
1971	20.24	3.25	0.42	4.07	27.99
1972	20.91	3.66	0.55	4.87	29.99
1973	21.02	4.38	0.62	4.92	30.93
1974	20.92	5.66	0.75	4.48	31.81
1975	20.59	6.74	0.91	6.36	34.60
1976	20.05	8.51	1.13	7.40	37.10
1977	19.23	10.04	1.28	6.31	36.86
1978	18.17	11.08	1.37	5.17	35.79
1979	17.13	11.78	1.50	4.01	34.42
1980	16.36	12.00	1.56	2.85	32.76

Sources: Table 2.7 and Appendix 2, Table 27.

Table 4.6. A comparison of average costs per student by type of education in Cuba and Canada, 1961

	Canada		Cuba	
	(Can.$)	Index	(pesos)	Index
Primary	300	100	54	100
Secondary	1,600	533	222*	411*
basic urban			139	257
basic rural			1,353	2,506
Higher education				
technical schools	3,600	1,200	748	1,385
Adult education				
(part-time)	(300)**	(100)**	58	107

* = 1962; ** = Usher has no estimate for adult education. The $300 figure used in my estimate of expenditures on adult education assumes that the cost per student is approximately the same as in primary education.

Sources: Canadian estimates: Usher (1980), Table 10.2; Cuban figures: Seers et al. (1964), p. 275.

Figure 4.4. The Cuban educational system

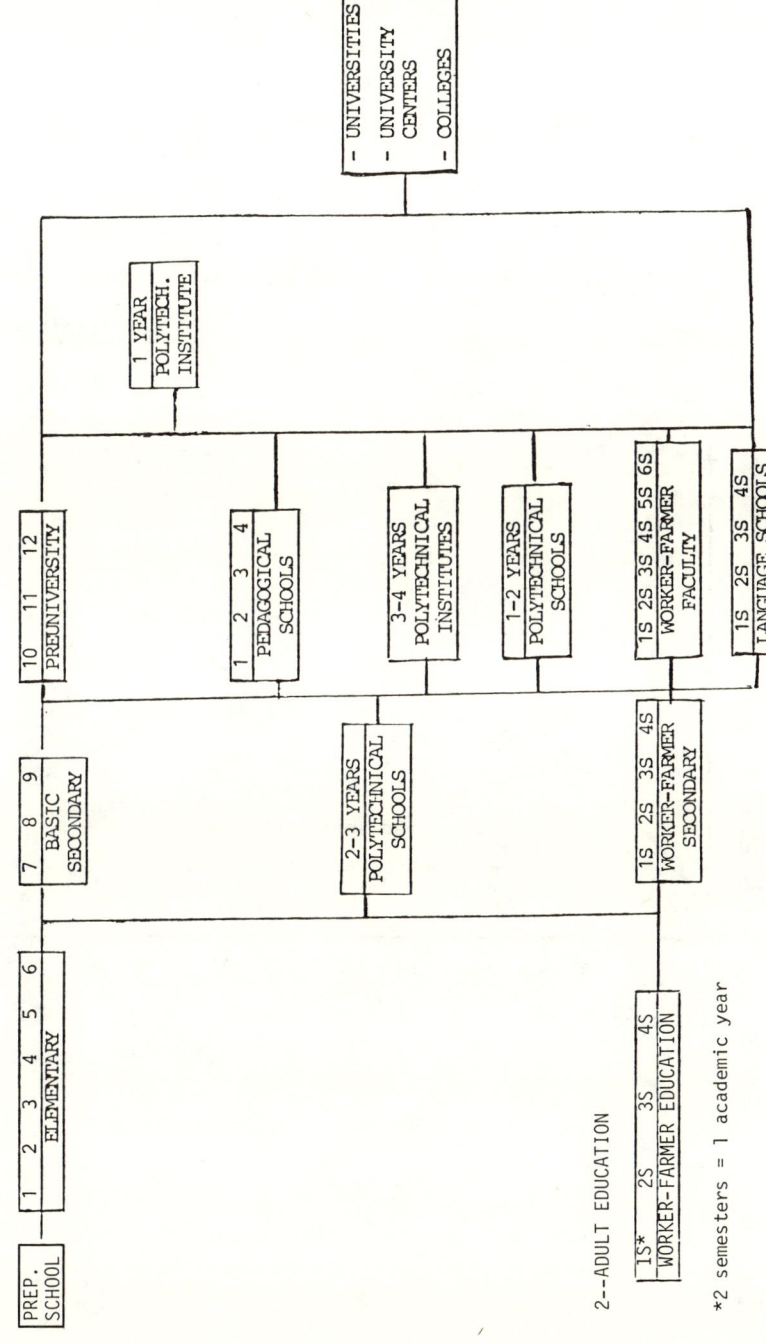

Source: Ministerio de Educación (1980).

Figure 4.5. Index of per capita expenditures on education, 1958-1980 (1963=100)

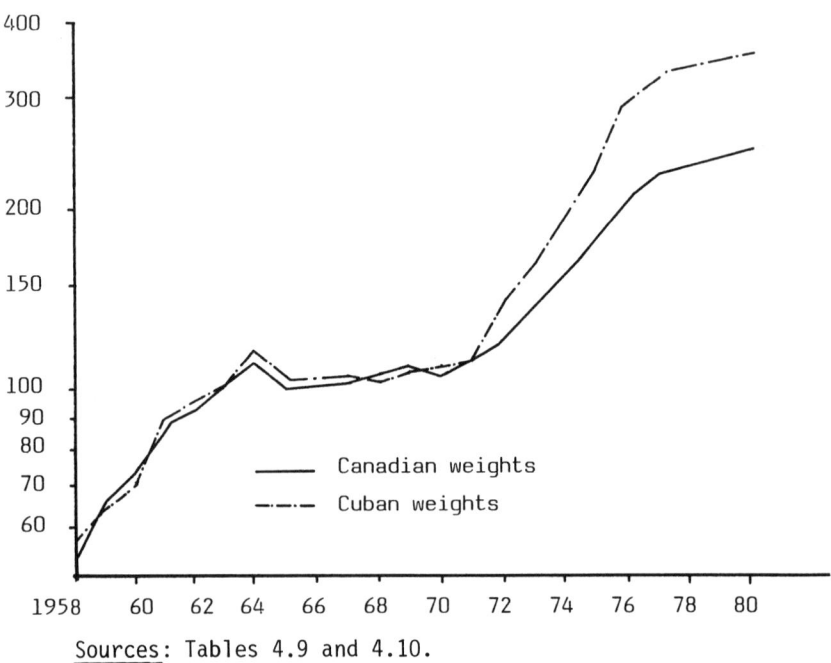

Sources: Tables 4.9 and 4.10.

Table 4.7. Basic needs indicators, health, 1958-1980

	Physicians		Dentists		Nurses		Hospital Beds	
	Number	Per 1,000 Inhabitants	Number	Per 1,000 Inhabitants	Number	Per 1,000 Inhabitants	Number	Per 1,000 Inhabitants
1958	6,257	0.93	2,100	0.31	5,000*	0.74	28,536	4.22
1959	6,943*	1.01	2,129*	0.31	5,431*	0.79	30,522	4.42
1960	6,773*	0.96	1,738*	0.25	5,862*	0.83	32,508	4.63
1961	6,330*	0.89	1,182*	0.17	6,293*	0.88	34,494	4.84
1962	6,570*	0.91	1,054*	0.15	6,724*	0.93	36,487	5.03
1963	6,743	0.91	978	0.13	7,156	0.97	36,479	4.92
1964	6,655	0.87	1,070	0.14	8,347	1.10	37,523	4.93
1965	6,238	0.80	1,200	0.15	9,637	1.23	38,696	4.95
1966	7,036	0.88	1,121	0.14	10,253	1.28	39,708	4.97
1967	6,608	0.81	1,081	0.13	12,459	1.53	40,816	5.01
1968	6,000	0.72	1,100	0.13	13,000	1.57	41,027	4.95
1969	6,028	0.72	1,248	0.15	14,372	1.71	41,706	4.95
1970	6,152	0.72	1,366	0.16	11,803	1.38	40,101	4.69
1971	6,204	0.71	1,149	0.13	13,155	1.51	40,321	4.64
1972	6,549	0.74	1,346	0.15	13,871	1.57	40,313	4.55
1973	7,043	0.78	1,746	0.19	17,210	1.90	41,019	4.54
1974	8,190	0.89	2,029	0.22	19,131	2.08	44,379	4.83
1975	9,328	1.00	2,319	0.25	21,193	2.27	42,712	4.58
1976	10,671	1.13	2,425	0.26	23,725	2.51	42,940	4.53
1977	13,908	1.45	3,130	0.33	24,891	2.60	42,519	4.43
1978	14,388	1.48	3,356	0.35	26,249	2.71	42,988	4.43
1979	15,038	1.54	3,549	0.36	26,457	2.71	43,883	4.49
1980	15,247	1.57	3,646	0.37	27,193	2.79	44,339	4.56

* = estimates based on information on the emigration of doctors during the first year after the revolution and the graduation of medical students in the same period

Sources: Table 2.7; BEC (1968, 1970, 1971); AEC (1974, 1979, 1981); Leyva (1972); Martínez Junco (1968); Ministerio de Salud (1980).

Table 4.8. Estimated unit costs in health services, Canadian and Cuban prices

	Canadian Prices (1961 dollars)	Cuban Prices (1968 pesos)
Physicians	26,000	3,300
Dentists	24,000	3,300
Nurses	25,000	2,400
Hospital beds	3,590	455

Sources: Canadian Prices: Usher (1980), Table 10.2 (f); Cuban Prices: information supplied by the Cuban Embassy in Stockholm (except for hospital beds).

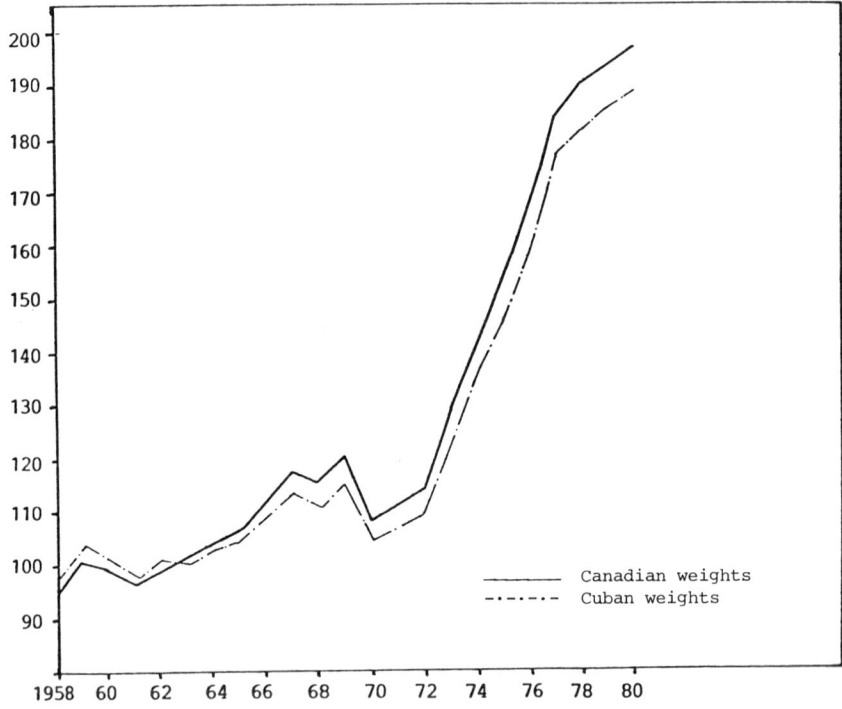

Figure 4.6. Index of per capita expenditures on health services, 1958-1980 (1963=100)

Sources: Tables 4.9 and 4.10.

Table 4.9. Composite basic needs index for Cuba, 1958-1980
(Cuban weights) (1963=100)

	Food & Beverages	Clothing	Housing	Education	Health	Total
1958	112.1	105.2	93.2	56.7	97.4	101.4
1959	120.8	126.7	94.7	64.1	103.3	111.3
1960	119.0	100.4	98.3	69.1	101.3	105.9
1961	117.3	72.0	99.9	89.6	97.6	101.1
1962	105.7	93.1	100.2	94.5	100.3	100.8
1963	100.0	100.0	100.0	100.0	100.0	100.0
1964	110.0	117.7	99.1	116.2	102.6	111.8
1965	110.8	117.8	98.3	103.6	104.3	110.9
1966	114.3	87.9	98.2	101.9	108.6	106.3
1967	124.0	88.0	97.9	103.4	113.1	111.3
1968	120.4	85.5	97.7	102.0	110.4	108.7
1969	117.3	74.3	97.5	102.8	115.4	105.2
1970	120.2	73.7	96.9	104.2	104.5	105.8
1971	130.0	88.6	96.1	110.1	106.3	114.3
1972	136.5	101.2	95.8	137.2	109.8	123.0
1973	136.4	101.2	96.0	159.8	122.9	126.0
1974	138.2	91.9	96.1	191.7	135.8	128.8
1975	142.5	108.1	96.3	230.9	145.8	138.9
1976	141.8	108.9	96.3	299.6	158.4	146.3
1977	132.4	108.9	97.0	325.8	176.8	145.6
1978	142.0	103.4	97.3	337.2	182.0	150.5
1979	144.3	119.6	98.3	349.6	185.1	156.7
1980	154.1	117.4	100.4	350.8	189.3	161.7

Source: Appendix 2, Table 28.

Table 4.10. Composite basic needs index for Cuba, 1958-1980
(Canadian weights) (1963=100)

	Food & Beverages	Clothing	Housing	Education	Health	Total
1958	108.3	105.2	93.2	52.7	95.6	88.6
1959	115.7	126.7	94.6	64.7	101.4	96.0
1960	114.7	100.4	98.2	70.9	100.4	97.0
1961	113.8	72.0	99.8	87.3	97.5	99.9
1962	105.6	93.1	100.1	92.1	100.0	99.6
1963	100.0	100.0	100.0	100.0	100.0	100.0
1964	108.4	113.9	99.0	111.8	104.5	106.6
1965	110.1	98.6	98.2	100.9	107.2	104.0
1966	114.9	95.3	98.2	101.3	111.8	106.2
1967	122.3	105.2	97.9	102.1	118.2	110.0
1968	120.2	101.0	97.7	103.5	115.9	109.2
1969	113.4	95.9	97.5	104.3	121.2	107.6
1970	115.3	82.2	96.9	103.3	108.4	105.6
1971	122.7	96.0	96.0	110.9	111.8	110.7
1972	125.5	107.8	95.7	123.3	115.2	115.6
1973	127.2	116.3	95.8	134.8	130.3	121.4
1974	133.0	111.6	96.0	153.5	142.3	129.6
1975	137.2	125.8	96.2	175.3	154.3	138.8
1976	138.1	116.9	96.2	205.3	167.8	148.2
1977	127.8	113.1	96.8	225.8	185.7	152.5
1978	134.9	114.4	97.1	230.9	191.6	157.1
1979	134.8	126.9	97.9	242.2	194.5	161.0
1980	150.7	112.7	100.2	242.4	198.3	166.8

Source: Appendix 2, Table 28.

104 *Basic Needs and Economic Growth*

Figure 4.7. Composite basic needs performance indexes, 1958-1980.

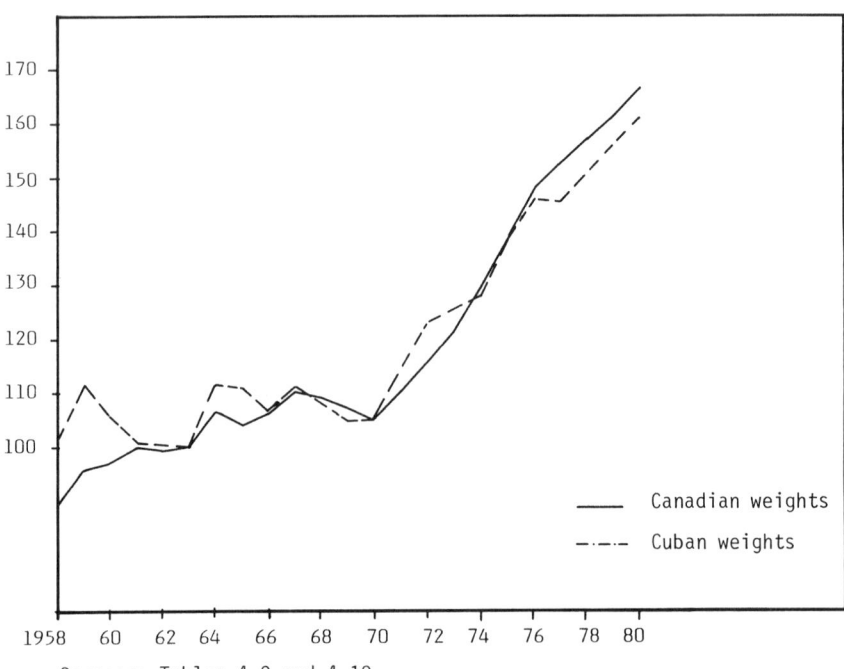

Sources: Tables 4.9 and 4.10.

Table 4.11. Comparison of per capita growth rates of TMP and basic needs, 1958-1980

		Annual Average Rates of Growth		
		Basic Needs (Excl. Food & Clothing)		Combined Index
	TMP/Capita (Cuban weights)	(Cuban weights)	(Canadian weights)	(Cuban weights)
1958-1961	0.8	5.0	6.3	1.7
1961-1965	-0.2	1.6	2.3	0.2
1966-1970	1.6	-0.1	0.0	1.2
1971-1975	8.2	9.1	7.2	8.5
1976-1980	2.9	3.1	3.3	3.0

Sources: Appendix 2, Tables 5, 7, 9, and 28.

5
Distribution of Income and Consumption

Income Distribution Before 1959

Two important aspects of a basic-needs-oriented strategy are the distribution of income and the distribution of consumption. Although there are no official figures to support the claim that a radical redistribution of income and assets has taken place in Cuba since the revolution, few observers of contemporary Cuba seem to doubt the claim. As a matter of fact, Dudley Seers considers that "the degree of equality in Cuba is now probably unique,"[1] and Robert Bernardo even argues that Cuba "is the first [country] to institutionalize the communist or egalitarian rule of production and distribution."[2] Although those claims may be somewhat exaggerated, they reflect the large number of redistributive reforms and laws enacted immediately after the revolution. However, before discussing the effects of those reforms, it is of interest to get at least some idea of the income situation in Cuba before 1959.

There are no official estimates of the distribution of income and assets in prerevolutionary Cuba, nor do I know of any unofficial estimates. What is evident, however, is that the distribution was very skewed, although not necessarily more skewed than in the rest of Latin America. Arthur MacEwan, for instance, derived a crude estimate of Cuba's prerevolutionary income distribution by simply taking the average quintile distribution for Mexico, Argentina, and Puerto Rico.[3] I have tried to estimate the income distribution around 1953 by beginning with the census of that year (which gives a detailed breakdown of the economically active population by branch and occupation)[4] and then ascribing an estimated annual income to each occupational and branch group by using a wage and salary survey done in Cuba in 1955[5] and scattered information for other income groups gathered from a number of books and publications. The result of this exercise is shown, together with MacEwan's hypothetical estimate, in Table 5.1.

The estimated income distribution in 1953 is a slightly modified version of an earlier estimate made by me[6]—the major difference is that here I have incorporated more information for the lower quintile and the upper decile groups which were very crudely estimated in the earlier version.[7] For the lowest quintile, I had originally assumed that the people who had declared that they were looking for work when the census was taken (1953) did not receive any income during that year, but that assumption now does not seem correct. Therefore, I have now assumed that those people, including those who were employed but without work when the survey was taken (see Table 5.2), earned 100 pesos, or roughly one-fifth the minimum wage. The only labor force now assigned zero income is made up of those people who were working without pay for a relative.

The annual income estimate for the lowest quintile may seem rather arbitrary, but it is based on the evidence that 8.8 percent of the labor force was working less than nineteen weeks per year and no less than 16.6 percent was working less than half the year.[8] The amount of unemployment and underemployment was thus conspicuous in prerevolutionary Cuba, and probably the situation was even worse than the figures in Table 5.2 indicate since the census was taken in January when the sugar crop was under way.[9] The income share of the lowest quintile is an overestimate rather than an underestimate if one considers the fact that the average annual income of agricultural workers in 1957 was only 92 pesos according to a survey done by the Catholic university in Havana.[10] In another study, Jacques Chonchol has estimated that one-third of the populace received roughly 5 percent of the income in 1953, a figure that coincides very closely with my own estimate.[11] In regards to the upper decile, my earlier estimate was based on a much too conservative assumption of average income in the higher income brackets. There are reports, for instance, that claim that the annual income of the big landowners was about 40,000 pesos on the average.[12] The figure in the upper percentile has thus been adjusted upwards, which slightly affects the total distribution of income. The skewness of the distribution, as measured by the Gini coefficient, remains almost the same, however—0.55 as compared with 0.56 in the earlier estimate.

Income Distribution in the 1960s

Raising the living standards of the rural proletariat was one of the first priorities of the revolutionary government after it came into power in January 1959. The Agrarian Reform Law was, of course, important, but almost immediately, the government also raised the living standard of some 350,000 *braceros* by offering them stable jobs and by almost doubling their annual income.[13] It has been estimated that total money wages rose from about 550 million pesos during the first nine months of 1958 to over 1 billion pesos during the corresponding period in 1961,[14] an increase that corresponds to about 20 percent of the average national income in 1959 and 1960.[15]

René Dumont reported that wages in the rural areas increased by about 20 percent during the first two years, and he warned that this "dangerous generosity" on the part of the Cuban revolutionary government would be bound to create an inflationary situation unless production increased at the same rate.[16] In retrospect, it seems that the Cuban leaders also had second thoughts about this very drastic increase in the purchasing power of the poorer classes or, as Che Guevara said in July 1963, "as regards income distribution, we gave from the first moment emphasis to satisfying social needs, paying more equal wages and salaries and increasing employment without sufficiently taking the state of our economy into consideration."[17]

But more than the rise in wages and salaries led to the rapid increase in purchasing power of the last bottom half of the income earners. According to one study, various decrees and measures in 1959 resulted in an increase in purchasing power of 382.5 million pesos in that year alone, of which 150 million pesos were the result of wage increases, 80 million were due to the reduction in rents, 100 million came from the general suppression of gambling (which had been an important activity in prerevolutionary Cuba), 15 million were due to lower prices for medicine, and another 15 million pesos were the result of a reduction in electricity rates.[18]

The problem in estimating the income redistribution that took place during the first redistributive phase after the revolution is that there are no official figures for income distribution in Cuba so that in trying to estimate this distribution, I have had to resort to average annual income figures by sector that were published after 1962.[19] Table 5.3 gives an estimate of the income distribution in Cuba in 1962. This year was chosen because it is the only year in the 1960s for which there are figures for the private sector—which was still important at that time, accounting for about 40 percent of the civilian labor force.[20] The state sector data are from official Cuban statistical sources, the wage data for the private sector are taken from an unofficial 1963 estimate by Juceplan,[21] and the corresponding private sector employment estimates are taken from a 1966 official Cuban publication.[22] All the data, however, refer to 1962.

In estimating the distribution of income, the following method was adopted: The number of people employed in each sector was divided into quartiles, and then an average income was calculated for each quartile and for each sector on the assumption that there was a normal distribution within each sector with a range of income from four to one. This assumption is arbitrary, and other studies claim that a span of three to one covered the great majority of the wage and salary rates.[23] However, this wage differential was only beginning to be introduced during 1962 and 1963—along lines similar to those practiced in the Soviet Union and China[24]—so it is doubtful that the effects of the new wage scales had been fully applied by 1962. For this reason, it has been assumed that the wage span was somewhat larger in that year.

The resulting distribution in Table 5.3 indicates that there was a massive redistribution of income immediately after the revolution, and it is estimated that the lowest 40 percent of the income earners increased their share from 6.5 percent before the revolution to 17.2 percent by 1962. There can be no doubt that the rural proletariat was the major group to benefit from the new regime. Surveys conducted between 1958 and 1961 show that the number of rural workers earning more than 75 pesos a month increased from 28.8 percent in April 1958 to 34.2 percent in April 1959 to 44.2 percent in the same month in 1960.[25] A labor census of April 1960 shows that 49 percent of the people interviewed earned less than 81 pesos per month; 16.7 percent earned between 81 and 101 pesos; 6.7 percent, between 101 and 121 pesos; 11.2 percent, between 121 and 151 pesos; 15.4 percent, between 151 and 500 pesos; and only 0.7 percent earned over 500 pesos per month.[26]

It should be pointed out that the figures in Table 5.3 refer to the distribution before taxes. If taxes were deducted, the distribution would be even more egalitarian since many tax laws were passed during the first years of the revolutionary government. The Tax Reform Law of July 1959 mainly affected the consumption of the higher income people as it substantially increased the taxes on luxury goods and services while leaving the income tax, a flat 3 percent tax, remarkably low. Only in August 1960 was a progressive income tax introduced for the first time in Cuba, and it exempted only those people who earned less than 200 pesos per month.[27]

O'Connor has established that between 1958 and 1961, income redistribution and employment creation resulted in an increase in real income on the order of 30 to 40 percent for perhaps 80 percent of the Cuban labor force.[28] This claim also seems to be partially substantiated by the figures in Table 5.4, which show the income total and average income for each decile group in 1953 and 1962. This estimate indicates that at least 60 percent of the labor force benefited from the reforms and that the real average wage for the bottom 40 percent more than doubled. The figures also imply that about 300 million pesos (or about 15 percent of the total income) were redistributed from the upper quintile to the lower three quintiles, which, incidentally, agrees with an estimate made by Felipe Pazos.[29]

MacEwan has also made some crude estimates of the distribution of family income in 1962 (see the third and fourth columns of Table 5.3)—actually two estimates based on different assumptions. As can be seen, there is a rather close agreement between his lower estimate (fourth column) and my own, although he may have somewhat overestimated the share accruing to the bottom quintiles.

Income Distribution in the 1970s

In the period 1962–1973, there was no doubt a drive toward narrowing income differentials, especially after the victory of moral over material incentives was proclaimed at the Twelfth Workers' Congress in 1966, but this is not the same as saying that existing wage scales actually changed. In fact, the same wage scales that were introduced in 1962-1963 were still being applied at the end of the 1970s, and they were not replaced until July 1980 (see Table 5.5). Egalitarianism in the 1960s was advanced instead through the elimination of bonuses, the renouncement of overtime pay, and voluntary, unpaid mobilization campaigns.[30] How much these actions really meant in egalitarian terms is difficult to evaluate, but an estimate of income distribution in 1973 (the year of the Thirteenth Workers' Congress when material incentives were reinstated), based on the same methods as the 1962 estimate except for the exclusion of the private sector,[31] shows that a rather insignificant redistribution took place, at least in relation to the 1959–1961 period (see Table 5.6). The major group to benefit in the later period was again the agricultural workers as their average annual income (in the state sector) increased from 954 pesos in 1962 to 1,416 in 1973, compared to a decrease in the industrial average from 1,941 to 1,603 pesos during the same period.[32] One explanation could be that agricultural workers were promoted to higher grades on the applicable wage scale at the same time as new industrial workers were being placed in lower grades.

Looking at the trend during the latter half of the 1970s, one would perhaps expect a regressive redistribution of income as a result of the new policy of encouraging productivity increases through material incentives. However, an estimate of the income distribution in 1978 (based on the same method as before but including the private sector) shows that the income differentials remained almost the same as in 1973, although they increased slightly for the bottom decile, but the assumption of a constant four-to-one wage span in each of the sectors over time is probably unrealistic. Since the wage scales did not change between 1963 and 1979, it would seem that the only redistribution that took

110   *Distribution of Income and Consumption*

place in this period was as a result of movements of workers up or down the existing wage scale (and in most cases up, one has to assume).

I thus decided to make an alternative estimate for 1978 based on the distribution of the state civilian labor force affected by the various wage scales (information not available for 1973). I then applied a hypothetical distribution of the number in each grade category within each wage scale (the different wage scales are shown in Table 5.5). This hypothetical distribution is based on Mesa-Lago's estimate of the distribution of the work force within each wage scale in the mid-1960s[33] with the important distinction that I have assumed that by 1978 there were no longer appreciable numbers of workers in grade one.[34] The result of this alternative estimate of income distribution in 1978 shows, perhaps surprisingly, a more egalitarian distribution than when one applies the other assumption (a four-to-one differential in each sector). One reason may be that the wage scales do not include bonuses and overtime pay (which were virtually abolished between 1966 and 1973), and the conclusion could be that the real income distribution in 1978 lies somewhere in between the two 1978 estimates.

An interesting question is how the new wage scales being introduced in Cuba (see Table 5.5) are likely to affect the existing distribution of income. One would perhaps expect a widening of the differentials in line with the new policy (after 1973) of reward according to work accomplished. The new wage scales as such, however, do not point in this direction. There generally is a narrowing of the gap between the highest and the lowest wage paid in each category, and in the case of the highest paid categories—technical personnel and executives—the gap has narrowed considerably as there is a ceiling of 450 pesos in each. What is important, however, is that these are the basic wages applied: They do not include bonuses, overtime pay, and other fringe benefits. But even if those extras were included, it is not at all certain that there would be a regressive income redistribution since the material incentives apply to the lowest paid people at least as much as to those at the top of the wage scale. Another fact is that the so-called historical wage (applicable to those people who had higher wages before the introduction of the new wage scales in 1962) has gradually lost its importance.[35] In 1962, no less than 79.9 percent had the right to such compensation, but by 1972, this share had fallen to 18.9 percent, and by the end of the 1970s, the share was probably less than 10 percent.[36]

To sum up, it is quite clear that there has been a radical redistribution of income in Cuba since the revolution with the major transfer of income going to the bottom quintiles during the first years after 1959 and more moderate transfers during the latter part of the 1960s and the 1970s. This trend is illustrated by so-called Lorenz curves in Figure 5.1.

Distribution of Consumption

The income distribution in a country does not necessarily give a true picture of the standard of living of various income groups and the figures in the preceding tables tend to exaggerate the standard of living of the upper quintiles because there have been only limited possibilities to spend extra income since 1962 because of the rationing introduced in that year for most consumer goods. On the other hand, the figures also tend to underestimate the standard of living of the same upper income groups since many people in this category also have other benefits connected with their work such as free cars or traveling abroad (for instance, in the case of technicians, executives, and military staff members).

In the absence of any published material on the distribution of consumption in Cuba,[37] I have done a small survey of my own. It does not pretend to be a true reflection of the actual consumption patterns in Cuba, but I have selected five households that represent different family compositions and different income groups. I simply asked members of these households to make detailed day-by-day annotations of all their expenditures during November 1980. A summary of the result is shown in Table 5.7.

The characteristics of the households were as follows:

Household A: Divorced mother, university teacher, monthly salary 248 pesos. Two children, 9 and 15 years old.

Household B: The woman is a primary school teacher, monthly salary 180 pesos. The man is a factory worker, monthly wage 128 pesos. Two children, 7 months and 6 years old.

Household C: The woman is a housewife. The man is a longshoreman, monthly wage 138 pesos, but he often works overtime, and in November 1980 he earned 169 pesos. There are three children, 2, 5, and 7 years old.

Household D: Female textile worker living alone; monthly salary 90 pesos; no children.

Household E: Retired worker living on his pension, 65 pesos; no children.

The incomes included in this survey ranged from 65 pesos in the case of the retired worker to 248 pesos in the case of the university teacher, and the wages fit the range of wages listed in Table 5.8 reasonably well. What is perhaps the most interesting finding of this survey is that all the households, except that of the retired worker, had money left over at the end of the month. The cost of food (except for meals outside

112 *Distribution of Income and Consumption*

the home)[38] accounted for a percentage of the total income ranging from 23 percent to 59 percent. Asked what the families did with their surplus money, the answer in all cases was that it was saved for the annual vacation or for future purchases of consumer durables.

The fact that food expenses account for such a relatively small share of the total income of households is easy to understand if one looks at the price examples in Table 5.9. The prices on rationed food have more or less remained the same since 1962, although the gradual liberation of many food products, now sold on the parallel market, probably means that a relatively higher share of a family's income is now being spent on food than was being spent some years ago. As late as 1980, however, it was claimed that government subsidies for food (including both retail sales and subsidized meals in the work places) amounted to 25 pesos per capita per month.[39]

Regional Differences in Income and Consumption

Finally, a few words should be said about regional differences with respect to income and consumption. Very little statistical information is available regarding regional inequalities in Cuba before the revolution, but a safe assumption is that they were very large, and a classical study by Lowry Nelson on living conditions in rural Cuba in the 1940s supports this assumption. According to a survey of Cuban farm families in 1945, which Nelson quotes, the average yearly expenditures per household differed among regions from 499 to 1,745 pesos.[40]

Unfortunately, not very much information is available on regional differences in income and consumption after the revolution either. The only years for which detailed information is available are 1978 and 1979 and some of these data are shown in Table 5.10. The figures reveal that the average income in the richest province, the city of Havana, was 12 percent above the national average and 27 percent above the average income of the poorest province, Guantánamo.[41] The most interesting finding, however, is that the differences in food consumption were larger than the differences in income. Thus, per capita food consumption in the city of Havana was almost one-third higher than the national average and 79 percent higher than in Guantánamo.

Although these differences are alarmingly large, it is most likely that there has been a trend toward a narrowing of the gap since the revolution. As an indication of this possibility, a 1960 survey showed that the average monthly income in the old province of La Habana (which included the city of Havana) was 14 percent above the national average and 40 percent above that of the poorest province (the old Oriente Province, which embraced the new provinces of Santiago de Cuba, Granma, and Guantánamo).[42]

Table 5.1. Estimates of Cuban income distribution in the 1950s

Deciles	Hypothetical Family Income (1959) %	Cumulative %	Wages and Salaries (1953) %	Cumulative %
0-10	} 5.7	na	0.6	0.6
11-20		5.7	1.5	2.1
21-30	} 8.9	na	1.9	4.0
31-40		14.6	2.5	6.5
41-50	} 12.5	na	4.3	10.8
51-60		27.1	6.8	17.6
61-70	} 18.3	na	10.6	28.2
71-80		45.4	13.9	42.1
81-90	} 54.6	na	19.1	61.2
91-100		100.0	38.8	100.0
(Top 5%)	(na)		(26.5)	
Gini coefficient*		0.47		0.55

* = a measure of the degree of inequality represented by the Lorenz curve (see Figure 5.1). In the case of perfect equality the coefficient (G) is zero, and in the opposite case, that of total inequality, it is one. The Gini coefficient is defined by the formula:

$$G = 1 - \sum_{i=1}^{n} f_i (g_{i-1} + g_i)/10,000, \text{ where}$$

n = total number of income groups
i = ordinal number of each group
f = percentage of the population in each income group
g = cumulative percentage of income received

Sources: Hypothetical distribution: MacEwan (1981), p. 229; 1953 distribution: Appendix 2, Table 29.

Table 5.2. Employment and unemployment, 1953

	Urban (000s)	%	Rural (000s)	%	Total (000s)	%
Employed with pay	1,069.9	86.6	709.3	86.1	1,779.2	86.4
Working without pay for a relative	33.8	2.7	48.7	5.9	82.5	4.0
Employed but without work at survey date	12.7	1.0	11.4	1.4	24.1	1.2
Looking for work	119.4	9.7	54.4	6.6	173.8	8.4
Total labor force	1,235.9	100.0	823.7	100.0	2,059.7	100.0

Note: Totals may not add exactly because of rounding.

Source: Censo de población, viviendas y electoral 1953 (1953), quoted in Mesa-Lago (1968a), p. 374.

114 Distribution of Income and Consumption

Table 5.3. Estimated income distribution, 1962

Deciles	Percentage Share	Cumulative Share	MacEwan's Estimates of 1962 Family Income alt.1(%)	alt.2(%)
0-10	2.5	2.5	11.4	9.5
11-20	3.7	6.2		
21-30	4.8	11.0	14.6	12.2
31-40	6.2	17.2		
41-50	6.8	24.0	16.1	13.5
51-60	9.5	33.5		
61-70	12.0	45.5	18.3	18.3
71-80	13.1	58.6		
81-90	18.4	77.0	39.6	46.5
91-100	23.0	100.0		
(Top 5%)	(12.7)			
Gini coefficient	0.35		0.27	0.35

Source: Appendix 2, Table 30, and MacEwan (1981).

Table 5.4. Estimated average annual income by income groups, 1953 and 1962 (current pesos)

Deciles	Total Personal Incomes (000 pesos)		Average Incomes (current pesos)	
	1953	1962	1953	1962
0-10	12,596	55,506	61 ⎫	250 ⎫
11-20	31,489	82,149	153 ⎬ 166	370 ⎬ 430
21-30	39,886	106,572	194 ⎪	480 ⎪
31-40	52,481	137,656	255 ⎭	620 ⎭
41-50	90,268	150,977	438	680
51-60	142,750	210,924	693	950
61-70	222,521	266,431	1,080	1,200
71-80	291,797	290,853	1,417	1,310
81-90	400,959	408,527	1,947	1,840
91-100	814,512	510,659	3,955	2,300
(Top 5%)	(556,304)	(281,972)	(5,300)	(2,539)
Total	2,099,259	2,220,254	1,019	1,255

Sources: Appendix 2, Tables 29 and 30.

Table 5.5. Wage scales applied in Cuba between 1963-1979 and after 1980 (pesos per month)

Grades	Agricultural Workers Old Wage Scale	Agricultural Workers New Wage Scale	Nonagricultural Workers Old Wage Scale	Nonagricultural Workers New Wage Scale	Administrative and Service Personnel Old Wage Scale	Administrative and Service Personnel New Wage Scale	Technical Personnel Old Wage Scale	Technical Personnel New Wage Scale	Executives Old Wage Scale	Executives New Wage Scale
1	71	82	82	93	75	85				
2	80	95	95	107	86	97				
3	91	111	111	122	100	111				
4	107	128	128	141	118	128	118	128	100	111
5	124		151	162	138	148	138	148	118	128
6	145		177	187	163	171	163	171	138	148
7	170		208	217	192	198	192	198	163	171
8			250		211		211	211	192	198
9				254		231	231	231	211	211
10							250	250	231	231
11							275	260	250	250
12							300	280	275	260
13							325	295	300	280
14							350	310	325	295
15							more	325	350	310
16							than	340	more	325
17							350	355	than	340
18								370	350	355
19								385		370
20								400		385
21								425		400
22								450		425
										450

Source: Comité Estatal de Trabajo y Seguridad Social, Resolución no. 476.

Distribution of Income and Consumption

Table 5.6. Income distribution estimates, 1973 and 1978

	1973		1978			
	Excl. Private Sector		Incl. Private Sector		Alt. Estimate	
Deciles	%	cum. %	%	cum. %	%	cum. %
0-10	2.9	2.9	3.4	3.4	5.1	5.1
11-20	4.9	7.8	4.4	7.8	5.9	11.0
21-30	5.4	13.2	5.3	13.1	6.5	17.5
31-40	7.1	20.3	7.1	20.2	7.3	24.8
41-50	8.7	29.0	9.3	29.5	8.0	32.8
51-60	10.5	39.5	10.4	39.9	8.5	41.3
61-70	12.5	52.0	12.6	52.5	9.9	51.2
71-80	13.5	65.5	14.1	66.6	12.8	64.0
81-90	15.1	80.6	15.3	81.9	14.9	78.9
91-100	19.4	100.0	18.1	100.0	21.1	100.0
(Top 5%)	(9.8)		(9.5)		(11.0)	
Gini coefficient	0.28		0.27		0.25	

Sources: AEC (1979), p. 58, Table 5.5, and Appendix 2, Tables 31 and 32.

Figure 5.1. Estimated income distribution in Cuba in 1953, 1962, and 1978 (Lorenz curves)

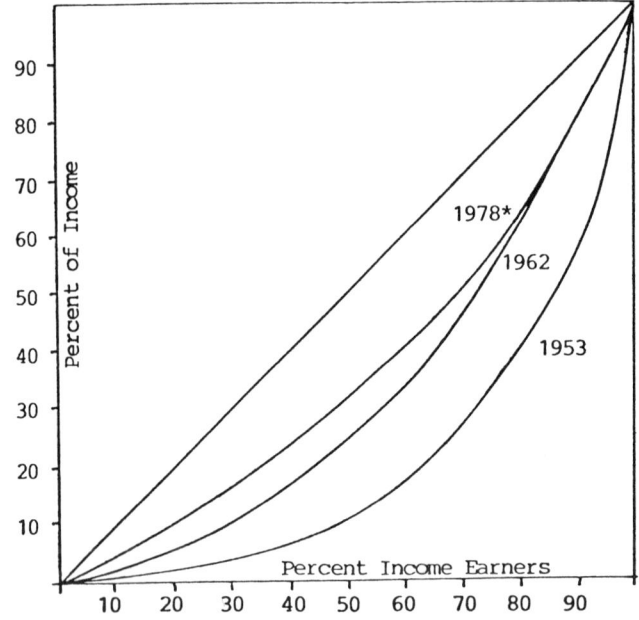

* = alternate estimate in Table 5.6.
Sources: Tables 5.1, 5.3, and 5.6.

Distribution of Income and Consumption 117

Table 5.7. Distribution of family expenditures by income groups and family size, Havana, November 1980

	Household A	Household B	Household C	Household D	Household E
Number of family members	3	4	5	1	1
adults	(1)	(2)	(2)	(1)	(1)
children	(2)	(2)	(3)		
income-earners	(1)	(2)	(1)	(1)	(1- retired)
Monthly income (pesos)	248+50*	180+128	169	90	65
Monthly expenditures (pesos)	182.86	270.92	135.04	70.45	65.11
Food	(69.96)	(74.80)	(99.84)	(46.25)	(18.95)
Rent		(30.00)			
Electricity & gas	(14.90)	(10.92)	(13.95)	(8.55)	(1.85)
Telephone	(6.25)		(6.25)		
Transport	(6.80)	(10.40)	(6.00)	(2.00)	
Meals outside, beverages, tobacco	(24.15)	(43.80)	(0.90)	(3.05)	(44.05)
Books & newspapers	(9.00)	(4.10)	(1.50)		
Other expenditures**	(51.80)	(96.90)	(6.60)	(10.60)	(0.26)
Savings***	115.14	37.08	33.96	19.55	0.11

* = allowance for children from ex-husband; ** = clothes, pocket money for children, leisure; *** = monthly income minus expenditures

Source: Survey by the author in Havana, November 1980.

Table 5.8. Examples of monthly wages in Havana, April 1979

	Monthly Wage/Salary		Monthly Wage/Salary
Specialized physician	350	Cook's aid	95
Physician	250	Chauffeur	138
Engineer	250-300	Ballet dancer, Cat. A	138
University teacher	248	Ballet dancer, Cat. B	163
Accountant	211	Secretary, Cat. A	138
Primary school teacher	180	Secretary, Cat. B	118
Head of personnel	163	Secretary, Cat. C	100
Longshoreman, Cat. A	163	Secretary, Cat. D	86
Longshoreman, Cat. B	138	Receptionist	86
Cook	128		

Source: Information collected by the author in Havana, April 1979.

Distribution of Income and Consumption

Table 5.9. Prices of rationed and liberated consumer goods in Havana, October 1980

Product	Ration (per family member and month)	Price (pesos/pound)
Rice	5 pounds	0.20
Black beans	1.25 pounds	0.17
Sugar	4 pounds	0.07
Beef	3/4 pound per nine days	0.55
Coffee	0.125 pounds	1.05
Lard	1.5 pounds	0.24
Butter	not rationed	2.40
Milk	1 liter to children under 7 per day	0.20/liter
Canned milk	3 cans (6 to children between 7 and 14)	0.20/can
Bread	not rationed	0.15
Eggs	not rationed	0.08 apiece
Fish	not rationed	0.40–0.60/kg
Beer	not rationed	0.60–1.20/bottle
Matches	not rationed	0.05/box
Cigarettes	4 packages + free sale on parallel market (adults only)	0.20/pkg. (ration); 1.60–1.80/pkg. (parallel market)
Wine (Bulgarian)	not rationed	6.00–8.00/bottle
Rum (Havana Club)	not rationed	16.80/bottle
Toothpaste	not rationed	0.65–1.00/tube
Radio	not rationed	50–150/unit
TV set	not rationed	750–900
Refrigerator	not rationed	700–800

Source: Information collected by the author in Havana, October 1980.

Table 5.10. Regional differences in income and consumption, 1978/1979

Provinces	Average Annual Wage/Salary 1978 (pesos)	(index)	Annual Per Capita Food Supply 1979 (pesos)	(index)
Ciudad de la Habana	1,874	112	266	132
Cienfuegos	1,770	105	186	92
Villa Clara	1,709	102	182	90
La Habana	1,693	101	236	129
Matanzas	1,683	100	225	112
Camagüey	1,645	98	232	115
Ciego de Ávila	1,627	97	176	87
Sancti Spíritus	1,608	96	157	78
Santiago de Cuba	1,608	96	184	91
Pinar del Río	1,560	96	191	95
Holguín	1,548	93	153	76
Las Tunas	1,545	92	140	69
Granma	1,486	88	159	79
Guantánamo	1,480	88	149	74
National average	1,680	100	201	100

Source: AEC (1979), pp. 57 and 132.

6
Cuban Growth and Equity in a Comparative Context

Cuba was deeply affected by the Depression in the 1930s, when very adverse terms of trade plunged the economy and the standards of living to the lowest levels since the beginning of the century. The economy then slowly recovered, and by the outbreak of World War II, it had almost reached pre-Depression levels. There was a period of rather rapid growth during the 1940s, which was followed by declining growth rates in the decade leading up to the 1959 revolution.

In spite of many claims to the contrary, there is no evidence that economic growth accelerated during the first years after the revolution. In fact, per capita growth was probably not much higher than in the 1950s. As a result of insufficiently installed productive capacity in the past and a massive redistribution of incomes during the first years after the revolution, a discrepancy between available resources and needs soon appeared. In spite of increasing investment levels, with higher amounts going to the productive areas, economic growth continued to be sluggish during most of the 1960s, and per capita income was probably only slightly higher in 1969 than in 1958. The 1970 *zafra* created disequilibriums in the economy, with many sectors being neglected and many resources being wasted. During the first half of the 1970s, however, economic growth accelerated because of investments made during the 1960s and especially because of new investments that were facilitated by favorable terms of trade, but the growth rate again declined during the latter part of the 1970s. It is estimated that per capita income grew at an average annual rate of 2.9 percent between 1958 and 1980, which means that the real product per capita almost doubled during the same period.

The most important aspect of economic growth in revolutionary Cuba is perhaps not that there has been sustained economic growth as such, but that the economy today is much more diversified than before. The Cuban economy in 1980 was much more industrialized than in 1960, and an important process of import substitution had taken place, especially during the 1970s.

Cuba's dependence on sugar exports is still exceedingly large, however, and sugar accounted for about the same share of total exports in 1980 as it had before the revolution. On the other hand, Cuba's dependence on exports in general seems to have diminished, and the Cuban economy is not as vulnerable as it was earlier to fluctuations in world market sugar prices—even if those fluctuations still play an important role in determining the success or failure of the Five-Year Plans (the somewhat disappointing results of the 1976–1980 plan is a case in point).

A strong emphasis was placed on the satisfaction of the most basic needs of the population after the revolution, and basic education especially expanded during the 1960s. In other basic need areas, there was a stagnation or even a decline during most of the 1960s, but in the 1970s, there was a virtual explosion in the expenditures devoted to basic needs—especially secondary education, health, and to a lesser extent, food. Areas that are still seriously neglected are clothing and housing, and those standards have barely surpassed the prerevolutionary levels even if the satisfaction of those needs is no doubt much more egalitarian today.

In terms of income distribution, it is clear that a massive redistribution took place immediately after the revolution, and the redistribution continued at a slower pace in the 1960s and the 1970s. New wage scales were introduced in 1980 that might effect income distribution in the long run since more importance is given to bonuses, overtime, and other fringe benefits; this importance is linked to the renewed priority given to material over moral incentives.

The revolutionary government's most spectacular success has no doubt been its commitment to reduce inequalities between the countryside and the towns. Thus, although the average 1962 wage in agriculture was only 49 percent of the average wage in industry, the difference between the two sectors had narrowed to 86 percent by 1980. During the same period, housing construction was concentrated in the rural areas, as were the installations of electricity, piped water, and sanitary facilities.

By the end of the 1970s, almost 350 small communities had been created throughout the island to bring the rural population together and special priority had been given to the less densely populated areas. In almost 450 communities that have 1,000 people or more, special programs for urban development planning are under way, and urban zoning plans provide the guidelines for future development. An integral part of this process has been the extension of compulsory secondary education to include practically everyone in the country. The secondary schools operate according to the principle of half-time work and half-time study, and all of the schools have their own agricultural land.

The programs to increase the standard of living of the rural people have no doubt helped to stem the flow of migrants to the big cities, and today only about one-fifth of the population is concentrated in the large metropolitan areas. This success in equalizing the living conditions between town and village is perhaps one of the most important lessons to be drawn from the Cuban experience.

The Cuban challenge of growth with equity may not be fully appreciated, however, if the results are not compared to the situation in other Latin American countries. I have therefore made an attempt to construct some comparable statistics on economic growth, structural changes, and income distribution in Cuba and some selected Latin American countries.

Table 6.1 shows the GDP per capita trends in Cuba and other Latin American countries between 1960 and 1982. The figures are expressed in the equivalent of U.S. dollars of 1980. The Cuban data are my own estimates presented in Table 2.7, and the figures for the other countries are taken from a report by the Interamerican Bank, which uses a conversion method that is very similar to my own (see note 51 in Chapter 2). The figures in the table show that the Cuban GDP per capita growth averaged 2.7 percent between 1961 and 1982, more or less the same rate recorded by the rest of the Latin American countries combined. One important difference, however, is that while growth was stagnant in Cuba in the 1960s, the per capita rate of growth was 3 percent in Latin America during the same decade. On the other hand, Cuba's per capita growth was considerably higher in the 1970s than the growth of the other countries in the hemisphere with the exception of Brazil, which had more or less the same rate as Cuba. Judging from the figures in the table, Cuba has suffered much less from the present international economic crisis that began in 1980 than most other countries in Latin America, including its neighbors in the Caribbean and Central America. Thus, while the GDP per capita in Central America decreased by 4.5 percent in 1981 and by another 7.8 percent in 1982, Cuba's GDP per capita increased by 8.5 percent in 1981 and by 1.3 percent in 1982.[1]

It has been argued, however, that in spite of Cuba's sustained rate of growth in the 1970s, there have been no profound structural changes in its basically sugar-dominated economy. The comparative data on economic structural changes in Table 6.2 do not give any credit to such a claim, however. As a matter of fact, none of the areas or countries cited appears to have undergone such drastic structural changes as Cuba since 1960. Thus, industrial activities (defined as mining, manufacturing, electrical energy, and construction) accounted for an estimated 46.4

percent of GDP in 1981, probably one of the highest figures in Latin America, and the change from 31.8 percent in 1961 apparently implies the most dramatic change in relation to GDP in Latin America. There may, of course, be a problem of definitions here in the sense that Cuba's concept of industrial activities is somewhat broader than that used in the rest of Latin America, but even so, the very drastic change in Cuba can only be explained by the accelerated growth of basic industry, capital goods, and the construction industry, particularly after 1971.

The fundamental changes that have taken place in Cuba's economy since the revolution have, however—as stressed before—also been accompanied by a radical redistribution of income to the benefit of the poorest people, which means that the per capita income of the poor must have grown at a more rapid pace than that of the rest of the population. In order to illustrate the importance of the income redistribution in Cuba, I have made an attempt to compare the income distribution development in Cuba with that of two other Latin American countries, Brazil and Peru (Table 6.3). Brazil was chosen because it is the country that experienced the most rapid growth in Latin America after 1960, and Peru was included because of the structural reforms introduced by the Velasco government between 1968 and 1975—reforms that aimed at radically transforming the economy of the country, including income distribution.

The result of this exercise is rather striking. Brazil is a good example of the limited effects of the so-called trickle-down policies. In spite of unprecedented growth in Brazil after 1960, the per capita income of the poorest 40 percent only doubled (from $197 to $401) in twenty years. In Cuba on the other hand, per capita income of the same income group increased by almost five times (from $182 to $865) in the same period of time. Peru has experienced slow growth, and its income disparities have increased, with the poorest 40 percent receiving not only relatively smaller shares of income but also living poorer in absolute terms (with income levels falling from $232 to $197 between 1961 and 1979). A tentative conclusion then seems to be that rapid growth as such does not necessarily increase the income levels of the poorer people dramatically, but the Cuban case also shows that income redistribution alone does not solve the situation of the poor unless the redistribution is accompanied by sustained economic growth of the country in the long run.

Table 6.1. GDP per capita and growth rates, Cuba and selected areas/countries in Latin America, 1960-1982

	GDP/Capita (US $ 1980)				Average Annual Rate of Growth			
	1960	1970	1978	1982	1960/70	1970/78	1978/82	1960/82
Cuba	887	867	1,395	1,600	-0.2	5.9	3.4	2.7
Caribbean[1] (Excl. Cuba)	595	784	932	959	2.8	2.2	0.7	2.2
Central America[2]	654	904	1,087	1,018	3.2	2.3	-1.6	2.0
Argentina	1,371	1,767	1,842	1,686	2.5	0.5	-2.2	0.9
Brazil	651	924	1,508	1,527	3.5	6.1	0.3	3.9
Mexico	975	1,376	1,689	1,897	3.4	2.6	2.9	3.0
Peru	910	1,142	1,226	1,268	2.3	0.9	0.8	1.5
Latin America (Excl. Cuba)	836	1,128	1,485	1,504	3.0	3.4	0.3	2.7

[1] Dominican Republic, Haiti, Jamaica, Trinidad and Tobago
[2] Costa Rica, El Salvador, Guatemala, Honduras, Nicaragua, Panama

Sources: Cuba: Table 2.7 and preliminary figures for 1982 (Granma Weekly, 9 January 1983); Other areas/countries: BID (1982), Table 3, and Iglesias (1983), Table 3.

Table 6.2. Economic structural changes in Cuba and selected areas/countries in Latin America between 1960 and 1981

	Share in GDP (Percent)				Average Annual Growth Rate 1960-1981	
	Primary Activities[1]		Industrial Activities[2]		Primary Activities	Industrial Activities
	1960	1981	1960	1981		
Cuba	18.2[3]	13.0	31.8[3]	46.4	2.7[4]	6.2[4]
Caribbean (excl. Cuba)	21.6	13.3	28.9	30.7	1.7	4.3
Central America	28.4	22.6	18.2	24.1	3.8	6.2
Argentina	15.5	13.7	32.5	36.3	2.2	3.3
Brazil	13.8	8.4	35.3	36.3	4.2	6.7
Mexico	16.3	8.9	28.5	35.4	3.7	7.7
Peru	18.3	11.7	35.1	36.9	1.9	4.3
Latin America (excl. Cuba)	16.4	10.8	32.5	34.6	3.4	5.7

[1] Agriculture, forestry, and fishing
[2] Mining, manufacturing, electric power, and construction
[3] 1961
[4] 1961-1981

Sources: Cuba: Table 2.7 and Appendix 2, Tables 7 and 9; Other areas/countries: BID (1982), Table 3, and Iglesias (1983), Table 3.

Table 6.3. Levels and growth of per capita income by strata--Brazil, Cuba, and Peru (equivalent of US$ 1980)

	GDP/Capita Dollars	Per Capita Income of Poorest 40%		Per Capita Income of Richest 5%	
		Dollars	Share of Total Inc.	Dollars	Share of Total Inc.
Brazil					
1960	651	197	11.5%	3,788	27.7%
1970	924	233	10.1%	6,450	34.9%
1980	1,652	401	9.9%	11,298	34.2%
Annual rate of growth					
1960-1970	3.5%	1.7%		5.3%	
1970-1980	5.9%	5.4%		5.6%	
Cuba					
1958*	866	182	6.5%	5,947	26.5%
1962	882	379	17.2%	2,237	12.7%
1973	996	506	20.3%	1,892	9.5%
1978	1,395	865	24.8%	3,068	11.0%
Annual rate of growth					
1958-1962	0.5%	18.3%		-24.4%	
1962-1973	1.1%	2.6%		-1.5%	
1973-1978	6.7%	10.7%		9.7%	
Peru					
1961	925	232	10.0%	4,810	26.0%
1972	1,163	234	9.0%	6,578	33.0%
1979	1,245	197	8.2%	7,255	37.3%
Annual rate of growth					
1961-1972	2.1%	0.1%		2.8%	
1972-1979	1.0%	-2.4%		1.4%	

* = based on the assumption that there was no change in income distribution between 1953 and 1958

Sources: Cuba: elaborated on the basis of the estimates in Chapter 5; Brazil (1960 and 1970) and Peru (1961 and 1972): Brundenius (1982); Brazil (1980): IBGE (1981); Peru (1979): World Bank (1980); GDP estimates in dollar equivalents (1980): BID (1982), Annex Table 3.

APPENDIX 1
The Development of the Cuban Labor Force, 1970–1980

Data on the development of the Cuban labor force after the revolution are extremely scarce. At the beginning of the 1960s, some sample surveys were taken, and published, but for the years after 1962 there is only scattered information on the deployment of the civilian labor force in official statistical publications[1] and occasional data on distribution by sector and sex in other publications.[2] The census results of 1970 give some important characteristics of the labor force in that year, which makes it possible to trace with reasonable accuracy the changes between 1959 and 1970. Since the section on labor force statistics in the *Anuario estadístico de Cuba* (AEC), published regularly since 1972, is extremely meager (usually only two pages), it is difficult to make reliable estimates of the components of the labor force, activity rates, sector participations, self-employment, unemployment, etc. Most estimates of this type have been guesswork even if Carmelo Mesa-Lago made brave attempts to overcome many of these difficulties.[3]

In March 1979, however, a rather detailed demographic survey was taken in Cuba in preparation for the 1981 census. This survey, *Encuesta demográfica nacional de 1979* (EDN) has been published and is thus available to foreign researchers.[4] The EDN and an accompanying analytical report[5] contain an important wealth of information and make possible new estimates of the development of the Cuban labor force, and the characteristics of that force, after 1970. I shall here present the main findings from such an exercise divided into five areas: (1) a comparison of the 1979 survey and the 1970 census with some references to earlier censuses and surveys, (2) estimates of unemployment, (3) characteristics of the female labor force, (4) the educational level of the labor force, and (5) a new estimate of the various components of the labor force in the period 1970–1980.

The 1979 Survey

The survey was taken 2-7 April 1979, and its results contain, in addition to general demographic information such as the distribution of the population by sex, age, region, and size of family, a few tables showing some characteristics of the occupied (employed) labor force. The accompanying analytical document, however, also contains some tables on the total labor force so that it is possible to deduce, through simple arithmetic, the unemployed labor force by sex. As shown in Table A1.1, the survey also shows the distribution of the occupied labor force by economic sector and type of occupation (state, private, or self-employed). The categorization is more or less the same as the one used in the 1970 census, which makes a comparison with the latter possible.

The most dramatic change between 1970 and 1979 took place in agriculture, as employment decreased in both relative and absolute terms. As a matter of fact, the sharp decrease in agricultural employment, almost 10 percent, is probably one of the greatest structural changes in employment that occurred in Latin America in the 1970s. In the same period, almost 218,000 new jobs were created in the industrial sector (mining, manufacturing, and construction), and there were no fewer than 492,000 new jobs in services, of which almost 200,000 were in social services (mostly education and public health). In contrast to the rest of Latin America, Cuba had an absolute decline of employment opportunities in commercial activities.

Another salient feature of Table A1.1 is the diminishing private sector. Non-state employment, which in 1962 was estimated to have represented 35.4 percent of total employment,[6] decreased to 12.5 percent in 1970 and by 1979 had shrunk to insignificant 6.6 percent, of which 78 percent was in agriculture.

If we now look at the employment trend over time (Table A1.2), we find, first of all, that the growth of the labor force accelerated after 1970, significantly outstripping population growth. The reason for this acceleration was not so much the so-called baby boom of the first half of the 1960s as the spectacular growth of the female labor force. Another important feature of Table A1.2 is the impressive growth of the industrial work force, which almost doubled in size between 1959 and 1979. The figures imply an annual growth rate of 3.4 percent after the revolution, although the rate decreased somewhat (3.0 percent) in the 1970s.

Unemployment

One of the most controversial issues concerning the labor force in postrevolutionary Cuba has been to what extent the Cuban government

Development of the Cuban Labor Force, 1970-1980   127

has been able to reduce unemployment, which was estimated to have affected 13.6 percent of the labor force in 1959.[7] The unemployment rate was successively reduced during the 1960s until it reached, according to the 1970 census, only 1.3 percent. Such an impressive figure would mean that unemployment had virtually been wiped out during the first decade after the revolution, but one should keep in mind that the labor force grew at a very moderate rate (1.6 percent), less than the rate of population growth. This fact no doubt concealed substantial proportions of so-called disguised unemployment, that is, available laborers (for instance, women) who for various reasons refrained from entering the labor force.

Little is known about the unemployment in Cuba since 1970, although Mesa-Lago has made a brave attempt to estimate the levels of unemployment between 1970 and 1978, basing his estimates on certain assumptions about the growth of the labor force. The conclusion of Mesa-Lago's exercise is that unemployment increased after 1970 to a peak of 3.9 percent in 1974, but it then decreased to a low of 1.3 percent in 1978.[8] However, one can estimate from official Cuban publications (the 1979 survey and the accompanying analytical document) that unemployment had increased to as much as 5.4 percent of the labor force by 1979. In Table A1.3, I have estimated unemployment rates for 1970-1980 for both the female and the male labor forces. To make the estimates, I used Cuban data on the occupied female labor force (from various sources) for the period 1970-1979 and then estimated the figures for the male occupied labor force by intrapolating the trend between the 1970 census figure and the 1979 survey figure (which implies an annual rate of growth of 1.0 percent). In order to calculate the growth of the total labor force by sex, I correlated the growth of the occupied labor force with the potential supply of labor, using official data on the population of working age and substracting the number of students of working age (working age in Cuba is 17-59 in the case of men and 17-54 in the case of women).

The resulting calculations indicate that unemployment grew continuously from 1970 until 1979. The major reason for this trend is no doubt the spectacular growth of the female labor force, especially after 1974. This latter growth is, in turn, the result of two phenomena: (1) the expansion of educational opportunities for both sexes without discrimination and (2) increased motivations for women to work. One reason for the low participation of women in economic activities in the late 1960s was, I think, largely due to insufficient material incentives to do so. If there was nothing to buy, why should the family gain extra money? With more material incentives (in both money terms and the supply of durable consumer goods) and increased child care facilities, Cuban women leaving the educational system in the 1970s were more strongly motivated to go out and work.

However, this trend of increasing female participation apparently comes into conflict with another overriding goal of the Cuban government in the 1970s, that of increasing labor productivity. The result was that the women have had to bear the brunt of the unemployment, especially since 1973 when the female share of unemployment accounted for over half of all unemployment for the first time (see Table A1.4). According to the 1979 survey, there was a total of 188,000 unemployed (non-occupied) persons in Cuba in 1973, of which 129,000 (68.6 percent) were women for a female unemployment rate of 12.0 percent. According to my estimates, however, the female employment rate reached a peak in 1976 when 13.6 percent of the women were unemployed, accounting for 74.2 percent of all the unemployed.

An important question is: To what extent have unemployment rates continued to go up, or have they started to decrease since 1979? When the final results of the 1981 census are published, we shall know for sure, but it would seem logical that the massive exodus of over 140,000 Cubans in 1980 must have had a positive effect on the unemployment rates.[9] I have made a very rough estimate of this effect (comparing official data on the working-age population for 1979 and 1980 with official data on emigration in 1980), and I have arrived at the conclusion that overall unemployment decreased from 188,000 in 1979 to 146,000 in 1980, with female unemployment falling from 12.0 percent to 7.8 percent and male unemployment stabilizing around 2.5 percent.

Female Labor Force

Since the female labor force is playing an increasing role in the Cuban economy, it could be worthwhile to take a closer look at some of its characteristics (Tables A1.5 and A1.6). The female work force more than doubled during the 1970s from 482,000 to more than 1 million (see Table A1.3), compared to an estimated female labor force of some 300,000 in 1960 (then constituting only 13.2 percent of the labor force). Almost one-third of the labor force today is composed of women, a figure that is close to the situation in the industrialized countries. Of the total of 671,000 new jobs created since 1970, no fewer than 470,000, or 70 percent, were occupied by women. However, the creation of new jobs has not been enough to absorb the total increase in the female labor force, which has resulted in increasing unemployment rates for women. But one should not draw the erroneous conclusion that the activity rate of women has fallen. If we relate the occupied female labor force to the potentially available female labor force (that is, take the female population of working age and subtract the full-time students), we find that the activity rate continuously increased during the whole of the 1970s—from 24.9 percent in 1970 to 44.5 percent in 1979 and an estimated 47.7 percent in 1980. There is still a long way to go before the female activity rate reaches the corresponding male rate of almost 100 percent, but the increase in the 1970s was impressive.

Another question about the female labor force is, Has there been a change in the pattern of sector distribution? Table A1.6 shows the distribution of the occupied female labor force in 1970 and 1979 and indicates what happened to the 470,000 new female workers in that period. As seen, an overwhelming majority, almost two-thirds of the new entrants, were absorbed into the service sector and only about one-third became engaged in all other activities. This distribution means that most of the jobs created in services such as education and health are occupied by women—a trend that is also very common in the socialist countries of Eastern Europe.

Educational Level of the Labor Force

The 1979 survey gives, for the first time since the revolution, some insight into the educational qualifications of the labor force, but unfortunately, the 1970 census has no similar information (at least not published) so a comparison with 1979 is not possible. The 1953 census, however, does contain a set of tables on the educational level of the total population by age groups, and a comparison between the 1953 census and the 1979 survey is shown in Table A1.7.

The table shows that the educational level of the population at large increased considerably between 1953 and 1979. The illiteracy rate decreased from 23.9 percent to 5.6 percent, the share of the population having at least six years of schooling increased from one-fourth to almost two-thirds, and the most spectacular growth occurred in the category of people having at least nine years of education, which increased from 6 percent to 41.4 percent of the population. In other words, four out of ten Cubans over the age of fourteen have now completed the equivalent of junior high school.

If we look at the qualifications of the occupied labor force, we find, not surprisingly, that the educational levels are higher than for the population as a whole. Thus, 75 percent of the work force has had more than six years of education—48.4 percent has had at least nine years; 21.6 percent, at least twelve years; and 4.5 percent has a university degree or the equivalent. With respect to sex, we find that the female workers are substantially better qualified than their male colleagues. At a first glance, this fact might seem surprising, but if we recall that the female labor force is much younger—because of the rapid increase in the number of girls graduating from the educational system—it is quite natural that the average level of qualification is higher among women.

Estimate of the Cuban Labor Force, 1970-1980

Carmelo Mesa-Lago has made many pioneering attempts to estimate the various components of the Cuban labor force since the revolution, and without his studies, our knowledge of the employment trends in postrevolutionary Cuba would be rather poor. In his latest study, Mesa-Lago has tried to estimate the figure for the most important categories of the labor force for the years 1962–1978,[10] but in making those estimates, he did not have access to the survey of 1979, which is the pillar on which my analysis and conclusions are based. I have therefore tried to revise Mesa-Lago's estimates for the period after 1970 in this light, and the results are shown in Table A1.8. The major difference between Mesa-Lago's and my estimates is that Mesa-Lago seems to have underestimated the growth of the labor force (probably as a result of not taking due consideration of the growth of the female labor force). Unemployment in Mesa-Lago's analysis results as a residual, and this fact implies that his estimates of unemployment rates turn out to be somewhat underestimated.

Table A1.1. Employment by economic sector and by occupational category, 1970 and 1979

	Total[3]	State	Private	1970[1] Small Peasants	Self-Employed[4]	Family Workers
Agriculture, fishing, and forestry	790,356	495,073	24,139	230,525	6,276	34,289
Manufacturing industry and mining	533,258	530,727	645		1,759	24
Construction industry	157,182	156,003	209		948	6
Transport	146,223	122,966	6,648		16,549	23
Communications	15,155	15,092	55		3	
Commerce	305,958	300,537	1,570		3,789	29
Services	621,957	620,716	586		490	19
Not elsewhere classified	63,220	47,292	1,340		284	5
Total	2,633,309	2,288,406	35,192	230,525	30,098	34,395

Table A1.1 (continued)

	Total	State	Private	1979[2] Small Peasants[5]	Self-Employed	Family Workers
Agriculture, fishing, and forestry	716,004	545,974	9,015	143,121	9,568	8,326
Manufacturing industry and mining	651,863	649,834	824	630	556	19
Construction industry	256,517	255,776	186	145	382	28
Transport Communications	202,729	195,809	1,417	120	5,383	
Commerce	265,506	264,509	71	478	425	23
Services	934,016	928,109	714	1,284	3,741	168
Not elsewhere classified	243,706	213,008	1,215	20,052	7,582	1,849
Total	3,270,341	3,053,019	13,442	165,830	27,637	10,413

[1] Total labor force
[2] Occupied labor force
[3] Including 14,693 who did not declare occupational category
[4] Including 108 patrones (owners)
[5] Including 5,705 cooperativistas (farmers organized in cooperatives)

Sources: Censo de población y viviendas 1970 (1975), Table 20, and Comité Estatal de Estadísticas, Dirección de Demografía, Encuesta demográfica nacional de 1979--metodología y tablas seleccionadas (Havana, April 1981), Table 7.

Table A1.2. Employment by sector and growth of labor force and population, 1953-1979

	1953 Census		1958-1959 Survey		1970 Census		1979[1] Survey	
	(000s)	(%)	(000s)	(%)	(000s)	(%)	(000s)	(%)
Employment by Sector								
Agriculture, fishing, and forestry	818.7	41.5	813.0	37.0	790.4	30.0	716.0	21.9
Industrial activities	410.6	20.8	461.3	21.0	690.4	26.3	908.4	27.8
(Construction)	(65.3)	(3.3)	(82.8)	(3.8)	(157.2)	(6.0)	(256.5)	(7.8)
Transport and communications	104.0	5.3	80.6	3.7	161.4	6.1	202.7	6.2
Commerce	232.3	11.8	284.3	12.9	306.0	11.6	265.5	8.1
Services	406.7	20.6	558.3	25.4	622.0	23.6	934.0	28.6
Not elsewhere classified					63.2	2.4	243.7	7.4
Total	1,972.3	100.0	2,197.5	100.0	2,633.3	100.0	3,270.3	100.0

	1953-1959	1959-1970	1970-1979
Annual Rates of Growth			
Labor force	1.8	1.6	2.4
Population	2.0	1.9	1.5

[1] Occupied labor force

Sources: Table A1.1 and Mesa-Lago (1972c).

Table A1.3. Total labor force, occupied labor force, and unemployed labor force by sex, 1960 and 1970–1980 (000s)

	Total Labor Force			Occupied Labor Force			Unemployed Labor Force		
	Both Sexes	Male	Female	Both Sexes	Male	Female	Both Sexes	Male	Female
1960	2,276	1,976	300	2,007	1,802	205	269	174	95
1970	2,633	2,151	482	2,599	2,123	476	34	28	6
1971	2,708	2,181	527	2,652	2,144	508	56	37	19
1972	2,787	2,211	576	2,709	2,166	543	78	45	33
1973	2,866	2,236	630	2,768	2,188	580	98	48	50
1974	2,947	2,259	688	2,831	2,210	621	116	49	67
1975	3,031	2,278	753	2,896	2,232	664	135	46	89
1976	3,117	2,294	823	2,966	2,255	711	151	39	112
1977	3,225	2,326	899	3,060	2,278	782	165	48	117
1978	3,339	2,356	983	3,161	2,301	860	178	55	123
1979	3,458	2,383	1,075	3,270	2,324	946	188	59	129
1980	3,527	2,419	1,108	3,381	2,359	1,022	146	60	86

Sources: 1960: Mesa-Lago (1981); 1970 and 1979: Censo de población y viviendas 1970 (1975), Table 20, and Comité Estatal de Estadísticas, Dirección de Demografía, Encuesta demográfica nacional de 1979–– metodología y tablas seleccionadas (Havana, April 1981), Table 7; 1971–1978 and 1980: author's estimates, methodology explained in text.

Table A1.4. Unemployed as percent of labor force

	Both Sexes	Male	Female
1970	1.3	1.3	1.2
1971	2.1	1.7	3.6
1972	2.8	2.0	5.7
1973	3.4	2.1	7.9
1974	3.9	2.2	9.7
1975	4.5	2.0	11.8
1976	4.8	1.7	13.6
1977	5.1	2.1	13.0
1978	5.3	2.3	12.5
1979	5.4	2.5	12.0
1980	4.1	2.5	7.8

Source: Table A1.3.

Table A1.5. Characteristics of the female labor force, 1970-1980

	Share of Labor Force (%)	Share of Occupied Labor Force (%)	Share of Unemployment (%)	Activity Rate (Occ. LF as % of Available LF)[1]
1970	18.3	18.3	17.6	24.9
1971	19.5	19.2	33.9	26.1
1972	20.7	20.0	42.3	27.5
1973	22.0	21.0	51.0	29.1
1974	23.3	21.9	57.8	31.1
1975	24.8	22.9	65.9	33.2
1976	26.4	24.0	74.2	35.5
1977	27.9	25.6	70.9	38.7
1978	29.4	27.2	69.1	41.6
1979	31.1	28.9	68.6	44.5
1980	31.4	30.2	58.9	47.7

[1] Available labor force equals population of working age (17-54) minus full-time students.

Source: Table A1.3.

Table A1.6. Employment of female labor force by sector, 1970 and 1979

	1970		1979		Increase 1970–1979	
	000s	%	000s	%	000s	%
Agriculture, forestry, & fishing	39.2	8.2	101.4	10.7	62.2	13.2
Industrial activities	105.0	22.1	181.2	19.2	76.2	16.2
(Construction)	(3.1)	(0.7)	(26.5)	(2.8)	(23.4)	(5.0)
Transport and communications	10.9	2.3	31.5	3.3	20.6	4.4
Commerce	110.5	23.2	110.7	11.7	0.2	0.1
Social services	202.3	42.5	351.8	37.2	149.5	31.8
Other services	7.9	1.7	169.4	17.9	161.5	34.3
Total	475.8	100.0	946.0	100.0	470.2	100.0

Note: Totals may not add exactly because of rounding.

Sources: Censo de población y viviendas 1970 (1975), Table 20, and Comité Estatal de Estadísticas, Dirección de Demografía, Encuesta demográfica nacional de 1979--metodología y tablas seleccionadas (Havana, April 1981), Table 7.

Table A1.7. Educational level of the population and of the labor force, 1953 and 1979

	Percentage of the Population Having Achieved Level of Education		Percentage of Occupied Labor Force Having Achieved Level of Education		
	1953	1979	1979		
	Both Sexes (Pop. over 15)	Both Sexes (Pop. over 14)	Both Sexes	Male	Female
University education	1.4%	3.3%	4.5%	4.0%	5.7%
At least 12 years	3.6%	18.7%	21.6%	17.7%	31.3%
At least 9 years	6.0%	41.4%	48.4%	43.4%	60.7%
At least 6 years	25.4%	65.3%	71.8%	68.1%	80.9%
Less than 6 years	74.6%	34.7%	28.2%	31.9%	19.1%
Of which illiterate	23.9%	5.6%	4.0%	3.7%	4.2%

Sources: Censo de población, viviendas y electoral 1953 (1953) and Comité Estatal de Estadísticas, Dirección de Demografía, Encuesta demográfica nacional de 1979—metodología y tablas seleccionadas (Havana, April 1981), Table 7.

Table A1.8. Labor force characteristics, 1970-1980 (000s)

	1970	1971	1972	1973	1974	1975	1976	1977	1978	1979	1980
Labor force	2,633	2,708	2,787	2,866	2,947	3,031	3,117	3,225	3,339	3,458	3,527
Unemployed	34	56	78	98	116	135	151	165	178	188	146
Occupied labor											
force	2,599	2,652	2,709	2,768	2,831	2,896	2,966	3,060	3,161	3,270	3,381
State	2,254	2,303	2,361	2,441	2,525	2,619	2,721	2,834	2,940	3,053	3,168
Civilian	2,064	2,082	2,126	2,246	2,313	2,394	2,469	2,621	2,733	2,768	2,849
Military	190	221	235	195	212	225	252	213	207	285	319
Nonstate	345	349	348	327	306	277	245	226	221	213	213
Agriculture	295	300	300	280	260	232	200	182	178	195	172
Other nonstate	50	49	48	47	46	45	45	44	43	42	41

Source: Author's calculations from data presented in Appendix 1, Tables 1 and 3.

APPENDIX 2
Statistical Tables

Table A2.1. Estimates of Cuban national income, 1903-1939

	A	B*	C**		D***	
			C1	C2	D1	D2
1903	193	1,837	324	176	na	na
1904	222	1,879	372	198	na	na
1905	264	1,927	439	228	443	230
1906	249	1,979	403	204	na	na
1907	250	2,034	383	188	356	175
1908	238	2,092	378	181	na	na
1909	300	2,154	444	206	450	209
1910	347	2,219	493	222	na	na
1911	295	2,287	445	199	424	185
1912	397	2,358	575	244	na	na
1913	379	2,431	543	223	540	222
1914	400	2,507	587	234	na	na
1915	519	2,585	747	289	na	na
1916	644	2,664	753	283	709	266
1917	678	2,746	577	210	na	na
1918	734	2,828	577	198	488	173
1919	862	2,912	622	214	535	184
1920	1,191	2,997	771	257	643	215
1921	588	3,083	602	195	na	na
1922	656	3,170	678	214	na	na
1923	761	3,257	756	232	795	244
1924	783	3,345	798	239	na	na
1925	708	3,432	684	199	na	na
1926	604	3,519	604	172	604	172
1927	648	3,606	679	188	na	na
1928	584	3,693	604	164	675	183
1929	571	3,778	599	159	644	170
1930	517	3,862	598	155	681	176
1931	392	3,946	537	136	621	157
1932	283	4,028	437	108	399	99
1933	294	4,109	446	109	441	107
1934	364	4,188	486	116	479	114
1935	435	4,264	544	128	563	132
1936	510	4,339	631	145	na	na
1937	614	4,411	711	161	866	196
1938	468	4,481	595	133	663	148
1939	488	4,547	633	139	734	161

A = Nominal national income (million current pesos)
B = Estimated population (000s)
C = Alienes's estimate of real national income:
    C1 = Million 1926 pesos
    C2 = Real national income per capita
D = New estimate of real national income
    D1 = Million 1926 pesos
    D2 = Real national income per capita
* = estimates by Alienes; ** = nominal national income deflated by U.S. wholesale prices; *** = nominal national income deflated by Cuban official cost of living (food) index

Sources: Alienes (1950), p. 52; new estimate by the author deflating nominal national income by cost of living (food) index as given by Zanetti and García (1976), p. 441.

Table A2.2. Output of raw sugar, sugar income, and Cuban share of world sugar production, 1900-1958

	Raw Sugar (thousand metric tons)	Income from Sugar (million current pesos)	Sugar Income as % of Nominal National Income	Cuban Share of World Sugar Production (%)
1900	300.0	19.0	na	2.7
1901	635.9	30.1	na	5.0
1902	876.0	34.9	na	7.4
1903	1,029.2	43.5	22.5	8.3
1904	1,071.9	60.8	27.4	9.3
1905	1,198.6	72.7	27.5	8.4
1906	1,214.6	56.0	22.5	8.6
1907	1,491.1	71.3	28.5	10.4
1908	991.2	55.2	23.2	6.8
1909	1,559.4	85.4	28.5	10.5
1910	1,859.2	109.9	31.7	11.0
1911	1,889.5	100.4	34.0	9.4
1912	1,953.6	110.8	27.9	10.6
1913	2,502.4	106.1	28.0	13.0
1914	2,676.7	153.6	38.4	14.4
1915	2,688.2	191.4	36.9	15.6
1916	3,126.5	297.0	46.1	17.7
1917	3,147.9	316.1	46.6	18.2
1918	3,578.8	329.9	44.9	21.9
1919	4,131.6	454.5	52.7	26.4
1920	3,849.0	1,005.5*	84.4*	22.2
1921	4,053.9	273.2	46.5	22.3
1922	4,156.0	255.0	38.9	22.6
1923	3,756.8	400.2	52.6	18.6
1924	4,237.7	368.5	47.1	17.7
1925	5,347.1	290.8	41.1	21.8
1926	5,082.0	245.3	40.6	21.2
1927	4,645.7	267.0	41.2	18.0
1928	4,164.7	198.0	33.9	15.1
1929	5,313.0	199.0	34.9	19.3
1930	4,813.0	129.0	25.0	16.8
1931	3,215.7	78.0	19.9	12.5
1932	2,683.5	42.0	14.8	11.5
1933	2,054.4	43.0	14.6	8.2
1934	2,324.4	60.6	16.6	9.2
1935	2,615.1	97.6	22.4	9.4

* = exceptional year

Table A2.2 (continued)

	Raw Sugar (thousand metric tons)	Income from Sugar (million current pesos)	Sugar Income as % of Nominal National Income	Cuban Share of World Sugar Production (%)
1936	2,634.7	113.0	22.3	8.9
1937	3,065.0	148.3	24.2	9.9
1938	3,044.4	106.4	22.7	10.4
1939	2,806.6	103.6	21.2	8.9
1940	2,883.8	103.8	24.1	9.1
1941	2,450.1	138.1	20.4	8.4
1942	3,446.7	224.7	31.2	13.7
1943	2,929.5	160.7	17.2	12.3
1944	4,300.9	230.6	19.0	18.8
1945	3,560.0	227.2	21.0	17.8
1946	4,060.5	305.4	23.3	21.7
1947	5,859.8	610.4	37.5	25.0
1948	6,055.4	550.0	33.3	23.9
1949	5,228.2	493.8	32.3	18.1
1950	5,557.5	630.1	39.1	18.5
1951	5,759.1	724.4	37.3	16.7
1952	7,224.6	797.1	39.3	19.4
1953	5,159.2	511.0	29.2	14.3
1954	4,890.4	500.7	27.9	12.3
1955	4,527.6	491.9	26.4	11.5
1956	4,743.7	495.0	24.3	11.6
1957	5,671.9	705.3	30.4	13.2
1958	4,780.6	632.3	29.5	12.6

Sources: Raw Sugar output: Zanetti and García (1976), pp. 433-434; Sugar Income: Guerra (1976), pp. 242-243, and J.-L. Rodríguez (1980), p. 189; Nominal National Income: Alienes (1950), p. 54, and J.-L. Rodríguez (1980), p. 184; Cuban Share of World Sugar: Thomas (1971), pp. 1563-1564.

Statistical Tables   143

Table A2.3. Growth estimates, 1930-1958

	Alienes Real National Income (1926 pesos)		Pérez-López Total Industrial Activities (1952 prices)		IBRD Mission Real National Income (1939 pesos)		Domínguez Real National Income (1937 pesos)		New Estimate Real National Income (1926 pesos)	
	Index (1939=100)	Annual Rate	Index (1939=100)	Annual Rate	Index (1939=100)	Annual Rate	Index (1939=100)	Annual Rate	Index (1939=100)	Annual Rate
1930	94		115						93	5.7
1931	85	-10.2	78	-32.0					85	-8.2
1932	69	-18.6	66	-16.1					54	-35.7
1933	70	2.1	58	-12.3					60	10.5
1934	77	9.0	66	13.8					65	8.6
1935	86	11.9	78	18.2					77	17.5
1936	100	16.0	90	15.4					na	na
1937	112	12.7	110	22.2			116		118	na
1938	94	-16.3	101	-7.2			88	-24.1	90	-23.4
1939	100	6.4	100	-1.0	100		100	11.4	100	10.7
1940	87	-13.4	107	7.0			89	-11.0	90	-9.9
1941	123	41.8	125	16.8			129	44.9	131	45.2
1942	114	-7.5	123	-1.2			99	-23.3	100	-23.3
1943	143	25.9	105	-14.6			117	18.2	119	18.8
1944	184	28.7	150	42.8			131	12.0	136	13.8
1945	171	-7.1	129	-14.0	121		100	-23.7	111	-27.8
1946	168	-1.7	139	7.8	138	14.0	113	13.0	118	6.5
1947	186	10.8	165	18.7	158	14.4	124	9.7	126	5.9
1948	163	-12.3	170	3.0	148	-6.3	109	-12.1	117	-7.8
1949			160	-5.9	154	4.1	116	6.4	125	6.9
1950			176	10.0			142	22.4	136	8.6
1951			184	4.5			145	2.1	148	8.9
1952			223	21.2			146	0.7	154	4.3
1953			195	-12.6			135	-7.5	136	-11.7

Table A2.3 (continued)

	Alienes Real National Income (1926 pesos)		Pérez-López Total Industrial Activities (1952 prices)		IBRD Mission Real National Income (1939 pesos)		Domínguez Real National Income (1937 pesos)		New Estimate Real National Income (1926 pesos)	
	Index (1939=100)	Annual Rate	Index (1939=100)	Annual Rate	Index (1939=100)	Annual Rate	Index (1939=100)	Annual Rate	Index (1939=100)	Annual Rate
1954			203	4.1			144	6.7	147	8.2
1955			211	3.9			152	5.6	157	6.3
1956			215	1.9			167	9.9	171	9.0
1957			229	6.5			178	6.6	185	8.2
1958			242	5.7			167	-6.2	164	-11.3

na = not available

Sources: Alienes (1950), p. 52; Pérez-López (1974), p. 70; IBRD (1952), p. 1046; Domínguez (1978), p. 74; new estimate by the author deflating nominal national income by cost of living (food) index as given by Zanetti and García (1976), p. 441.

Table A2.4. Estimates of Cuban national income, 1939-1958

	Nominal National Income (m. current pesos)	Real National Income (m. 1926 pesos)	Estimated Population (mid-year, in 000s)	Real Income Per Capita (pesos)
1939	488	734	4,547	161
1940	431	661	4,611	143
1941	678	960	4,672	205
1942	720	736	4,729	156
1943	933	874	4,782	183
1944	1,212	995	5,084	203
1945	1,125	818	5,191	163
1946	1,313	871	5,300	169
1947	1,626	922	5,411	175
1948	1,651	859	5,525	159
1949	1,530	918	5,641	165
1950	1,611	997	5,759	175
1951	1,944	1,085	5,883	186
1952	2,030	1,132	6,003	189
1953	1,753	1,000	6,129	163
1954	1,793	1,082	6,252	173
1955	1,866	1,150	6,377	180
1956	2,034	1,254	6,505	193
1957	2,321	1,357	6,635	205
1958	2,140	1,204	6,763	178

Sources: Nominal National Income: Alienes (1950), p. 52; IBRD (1952), p. 1043; and J.-L. Rodríguez (1980), p. 190; Real National Income: nominal national income deflated by cost of living index given in Zanetti and García (1976), p. 441-442; Estimated Population: AEC (1974) and Chavez (1976).

Appendix 2

Table A2.5. Total material production at factor cost, 1946-1961 (million 1952 pesos)

	1946	1947	1948	1949	1950	1951	1952	1953
Agriculture	461.7	525.2	532.6	498.2	553.7	557.4	650.2	533.4
Sugar	(228.7)	(329.8)	(341.3)	(294.7)	(313.0)	(324.5)	(430.0)	(294.7)
Nonsugar	(233.0)	(195.4)	(191.3)	(203.5)	(240.7)	(232.9)	(220.2)	(238.7)
Mining	17.8	12.0	10.8	11.8	12.6	15.7	22.8	28.4
Manufacturing	381.5	434.1	425.7	423.7	480.5	494.9	582.6	517.0
Sugar	(134.9)	(193.4)	(185.1)	(174.7)	(184.8)	(191.7)	(241.2)	(173.0)
Nonsugar	(246.6)	(240.7)	(240.6)	(249.0)	(295.7)	(303.2)	(341.4)	(344.0)
Electricity & gas	17.0	18.3	20.5	22.1	24.3	26.8	29.4	32.2
Construction	55.7	55.7	65.9	72.1	80.1	88.9	75.1	81.2
Total material production	933.7	1,045.3	1,055.5	1,027.5	1,151.2	1,183.7	1,360.1	1,192.2

Table A2.5 (continued)

	1954	1955	1956	1957	1958	1959	1960	1961
Agriculture	532.3	508.9	527.5	594.7	588.9	616.6	627.3	671.6
Sugar	(283.8)	(251.4)	(267.6)	(323.0)	(330.1)	(346.9)	(343.0)	(392.2)
Nonsugar	(248.5)	(257.5)	(259.9)	(271.7)	(258.8)	(269.7)	(284.3)	(279.4)
Mining	24.9	28.0	25.2	26.2	26.5	21.6	15.1	13.6
Manufacturing	540.9	554.6	587.3	600.0	659.8	706.1	702.9	694.7
Sugar	(184.4)	(188.2)	(175.8)	(188.1)	(202.8)	(209.0)	(205.5)	(237.2)
Nonsugar	(356.5)	(366.4)	(411.5)	(441.9)	(457.0)	(497.1)	(497.4)	(457.5)
Electricity & gas	34.8	38.4	42.3	43.3	46.7	46.4	48.1	48.2
Construction	101.1	90.4	96.1	99.1	98.1	89.7	108.5	116.2
Total material production	1,234.0	1,220.3	1,278.4	1,393.3	1,420.0	1,480.4	1,501.9	1,544.3

Sources: Estimates explained in text.

Table A2.6. Annual growth rates of total material production by branches, 1947-1961

	1947	1948	1949	1950	1951	1952	1953	1954	1955	1956	1957	1958	1959	1960	1961
Agriculture	13.8	1.4	-6.5	11.1	0.7	16.6	-18.0	-0.2	-4.4	3.7	12.7	-0.9	4.7	1.7	7.1
Sugar	44.2	3.5	-13.7	6.2	3.7	32.5	-31.5	-3.7	-11.4	6.4	20.7	2.2	5.1	-1.1	14.3
Nonsugar	-16.1	-2.1	6.4	18.3	-3.2	-5.5	8.4	4.1	3.6	0.9	4.5	-4.7	4.2	5.4	-1.7
Mining	-32.6	-10.0	9.3	6.8	24.6	45.2	24.6	-12.3	12.4	-10.0	4.0	1.1	-18.5	-30.1	-9.9
Manufacturing	13.8	-1.9	-0.5	13.5	3.0	17.7	-11.3	4.6	2.5	5.9	7.2	4.7	7.0	-0.5	-1.2
Beverages	-2.6	3.2	2.4	9.3	13.4	12.6	-10.8	0.1	0.6	4.1	2.6	-4.4	17.8	-5.2	-5.5
Tobacco	5.5	3.3	-3.3	-2.5	3.3	7.5	-3.6	-6.5	4.0	7.1	8.5	-5.8	2.0	-13.6	-15.7
Textiles	-5.0	-17.6	21.4	105.0	-27.4	11.6	-9.4	26.2	-7.6	11.9	8.2	2.5	27.2	-17.1	-25.6
Processed foods	0.0	0.0	11.1	6.6	-4.1	37.8	29.4	0.4	7.0	12.2	8.6	-1.7	6.4	11.6	-19.7
Sugar	43.3	-4.3	-5.6	5.7	3.7	25.8	-29.3	6.6	2.1	-6.6	7.0	7.8	3.1	-1.7	15.4
Shoemaking	44.6	-23.1	-15.6	9.5	1.2	-0.6	12.0	7.3	6.8	10.3	10.0	4.6	4.3	-15.6	-49.6
Rubber products	8.6	-6.4	-9.4	55.9	24.8	-13.3	-11.0	19.2	-0.2	26.9	17.6	63.7	-0.3	-0.2	5.6
Paper & paperboard	-58.8	30.0	-14.8	55.1	4.8	-3.1	14.7	3.8	5.1	12.3	3.6	1.3	26.5	-1.5	36.1
Construction materials	15.1	3.1	9.6	1.3	21.1	9.7	-3.2	3.3	8.4	29.8	8.9	11.0	-8.6	21.0	7.1
Electricity & gas	7.6	12.0	7.8	10.0	10.3	9.7	9.5	8.1	10.3	10.2	2.4	7.9	-0.8	3.7	0.2
Construction	0.0	18.3	9.4	11.1	11.1	-15.5	8.1	24.5	-10.6	6.3	3.1	-1.0	-8.6	21.0	7.1
Total material production	12.0	1.0	-2.7	12.1	2.8	14.9	-12.3	3.5	-1.1	4.8	9.0	1.9	4.3	1.5	2.8

Source: Appendix 2, Table 5.

Table A2.7. Total material production at factor cost, 1961-1968 (constant prices in million pesos)

	1961	1962	1963	1964	1965	1966	1967	1968
Agriculture	836.8	742.3	699.6	736.5	829.8	786.8	848.9	860.0
Sugarcane	(362.8)	(245.0)	(214.5)	(242.0)	(334.7)	(245.7)	(325.7)	(327.3)
Nonsugar agriculture	(245.6)	(264.7)	(246.6)	(232.4)	(215.4)	(249.0)	(243.2)	(259.3)
Livestock	(207.8)	(205.3)	(214.7)	(239.2)	(255.3)	(261.9)	(238.5)	(208.1)
Forestry	(8.3)	(10.9)	(5.5)	(5.4)	(6.1)	(6.0)	(9.0)	(34.4)
Fishing	(12.3)	(16.4)	(16.2)	(17.5)	(18.3)	(24.2)	(32.5)	(30.9)
Mining	33.8	56.6	50.9	54.6	63.1	58.2	54.0	60.8
Manufacturing	1,124.9	1,129.3	1,112.6	1,153.1	1,190.4	1,166.9	1,314.0	1,276.3
Metallurgy	(73.1)	(75.4)	(74.5)	(76.3)	(68.0)	(71.9)	(76.4)	(93.9)
Construction materials	(83.4)	(76.1)	(78.1)	(67.8)	(74.5)	(70.5)	(91.6)	(67.6)
Petroleum	(114.0)	(136.5)	(132.1)	(132.2)	(142.0)	(144.4)	(147.7)	(135.2)
Chemicals	(118.8)	(153.0)	(155.2)	(166.6)	(156.9)	(166.0)	(208.7)	(229.4)
Textiles & leather	(131.8)	(139.9)	(153.8)	(161.7)	(148.8)	(145.9)	(150.3)	(136.6)
Sugar	(216.0)	(153.7)	(128.1)	(146.7)	(200.4)	(148.4)	(209.4)	(172.5)
Food	(205.0)	(208.6)	(204.1)	(208.4)	(200.6)	(203.2)	(205.8)	(267.8)
Beverages & tobacco	(110.7)	(108.3)	(111.7)	(117.4)	(112.7)	(117.5)	(127.7)	(120.7)
Other industry	(72.1)	(77.8)	(75.0)	(76.0)	(86.5)	(99.1)	(96.4)	(52.6)
Electricity	67.4	66.6	71.0	76.1	79.9	84.6	85.7	91.5
Construction	239.9	253.1	238.5	287.0	357.0	354.0	408.0	359.6
Total material production	2,302.8	2,247.9	2,172.6	2,397.3	2,520.2	2,450.5	2,711.4	2,648.2

Source: Estimates explained in text.

150 Appendix 2

Table A2.8. Annual growth rates of total material production by branches, 1962-1968

	1962	1963	1964	1965	1966	1967	1968
Agriculture, Forestry, & Fishing	-11.3	-5.8	5.3	12.7	-5.2	7.9	1.3
Sugarcane	-32.5	-6.8	12.8	38.3	-26.6	32.6	0.5
Nonsugar agriculture	7.8	-6.8	-5.8	-7.3	15.6	-2.3	6.6
Livestock	-1.2	4.6	11.4	6.7	2.6	-8.9	-12.7
Forestry	31.3	-49.5	-1.8	13.0	-1.6	50.0	282.2
Fishing	33.3	-1.2	8.0	4.6	32.2	34.3	-4.9
Mining	67.5	10.1	7.3	15.6	-7.8	-7.2	12.6
Manufacturing	0.4	-1.5	3.6	3.2	-2.0	12.6	-2.9
Metallurgy & mechanical industry	3.1	-1.2	2.4	-10.9	5.7	6.3	22.9
Construction materials	-8.8	2.6	-13.2	9.9	-5.4	29.9	-26.2
Petroleum	19.7	-3.2	0.1	7.4	1.7	2.3	-8.5
Chemicals	28.8	1.4	7.3	-5.8	2.6	29.6	9.9
Textiles & leather	6.1	9.9	5.1	-8.0	-1.9	3.0	-9.1
Sugar	-28.8	-16.7	14.5	36.6	-25.9	41.1	-17.6
Food	1.8	-2.2	2.1	-3.7	1.3	1.3	30.1
Beverages & tobacco	-2.2	3.1	5.1	-4.0	4.3	8.7	-5.5
Other industry	7.9	-3.6	1.3	13.8	14.6	-3.0	-45.3
Electricity	-1.2	6.6	7.2	5.0	5.9	1.3	6.8
Construction	5.5	-5.8	20.3	24.4	-0.8	15.5	-12.0
Total material production	-2.4	-3.3	6.2	9.2	-2.8	10.6	-2.3

Source: Appendix 2, Table 7.

Table A2.9. Total material production at factor cost, 1968-1980 (constant prices in million pesos)

	1968	1969	1970	1971	1972	1973
Agriculture	860.0	835.5	953.7	849.5	858.2	892.9
Sugarcane	(327.3)	(361.1)	(483.6)	(365.2)	(319.3)	(331.4)
Nonsugar agriculture	(259.3)	(233.3)	(207.7)	(213.4)	(241.1)	(251.5)
Livestock	(208.1)	(194.8)	(204.6)	(194.4)	(215.2)	(221.6)
Forestry	(34.4)	(22.6)	(15.3)	(21.5)	(24.7)	(30.3)
Fishing	(30.9)	(33.7)	(42.5)	(55.0)	(57.9)	(58.1)
Mining	60.8	55.9	59.2	59.2	62.8	64.8
Manufacturing	1,276.3	1,257.3	1,561.5	1,658.4	1,760.3	1,980.1
Metallurgy	(93.9)	(87.1)	(131.2)	(159.4)	(184.8)	(248.8)
Construction materials	(67.6)	(47.2)	(50.5)	(74.8)	(100.1)	(117.5)
Petroleum	(135.2)	(142.3)	(155.3)	(160.5)	(175.6)	(200.1)
Chemicals	(229.4)	(238.5)	(304.6)	(340.5)	(358.2)	(390.9)
Textiles & leather	(136.6)	(125.3)	(104.3)	(134.8)	(150.2)	(165.8)
Sugar	(172.5)	(187.6)	(254.3)	(234.5)	(186.2)	(208.1)
Food	(267.8)	(280.5)	(343.2)	(358.4)	(385.9)	(407.4)
Beverages & tobacco	(120.7)	(96.7)	(153.2)	(127.0)	(146.9)	(160.1)
Other industry	(52.6)	(52.1)	(64.9)	(68.5)	(72.4)	(81.4)
Electricity	91.5	99.1	103.0	106.0	112.8	122.6
Construction	359.6	306.4	298.4	392.5	549.6	731.2
Total material production	2,648.2	2,554.2	2,975.8	3,065.6	3,343.7	3,791.6

* = after 1976 "fishing" is no longer shown as a primary activity but as a separate category under Industry; here, the same growth index has been applied to Fishing

Table A2.9 (continued)

	1974	1975	1976	1977	1978	1979	1980
Agriculture	950.0	982.0	1,042.8	1,082.5	1,183.7	1,194.6	1,231.7
Sugarcane	(341.7)	(354.4)	(362.1)	(414.4)	(477.3)	(481.0)	(392.9)
Nonsugar agriculture	(290.7)	(300.0)	(323.8)	(305.3)	(318.6)	(328.0)	(417.5)
Livestock	(222.9)	(241.4)	(255.0)	(262.9)	(274.9)	(282.5)	(297.2)
Forestry	(32.9)	(30.6)	(29.6)	(29.7)	(32.4)	(29.9)	(33.7)
Fishing	(61.8)	(55.6)	(72.3)	(70.2)*	(80.5)*	(73.2)*	(90.4)*
Mining	64.9	70.5	66.5	65.2	67.4	64.8	74.2
Manufacturing	2,148.9	2,422.8	2,502.0	2,516.4	2,740.3	2,807.3	2,750.0
Metallurgy	(309.3)	(392.1)	(435.4)	(477.0)	(535.4)	(586.0)	(520.4)
Construction materials	(120.8)	(137.5)	(143.9)	(153.7)	(158.2)	(158.5)	(161.3)
Petroleum	(191.8)	(208.9)	(200.8)	(196.8)	(205.9)	(206.4)	(204.5)
Chemicals	(420.0)	(471.5)	(470.5)	(405.6)	(459.8)	(482.0)	(500.9)
Textiles & leather	(179.1)	(215.2)	(223.4)	(225.9)	(251.2)	(246.9)	(239.6)
Sugar	(223.9)	(237.5)	(231.0)	(260.6)	(298.6)	(308.5)	(279.5)
Food	(435.0)	(460.2)	(468.2)	(482.2)	(496.3)	(484.1)	(533.3)
Beverages & tobacco	(180.5)	(200.2)	(225.9)	(211.2)	(222.2)	(219.3)	(197.4)
Other industry	(88.5)	(99.7)	(102.9)	(103.4)	(112.7)	(115.6)	(113.1)
Electricity	126.8	138.2	151.6	153.3	167.1	170.3	179.2
Construction	806.3	962.4	1,020.4	1,121.0	1,203.6	1,213.2	1,230.2
Total material production	4,096.9	4,575.9	4,783.3	4,983.3	5,362.1	5,450.2	5,580.3

Source: Estimates explained in text.

Statistical Tables 153

Table A2.10. Annual growth rates of total material production by branches, 1969-1980

	1969	1970	1971	1972	1973	1974	1975	1976	1977	1978	1979	1980
Agriculture, forestry & fishing	-2.8	14.1	-10.1	1.0	4.0	6.4	3.4	6.2	3.8	9.3	0.9	3.1
Sugarcane	10.3	33.9	-24.5	-12.6	3.8	3.1	3.7	2.2	14.4	15.2	0.8	-18.3
Nonsugar agriculture	-10.0	-7.0	2.7	13.0	4.3	15.6	3.2	7.9	-5.7	4.4	3.0	27.3
Livestock	-6.4	5.0	-5.0	10.7	3.0	0.6	8.3	5.6	3.1	4.6	2.8	5.2
Forestry	-34.3	-32.3	40.5	14.9	22.7	8.6	-7.0	-3.3	0.3	9.1	-8.7	12.7
Fishing	9.1	26.1	29.4	5.3	0.3	6.4	-10.0	30.0	-12.9	14.7	-9.1	23.5
Mining	-8.1	5.9	0.0	6.1	3.2	0.2	8.6	-5.7	-2.0	3.4	-3.9	14.5
Manufacturing	-1.5	24.2	6.2	6.1	12.5	8.5	12.7	3.3	0.6	8.9	2.4	-2.0
Metallurgy & mechanical industry	-7.2	50.6	21.5	15.9	34.6	24.3	26.8	11.0	9.6	12.2	9.5	-11.2
Construction materials	-30.2	7.0	48.1	33.8	17.4	3.0	13.8	4.7	6.8	2.9	0.2	1.8
Petroleum	5.3	9.1	3.3	9.4	14.0	-4.1	8.9	-3.9	-2.0	4.6	0.2	-0.9
Chemicals	4.0	27.7	11.8	5.2	9.1	7.4	12.3	-0.2	-13.8	13.4	4.8	3.9
Textiles & leather	-8.3	-16.8	29.2	11.4	10.4	8.0	20.2	3.8	1.1	11.2	-1.7	-3.0
Sugar	8.8	35.6	-7.8	-20.6	11.8	7.6	6.1	-2.7	12.8	14.6	3.3	-9.4
Food	4.7	22.4	4.4	7.7	5.6	6.8	5.8	1.7	3.0	2.9	-2.5	10.2
Beverages & tobacco	-19.9	58.4	-17.1	15.7	9.0	12.7	10.9	12.8	-6.5	5.2	-1.3	-10.0
Other industry	-1.0	24.6	5.5	5.7	12.4	8.7	12.7	3.2	0.5	9.0	2.6	-2.2
Electricity	8.3	3.9	2.9	6.4	8.7	3.4	9.0	9.7	1.1	9.0	1.9	5.2
Construction	-14.7	-2.6	31.5	40.0	33.0	10.3	19.4	6.0	9.9	7.4	0.8	1.4
Total material production	-3.5	16.5	3.0	9.1	13.4	8.1	11.7	4.5	3.2	8.6	1.6	0.3

Source: Appendix 2, Table 9.

Appendix 2

Table A2.11. Output of transport equipment and machinery (except electrical), 1958-1980

	Transport Equipment				Machinery (except electrical)			
	Buses (units)	Fishing Boats (units)	Wagons for Sugarcane (units)	Trailers (units)	Combines (units)	Water Pumps (units)	Inputs for Sugar Industry (m. pesos)	Inputs for Acopios* (m. pesos)
1958						na	na	
1959						na	na	
1960						na	na	
1961						na	na	
1962						na	na	
1963		23	1,134			na	na	
1964		26	1,752			na	na	
1965		23	2,000			na	na	
1966		23	678			na	na	
1967		7	723			na	na	
1968			5,181			1,858	30.7	1.8
1969			24			1,605	39.7	25.5
1970	300	36	1,606	52		1,497	28.2	102.2
1971	800	53	1,650	105		4,256	59.8	225.9
1972	575	87	3,906	51		5,742	28.7	40.5
1973	1,137	105	3,000	50		8,812	40.4	25.1
1974	1,255	131	3,600	50		14,130	73.5	10.0
1975	1,718	137	3,600	90		14,851	97.0	9.8
1976	1,266	156	3,600	283		3,672	81.3	
1977	1,970	152	3,000		30	1,201	94.3	
1978	1,805	139	3,000	100	165	511	860.9	
1979	2,440	93	3,900	140	360	585	608.0	
1980	1,846	120	3,410	na	501	3,415	na	

*agricultural distribution centers run by the state; na = not available

Sources: 1963-1967: BEC (1968, 1970); 1968-1974: AEC (1974); 1975-1978: AEC (1978); 1979-1980: AEC (1979) and BEM (March 1981).

Table A2.12. Output of electrical equipment, electric power, and mining industry, 1958-1980

	Electrical Equipment				Electric Power (million kWh)	Mining Industry		
	Electrical Cables (km)	Telephone Cables (km)	Batteries (units)	Electrical Wires (mt)		Copper Concentrates (000mt)*	Nickel (000mt)*	Refractory Chrome (000mt)*
1958	na	na	na	na	2,589	17.9	17.9	na
1959	na	na	na	na	2,806	17.8	18.0	na
1960	na	na	na	na	2,981	11.8	12.8	na
1961	na	na	na	na	3,030	5.0	14.8	na
1962	na	na	na	na	2,998	5.5	16.6	na
1963	25,680	3,501	113.9	na	2,572	6.8	19.8	56.6
1964	16,800	3,463	125.7	na	2,770	5.5	22.9	32.9
1965	23,589	4,944	102.1	na	2,926	6.0	28.2	41.0
1966	17,187	4,829	62.4	na	3,316	5.4	27.9	37.5
1967	15,323	3,703	88.9	na	3,658	5.2	32.4	43.0
1968	14,701	3,385	96.9	1,167	3,789	5.3	37.3	48.5
1969	12,654	4,137	90.5	1,175	3,585**	3.8	35.4	45.3
1970	13,122	4,631	95.2	825	4,888	0.4	36.8	22.8
1971	19,894	7,923	90.4	1,144	5,021	--	36.5	13.9
1972	19,174	5,192	108.3	1,330	5,265	1.8	36.8	37.1
1973	32,869	4,060	111.6	1,022	5,703	2.1	35.2	37.2
1974	28,951	4,767	126.4	1,164	6,018	2.9	33.9	37.7
1975	27,287	4,635	139.4	1,332	6,583	2.8	37.3	36.1
1976	30,273	2,780	98.8	975	7,191	2.9	37.0	19.1
1977	21,356	3,658	97.4	657	7,707	2.6	36.8	20.4
1978	26,313	3,108	136.6	1,388	8,481	2.8	34.8	28.8
1979	42,046	3,753	177.9	2,362	9,401	2.8	32.3	28.2
1980	38,000	6,667	301.9	2,547	9,896	3.3	38.2	28.5

na = not available; * = metal content; ** = excluding autogeneration in sugar industry

Sources: 1958-1962: Mesa-Lago (1971c) and ECLA (1965); 1963-1967: BEC (1968, 1970); 1968-1974: AEC (1974); 1975-1978: AEC (1978); 1979-1980: AEC (1979) and BEM (March 1981).

Table A2.13. Output of metallurgy and metal products, petroleum products, and raw sugar, 1958–1980

	Metallurgy & Metal Products				Petroleum Products			
	Crude Steel (000mt)	Corrugated Steel (000mt)	Steel Balks	Aluminum Tins (m. units)	Refined Oil (000mt)	Fuel Oil (000mt)	Gasoline (000mt)	Raw Sugar (000mt)
1958	30*	na	na	na	na	na	na	5,781
1959	na	na	na	na	na	na	na	5,964
1960	na	na	na	na	na	1,379	599	5,862
1961	107.4	103.8	na	na	3,001	1,392	656	6,767
1962	55.0	122.1	na	na	3,673	1,995	766	4,815
1963	62.9	82.5	41.3	27.3	3,691	2,221	719	3,821
1964	52.2	49.8	53.2	30.3	3,454	1,953	751	4,590
1965	36.0	26.3		25.7	3,569	1,899	810	6,082
1966	66.6	74.9	62.6	29.9	3,699	1,973	778	4,867
1967	102.4	88.9	98.7	38.5	3,817	1,930	854	6,236
1968	119.8	103.9	109.5	34.0	3,879	1,941	713	5,315
1969	119.2	87.1	100.2	38.5	4,140	2,670	747	5,534
1970	140.0	85.0	105.7	31.7	4,308	2,367	746	7,559
1971	110.8	95.3	111.1	43.8	4,350	2,376	712	5,950
1972	186.6	145.1	162.7	51.9	4,745	2,526	803	4,688
1973	220.7	189.1	194.4	52.0	5,346	2,673	911	5,383
1974	250.3	205.4	215.2	54.9	5,567	2,769	868	5,926
1975	298.4	242.6	260.6	52.2	5,976	2,822	947	6,427
1976	250.3	229.7	235.3	53.0	6,129	2,936	909	6,151
1977	330.5	292.4	289.2	53.1	6,324	3,210	833	6,953
1978	323.6	292.8	263.1	59.3	6,359	3,101	887	7,661
1979	327.8	313.5	303.3	39.2	6,371	3,213	872	7,800
1980	303.8	260.2	248.3	na	6,334	3,018	816	7,075

* = speech by Fidel Castro on 26 July 1977, quoted in Fabian (1981), p. 663; na = not available

Sources: 1958–1962: Mesa-Lago (1971c) and ECLA (1965); 1963–1967: BEC (1968, 1970); 1968–1974: AEC (1974); 1975–1978: AEC (1978); 1979–1980: AEC (1979) and BEM (March 1981).

Table A2.14. Output of sulphuric acid, rayon tire cords, fertilizers, insecticides, herbicides, paper pulp, newsprint, tires, and matches, 1958-1980

	Sulphuric Acid (mt)	Rayon Tire Cords (mt)	Fertilizers (000mt)	Insecticides (mt)	Herbicides (mt)	Paper Pulp (000mt)	Newsprint (000mt)	Tires (000 units)	Matches (m. boxes)
1958	34*	4,700	266*			na	na	264.9	na
1959	na	na	na			na	na	na	na
1960	44	7,500	300			na	na	343.0	na
1961	59	1,800	406	1,400	200	na	na	362.0	192.5
1962	139	2,500	519	4,800	300	na	na	391.0	221.1
1963	139	1,055	439	2,523	1,412	na	16.8	363.6	245.9
1964	190	1,487	430	1,926	9	na	22.7	450.8	273.0
1965	202	1,044	473	2,461	847	na	18.8	197.1	277.9
1966	230	1,526	514	2,288	255	na	16.4	305.7	322.7
1967	270	1,857	788	3,651	1,532	na	18.9	413.9	333.6
1968	322	540	860	2,486	786	32.4	20.9	147.7	382.8
1969	326	1,402	695	4,164	1,048	32.6	19.9	356.4	395.6
1970	322	1,131	577	1,414	2,203	33.7	18.9	301.9	370.7
1971	368	1,425	565	2,988	2,594	36.0	22.0	751.2	428.2
1972	400	1,521	620	3,416	2,738	35.0	24.7	381.1	457.2
1973	385	1,268	663	4,424	2,715	43.0	26.9	371.5	439.6
1974	384	1,674	728	5,200	2,766	42.6	28.5	390.8	414.3
1975	418	2,154	749	5,426	3,102	36.3	32.0	367.8	424.4
1976	392	1,637	798	3,591	3,118	40.9	32.3	266.4	425.1
1977	375	440	863	2,660	na	37.5	31.3	171.9	430.8
1978	347	1,415	945	3,013	na	33.9	35.6	294.5	414.1
1979	297	1,586	873	4,414	na	29.5	34.9	302.0	370.5
1980	402	1,648	1,059	na	na	29.9	36.7	386.6	383.4

* = 1957; na = not available

Sources: 1958-1962: Mesa-Lago (1971c) and ECLA (1965); 1963-1967: BEC (1968, 1970); 1968-1974: AEC (1974); 1975-1978: AEC (1978); 1979-1980: AEC (1979) and BEM (March 1981).

Appendix 2

Table A2.15. Output of construction materials and durable consumer goods, 1958-1980

	Construction Materials			Durable Consumer Goods			
	Cement (000mt)	Concrete (prefabricated) (000 m³)	Bricks (000 units)	Refrigerators (units)	Gas Stoves (units)	Kerosene Stoves (units)	Radio Rec. (units)	TV Sets (units)
1958	736	na	na		na		na	
1959	673	na	na		na		na	
1960	813	na	na		na		na	
1961	871	na	na		na		na	
1962	779	na	na		na		na	
1963	812	341	67,849		8,727		38,569	
1964	806	350	66,546	1,093	29,645		41,642	
1965	801	361	64,322	11,871	10,228		81,861	
1966	750	340	52,599	1,711	46,024		43,068	
1967	835	378	74,146	730	34,878		7,312	
1968	780	162	48,148	19	6,440		20,853	
1969	680	113	27,203	2,080	4,155			
1970	742	134	31,389	5,841	6,009	500		
1971	1,088	256	46,061	20,168	30,010	2,150	19,135	
1972	1,474	582	70,727	30,097	30,000	25,381	12,706	
1973	1,757	734	64,855	40,220	40,112	50,800	31,283	
1974	1,814	828	66,691	42,001	45,079	72,250	23,928	
1975	2,083	981	76,861	50,012	53,627	100,000	42,223	25,600
1976	2,501	919	99,943	43,687	49,327	104,000	112,635	28,000
1977	2,656	915	113,361	46,274	51,717	79,000	92,352	33,000
1978	2,712	894	115,424	45,573	51,233	102,465	120,005	51,166
1979	2,613	883	115,133	55,622	35,652	73,272	120,628	52,414
1980				25,002	na	107,127	143,272	40,290
						107,100	200,000	

na = not available

Sources: 1958-1962: Mesa-Lago (1971c) and ECLA (1965); 1963-1967: BEC (1968, 1970); 1968-1974: AEC (1974); 1975-1978: AEC (1978); 1979-1980: AEC (1979) and BEM (March 1981).

Table A2.16. Output of nondurable consumer goods, 1958-1980

	Leather Shoes (000 units)	Cotton Cloth (million m^2)	Rayon Cloth (million m^2)	Rice[1] (000mt)	Wheat Flour (000mt)	Beef[2] (000mt)	Pork[2] (000mt)	Condensed and Evaporated Milk (000mt)
1958	20,000[3]	na	na	169.5[5]	66.0	93.8[6]	7.6[6]	35.1[7]
1959	16,700	na	na	218.4[5]	na	102.0[6]	8.0[6]	na
1960	10,203	99.4[4]	na	216.4[5]	106.6	87.7[6]	7.4[6]	na
1961	3,398	98.7[4]	na	138.7[5]	106.3	83.1[6]	8.2[6]	na
1962	7,085	117.9[4]	na	138.6[5]	142.5	75.0[6]	8.6[6]	39.3
1963	11,522	89.7	21.6	136.7[5]	133.3	72.8	8.0	49.3
1964	12,811	105.2	21.7	83.1	126.9	86.1	9.4	45.9
1965	11,003	95.9	21.2	46.1	137.3	97.7	9.9	56.6
1966	12,643	108.4	6.4	43.2	131.5	108.5	6.1	60.9
1967	13,674	112.5	6.2	45.8	130.8	99.7	5.5	65.7
1968	13,673	105.2	5.3	51.1	137.6	110.8	5.0	68.3
1969	13,261	91.3	4.4	87.9	147.9	104.5	2.6	69.2
1970	12,052	75.7	2.2	182.8	159.7	104.9	7.6	68.1
1971	14,217	87.1	8.1	134.4	175.3	100.8	10.0	77.9
1972	14,390	98.0	7.4	184.7	177.6	99.0	11.4	49.4
1973	14,760	117.1	6.8	139.5	178.4	84.6	12.9	58.6
1974	13,512	127.9	3.8	206.5	184.3	69.8	19.0	57.3
1975	15,513	137.6	6.3	222.8	176.1	67.7	24.2	62.1
1976	14,979	134.1	5.1	210.9	165.4	80.5	29.1	62.1
1977	13,449	148.9	2.7	241.4	176.4	87.5	33.7	63.2
1978	14,685	154.4	1.5	238.4	174.9	83.4	34.9	63.0
1979	13,759	148.4	1.5	202.6	160.5	78.8	34.0	65.2
1980	12,927	157.4	na	225.2	271.0	80.3	34.2	66.3

na = not available
[1]Hulled rice; [2]Net weight; [3]Including rubber shoes; [4]Tons converted into million m^2; [5]Paddy converted into hulled rice; [6]Carcass weight converted into net weight; [7]Cases of cans converted into tons

Sources: 1958-1962: Mesa-Lago (1971c) and ECLA (1965); 1963-1967: BEC (1968, 1970); 1968-1974: AEC (1974); 1975-1978: AEC (1978); 1979-1980: AEC (1979) and BEM (March 1981).
(Pérez-López [1974], p. 116)

Table A2.17. Estimates of Cuban labor force and its distribution, 1962-1978

	Total Population (mid-year)	Total Labor Force	Unemployed	Employed Labor Force	Armed Forces	Total Civilian Labor Force		
						Total	State	Private
1962	7,254	2,401	215	2,186	363	1,823	1,083	740
1963	7,415	2,431	198	2,232	382	1,851	1,238	613
1964	7,612	2,456	185	2,271	386	1,885	1,369	516
1965	7,810	2,490	163	2,327	367	1,960	1,452	508
1966	7,985	2,508	155	2,253	360	1,993	1,517	476
1967	8,139	2,549	135	2,414	350	2,064	1,604	460
1968	8,284	2,579	110	2,477	325	2,152	1,768	384
1969	8,421	2,608	75	2,533	275	2,258	1,895	363
1970	8,551	2,638	34	2,604	200	2,404	2,064	340
1971	8,691	2,652	55	2,597	195	2,402	2,082	320
1972	8,859	2,680	64	2,616	190	2,426	2,126	300
1973	9,035	2,795	84	2,711	185	2,526	2,246	260
1974	9,192	2,869	111	2,758	185	2,573	2,313	260
1975	9,335	2,923	90	2,833	210	2,683	2,391	232
1976	9,471	2,974	85	2,889	220	2,669	2,469	200
1977	9,593	3,088	60	3,028	225	2,803	2,621	175
1978	9,694	3,178	40	3,138	230	2,908	2,733	175

Table A2.17 (continued)

	Agriculture Total+	Agriculture	Industry	Construction	Transport & Communications	Trade	Services & Others
1962	841	297	267	104	74	132	209
1963	705	305	289	97	83	205	259
1964	766	386	303	108	82	216	274
1965	803	433	309	117	84	214	295
1966	810	450	323	118	82	235	309
1967	na	na	na	na	na	na	na
1968	na	na	na	na	na	na	na
1969	na	na	na	na	na	na	na
1970	712*	495*	479	140	125	272	560
1971	892	604	440	133	175	168	562
1972	907	637	438	154	177	166	554
1973	923	670	453	177	182	177	587
1974	910	675	467	183	186	184	618
1975	894	685	472	208	187	179	660
1976	865	685	477	243	199	179	686
1977	799	636	567	300	179	282	657
1978	865	660	553	319	183	296	722

+Includes estimate for private sector; data in other columns are for state sector only
*Census figure, does not include people mobilized for 1969-1970 zafra

Sources: Mesa-Lago (1981), Table 26, p. 111; AEC (1978, 1979); 1970 figures estimated from census data.

The data in this table partly contradict data in Appendix 1, which are more recent, but this table is included for purposes of comparison.

Table A2.18. Per capita consumption of food and beverages in Cuba, 1963–1971 (kgs)

	1963	1964	1965	1966	1967	1968	1969	1970	1971
Beef	8.5	10.0	11.2	12.3	12.2	12.5	11.2	11.4	11.1
Pork	0.2	0.3	0.3	0.2	0.2	0.2	0.1	0.6	0.6
Offal	1.1	3.3	3.5	3.2	2.9	3.5	3.1	3.1	3.0
Canned meat	5.8	4.4	2.5	1.9	3.0	2.8	3.3	2.6	4.4
Poultry	4.2	4.7	3.9	2.7	2.4	2.4	1.9	1.8	2.1
Eggs (units)	101	109	113	125	142	144	153	160	164
Beans	9.4	10.3	9.9	9.9	10.9	9.7	9.9	9.4	10.2
Butter	0.4	0.3	0.3	0.4	0.4	0.2	*	*	*
Lard	5.4	7.1	6.1	5.8	5.2	4.7	5.5	8.0	7.7
Vegetable oil	4.6	4.5	4.9	5.5	6.2	7.2	6.1	3.8	5.0
Potatoes	15.4	15.0	13.6	17.6	16.7	16.0	14.9	12.5	11.3
Sweet potatoes	11.1	10.2	11.1	18.5	10.5	10.8	5.3	2.4	4.6
Malanga	5.6	5.2	6.3	8.4	4.9	4.9	3.8	1.3	1.4
Manioc	8.5	6.7	5.5	8.3	4.4	5.4	4.2	2.4	3.0
Plantains	9.3	10.0	8.8	8.5	6.8	8.6	10.3	4.4	4.7
Ñame	1.1	1.1	0.7	1.3	0.6	0.19	0.6	0.22	0.13
Pumpkins	6.2	9.5	6.8	5.0	5.5	2.1	1.7	2.3	4.1
Rice	36.8	42.4	41.8	26.1	26.5	24.5	32.6	41.7	45.0
Wheat	24.3	22.3	15.2	15.6	14.5	13.7	10.2	8.6	7.8
Bread	7.5	19.2	23.6	33.0	38.8	43.7	44.7	45.3	44.7
Spaghetti	2.7	3.0	3.4	4.2	4.7	4.8	5.5	5.2	5.0
Cornmeal	0.8	3.2	2.0	0.5	0.3	0.2	0.1	0.1	0.2
Coffee	4.6	3.1	3.4	2.8	2.9	2.9	3.1	3.2	3.1

Table A2.18 (continued)

	1963	1964	1965	1966	1967	1968	1969	1970	1971
Sugar	30.9	38.9	47.3	52.8	59.9	66.1	44.2	46.5	46.8
Tomatoes	12.0	14.1	14.8	16.0	19.1	11.4	5.2	6.8	9.5
Onions	2.7	4.1	3.0	3.5	3.7	2.9	2.7	2.3	3.0
Cucumber	0.7	1.2	1.9	1.5	1.6	1.4	1.0	1.2	2.2
Cabbage	1.7	1.6	1.6	1.7	2.0	1.8	1.8	1.2	2.2
Citrus fruits	14.0	15.1	13.9	18.8	15.8	17.1	14.7	14.8	10.5
Pineapple	5.6	4.2	2.0	1.2	0.8	0.9	1.2	1.7	2.4
Bananas	5.8	4.3	4.6	3.3	3.4	2.9	3.3	5.1	5.9
Other fruits[1]	9.3	10.0	14.5	15.4	17.4	22.6	12.3	7.6	11.0
Fresh & frozen fish	3.5[3]	3.5	3.6	3.7	6.0	6.0	6.3	8.8	8.7
Canned fish	0.5	0.7	1.7	1.0	1.0	0.9	1.1	1.1	0.9
Fluid milk	19.5	21.1	26.2	37.9	43.5	44.0	51.7	55.2	57.7
Condensed milk	8.2	8.3	8.5	7.9	8.7	8.7	8.7	8.5	8.0
Evaporated milk	0.7	0.6	1.6	1.6	1.6	1.4	1.6	1.5	1.4
Yogurt	*	0.11	0.4	0.9	1.2	1.4	1.6	1.8	2.1
Cheese	0.61	0.52	0.33	0.30	0.21	0.32	0.62	0.39	0.46
Ice cream	0.9	1.0	1.2	1.6	2.3	1.6	2.3	2.2	3.1
Soft drinks[2]	51.7	49.8	47.1	44.0	44.1	43.5	35.9	28.0	28.9
Light beer[2]	12.0	13.6	12.8	13.6	16.7	9.5	7.8	11.1	15.1
Dark beer[2]	3.3	3.0	2.2	2.4	2.9	5.7	7.1	5.2	6.5

Table A2.18 (continued)

	1972	1973	1974	1975	1976	1977	1978	1979	1980
Beef	10.5	8.7	6.9	6.4	7.7	8.4	8.3	8.1	8.3
Pork	0.8	1.0	1.4	1.0	0.9	1.9	2.2	2.4	2.4
Offal	2.9	2.4	2.0	1.8	2.1	2.3	2.3	2.2	2.1
Canned meat	5.0	4.9	6.9	7.9	4.8	5.7	5.3	5.8	6.7
Poultry	2.6	2.9	4.7	7.2	6.5	5.9	7.0	7.4	8.8
Eggs (units)	167	172	177	186	175	174	178	184	212
Beans	10.0	9.9	10.2	10.3	11.1	10.2	10.7	9.5	12.5
Butter	0.3	0.6	0.6	0.5	0.5	0.5	1.0	0.8	0.7
Lard	6.6	6.8	7.5	8.8	8.3	7.4	8.8	7.6	7.7
Vegetable oil	5.5	5.1	4.9	4.1	4.8	5.1	4.5	5.5	5.3
Potatoes	9.5	7.4	11.5	13.5	15.9	15.8	19.5	18.3	22.3
Sweet potatoes	7.0	9.2	8.6	8.7	7.8	6.1	5.5	7.8	9.5
Malanga	2.7	1.9	2.5	3.6	3.6	5.7	10.8	10.0	12.2
Manioc	7.0	7.4	6.8	8.0	8.0	8.1	8.3	7.0	8.5
Plantains	11.4	16.1	10.2	8.9	10.3	8.1	8.6	7.2	7.1
Name	0.24	0.3	0.3	0.5	0.8	0.9	0.6	0.8	1.0
Pumpkins	3.2	4.6	4.7	6.6	3.3	2.4	3.0	2.3	2.6
Rice	43.7	42.4	43.7	44.6	41.0	37.7	39.6	39.7	42.2
Wheat	7.8	7.0	6.3	6.6	4.9	5.8	5.5	11.0	17.6
Bread	44.4	40.1	45.7	44.0	43.8	31.0	39.3	40.4	40.9
Spaghetti	5.7	5.8	5.6	5.8	5.6	5.2	5.3	5.3	6.1
Cornmeal	*	0.1	1.0	1.1	4.9	5.4	4.9	3.2	3.2
Coffee	3.0	3.0	3.0	3.0	2.7	1.6	1.8	1.8	2.1
Sugar	37.4	33.1	36.5	30.8	36.1	36.8	37.0	38.2	38.2
Tomatoes	6.2	10.7	18.9	18.3	19.7	14.7	13.1	14.0	15.7
Onions	1.7	2.1	2.1	1.9	1.8	1.9	1.8	1.8	2.1
Cucumber	2.5	3.4	3.2	4.3	3.1	2.5	2.8	2.8	2.8

Table A2.18 (continued)

	1972	1973	1974	1975	1976	1977	1978	1979	1980
Cabbage	1.9	2.3	2.4	2.5	3.5	1.6	2.0	2.0	2.0
Citrus fruits	12.3	12.3	11.6	12.4	13.4	12.0	11.0	9.4	15.8
Pineapple	3.6	3.4	3.3	2.4	2.3	1.8	1.9	2.0	3.4
Bananas	7.8	7.6	8.4	10.6	12.4	12.8	14.4	13.2	13.0
Other fruits[1]	11.6	16.1	18.4	17.9	19.9	18.8	15.5	16.6	27.7
Fresh & frozen fish	9.6	10.2	9.5	8.9	8.8	8.9	10.1	8.3	11.3
Canned fish	0.7	0.4	0.9	1.7	1.0	0.6	0.5	0.5	0.7
Fluid milk	59.3	62.5	64.2	65.1	66.1	62.6	72.0	71.5	72.2
Condensed milk	6.9	6.9	6.1	6.9	7.2	6.5	6.8	5.9	6.1
Evaporated milk	1.6	1.7	1.5	1.7	1.6	1.8	1.8	2.6	2.6
Yogurt	2.4	2.6	2.9	4.2	5.4	6.3	5.6	5.0	5.0
Cheese	0.45	0.8	0.9	1.2	1.1	1.3	1.3	1.6	1.7
Ice cream	3.3	3.5	3.4	3.8	4.1	4.2	4.2	4.7	4.3
Soft drinks[2]	33.4	33.6	24.6	20.9	21.7	15.6	18.6	18.9	25.6
Light beer[2]	18.8	20.5	19.6	22.4	23.2	23.0	23.8	23.6	24.3
Dark beer[2]	6.6	5.5	5.2	4.5	3.9	2.7	1.8	2.3	2.4

* = less than 0.1 kg

[1] Mango, guava, avocado, papaya, mammee, and coconut
[2] Liters
[3] Estimate

Sources: Calculated from data in BEC (1968, 1970, 1971), AEC (1974, 1979), and BEM (March 1981).

Table A2.19. Prices of basic needs goods, Cuba 1977 and Canada 1961

	Cuba 1977 (pesos/kg)	Canada 1961 (dollars/kg)
Beef	1.78	1.80
Pork	1.65	1.75
Offal	1.21	0.22
Canned meat	0.90	1.04
Poultry	1.10	1.55
Eggs (units)	0.08	0.03
Black beans	0.37	0.62
Butter	6.60	1.54
Lard	0.53	0.51
Vegetable oil	0.73	0.68*
Potatoes	0.15	0.11
Sweet potatoes	0.13	0.37
Malanga	0.22	0.11**
Manioc	0.13	0.11**
Plantains	0.15	0.22**
Ñame	0.18	0.11**
Pumpkins	0.13	0.11**
Rice	0.42	0.46
Wheat flour	0.22	0.20
Bread	0.50	0.55
Spaghetti	0.66	0.55**
Cornmeal	0.33	0.20
Coffee	2.09	2.64
Sugar	0.15	0.21
Tomatoes	0.18	0.55
Onions	0.31	0.25
Cucumber	0.24	0.33
Cabbage	0.18	0.20
Citrus fruits	0.13	0.44
Pineapple	0.15	0.24
Banana	0.15	0.41
Other fruits	0.14	0.41**
Fresh & frozen fish	0.88	1.06
Canned fish	1.54	0.79
Fluid milk (liter)	0.26	0.26
Condensed milk	0.44	0.77
Evaporated milk	0.46	0.35
Yogurt (liter)	0.44	1.09
Cheese	0.55	1.60
Ice cream (liter)	0.95	1.09
Soft drinks (liter)	0.24	0.25
Light beer (liter)	1.71	0.66
Dark beer (liter)	2.29	0.66

Table A2.19 (continued)

	Cuba 1977 (pesos/kg)	Canada 1961 (dollars/kg)
Cotton cloth (m^2)	1.50	na
Rayon cloth (m^2)	10.00	na
Underwear	1.55	0.67
Blouses	4.74	1.87
Shirts	5.22	1.85
Pants	15.00	4.75
Skirts	5.12	3.40
Suits	78.22	31.27
Dresses	15.88	6.78
Leather shoes (pairs)	12.77	4.18

* = margarine; ** = imputed value; na = not available

<u>Sources</u>: Cuba: CEP (1981); Canada: Usher (1980), pp. 200-201.

Appendix 2

Table A2.20. Estimated per capita expenditures on food and beverages, 1963-1980 (Cuban 1977 pesos)

	1963	1964	1965	1966	1967	1968	1969	1970	1971
Meat products	26.63	31.42	31.22	30.77	30.90	31.98	28.92	29.35	30.65
Eggs	8.08	8.72	9.04	10.00	11.36	11.52	12.24	12.80	13.12
Pulses	3.48	3.81	3.66	3.65	4.03	3.59	3.68	3.48	3.77
Oils & fats	8.86	9.03	8.79	9.73	9.93	9.07	7.37	7.01	7.73
Tubers	8.50	8.53	7.92	10.14	7.38	7.17	6.20	4.15	4.26
Cereals	26.60	35.36	35.60	33.83	36.92	38.39	41.94	45.51	46.34
Coffee	9.61	6.48	7.11	5.85	6.06	6.12	6.48	6.69	6.48
Sugar	4.64	5.84	7.10	7.92	8.99	9.92	6.63	6.98	7.02
Vegetables	3.47	4.39	4.34	4.64	5.33	3.61	2.34	2.44	3.57
Fruits	4.83	4.64	4.83	5.28	5.12	5.96	4.31	4.01	4.16
Fish	3.85	4.16	5.79	4.80	6.82	6.67	7.23	9.43	9.05
Milk products	10.20	10.71	12.79	16.16	18.79	18.23	21.24	21.87	23.28
Total food	118.75	133.09	138.19	142.77	151.63	152.23	148.58	153.72	159.43
Total beverages	40.49	42.08	38.23	39.32	45.78	39.74	38.22	37.61	47.65
Total food & beverages	159.24	175.17	176.42	182.09	197.41	191.77	186.80	191.33	207.08

Table A2.20 (continued)

	1972	1973	1974	1975	1976	1977	1978	1979	1980
Meat products	30.88	27.64	28.39	30.25	29.21	32.49	33.65	34.40	36.98
Eggs	13.36	13.76	14.16	14.88	14.00	13.92	14.24	14.72	16.96
Pulses	3.70	3.67	3.77	3.81	4.11	3.77	3.96	3.52	4.63
Oils & fats	9.50	11.28	11.52	10.95	11.20	10.94	14.55	13.33	12.57
Tubers	6.01	6.76	6.47	7.28	7.35	7.15	8.90	8.39	9.98
Cereals	46.03	43.26	46.66	46.37	45.52	37.82	42.61	43.85	47.13
Coffee	6.33	6.27	6.31	6.35	5.64	3.34	3.76	3.76	4.39
Sugar	5.61	4.97	5.48	4.62	5.42	5.52	5.55	7.73	5.73
Vegetables	2.59	3.81	5.25	5.36	5.48	4.13	3.95	4.11	4.51
Fruits	4.93	5.50	5.85	6.07	6.74	6.38	6.05	5.82	8.39
Fish	9.53	9.60	9.75	10.45	9.28	8.75	9.86	8.07	11.02
Milk products	23.65	24.98	25.07	26.87	27.99	27.45	29.71	29.94	29.92
Total food	162.12	161.50	168.68	173.26	171.94	161.66	176.79	179.64	192.21
Total beverages	55.28	55.72	51.33	53.63	53.81	49.25	49.28	50.17	53.19
Total food & beverages	217.40	217.22	220.01	226.89	225.75	210.91	226.07	229.81	245.40

Sources: Appendix 2, Table 18; prices from CEP (1981).

Table A2.21. Estimated per capita expenditures on food and beverages, 1963–1980 (constant shadow prices)*

	1963	1964	1965	1966	1967	1968	1969	1970	1971
Meat products	28.47	31.11	30.14	29.40	29.83	30.18	27.45	27.81	29.53
Eggs	2.83	3.05	3.16	3.50	3.98	4.03	4.28	4.48	4.59
Pulses	5.83	6.39	6.14	6.13	6.76	6.01	6.16	5.83	6.32
Oils & fats	6.44	7.19	6.90	7.25	7.84	7.59	6.69	6.69	7.35
Tubers	10.21	10.10	9.68	13.18	8.92	9.03	7.00	3.91	4.91
Cereals	27.49	36.74	37.44	35.65	36.92	40.67	44.60	48.62	49.54
Coffee	12.14	8.18	7.92	7.39	7.66	7.74	8.18	8.45	8.18
Sugar	6.49	8.17	9.93	11.09	12.58	13.88	9.28	9.81	9.83
Vegetables	7.85	9.51	9.84	10.52	12.37	7.82	4.23	4.96	7.15
Fruits	13.69	13.51	14.44	16.22	15.66	18.20	13.79	12.13	12.14
Fish	4.11	4.26	5.16	4.71	7.15	7.07	7.55	10.20	9.93
Milk products	13.59	14.10	16.20	19.69	21.96	22.44	25.94	26.41	28.06
Total food	139.14	152.31	156.95	164.73	174.33	174.66	165.15	169.30	177.53
Total beverages	23.03	23.41	21.68	21.56	23.96	20.31	18.82	17.76	21.49
Total food & beverages	162.17	175.72	178.63	186.29	198.29	194.97	183.97	187.06	199.02

Table A2.21 (continued)

	1972	1973	1974	1975	1976	1977	1978	1979	1980
Meat products	30.22	27.52	29.78	32.96	30.89	34.03	35.65	36.75	40.22
Eggs	4.68	4.82	4.96	5.21	4.90	4.87	4.98	5.15	5.94
Pulses	6.20	6.15	6.32	6.39	6.88	6.32	6.63	5.89	7.75
Oils & fats	7.51	7.82	8.07	8.08	8.21	8.01	9.00	8.83	8.59
Tubers	7.59	8.21	8.27	8.63	8.95	8.06	8.58	8.70	10.21
Cereals	48.14	46.08	49.73	49.36	47.92	39.44	44.70	46.17	49.36
Coffee	8.00	7.92	7.97	8.03	7.13	4.22	4.75	4.75	5.54
Sugar	7.85	6.95	7.67	6.47	7.58	7.73	7.77	8.02	8.02
Vegetables	5.05	8.00	12.47	12.45	13.01	9.72	8.98	9.48	10.49
Fruits	14.23	15.95	16.87	17.73	19.69	18.69	17.78	16.84	24.46
Fish	10.73	11.13	10.78	10.77	10.12	9.90	11.11	9.20	12.53
Milk products	28.23	30.09	30.23	33.48	35.41	35.45	37.35	37.03	37.21
Total food	178.43	180.64	193.12	199.56	200.69	186.42	197.28	196.81	220.32
Total beverages	25.12	25.56	22.52	22.98	23.31	20.86	21.55	21.83	24.02
Total food & beverages	203.55	206.20	215.64	2222.54	224.00	207.28	218.83	218.64	244.34

* = Canadian 1961 dollars

Sources: Appendix 2, Table 18; prices from Usher (1980), Table 10.

172   Appendix 2

Table A2.22. Estimated per capita expenditures on clothing, 1963-1980 (Cuban 1978 pesos)

	Cotton Cloth	Rayon Cloth	Under-wear	Blouses	Shirts	Pants	Skirts	Suits	Dresses	Leather Shoes	Total Clothing
1963	10.95	10.70	9.61	1.33	5.43	9.30	0.66	0.94	1.72	19.92	70.56
1964	11.97	16.10	12.25	1.52	5.79	9.30	0.77	1.72	2.21	21.45	83.08
1965	11.04	24.20	9.92	1.28	5.95	8.85	0.77	1.49	1.60	18.01	83.11
1966	7.47	7.90	9.15	1.28	5.01	8.10	0.72	1.02	1.16	20.18	61.99
1967	5.93	4.50	10.08	1.28	5.27	10.65	0.72	1.02	1.19	21.45	62.09
1968	4.35	3.80	8.84	1.04	4.59	14.10	0.67	0.86	1.03	21.07	60.35
1969	2.84	1.70	7.29	0.95	4.49	13.05	0.92	0.47	0.67	20.05	52.43
1970	3.02	8.00	7.13	0.71	3.71	10.35	0.72	0.08	0.27	18.01	52.00
1971	3.65	11.20	8.53	0.95	4.23	11.40	0.82	0.39	0.41	20.94	62.54
1972	4.35	13.40	8.99	1.04	5.32	15.60	1.02	0.47	0.51	20.69	71.39
1973	3.93	9.20	9.46	1.33	6.06	18.60	0.82	0.55	0.62	20.82	71.39
1974	2.28	7.50	10.54	1.04	5.59	16.80	1.13	0.63	0.56	18.77	64.84
1975	4.28	9.70	11.16	1.09	7.10	19.20	1.23	0.63	0.70	21.20	76.29
1976	3.86	14.50	9.92	1.28	6.68	18.45	0.72	0.63	0.59	20.18	76.81
1977	4.16	16.40	9.46	1.28	7.10	19.50	0.92	0.63	0.78	16.60	76.83
1978	4.17	12.30	10.70	1.23	6.58	16.20	0.97	0.39	0.86	19.54	72.94
1979	5.85	20.60	10.54	1.52	8.46	22.20	1.23	0.31	0.65	18.01	89.37
1980	6.20	20.60	10.23	1.14	7.83	18.15	0.72	0.31	0.65	16.98	82.81

Source: Appendix 2, Table 19.

Table A2.23. Estimated per capita expenditures on clothing, 1963-1980 (Canadian 1961 dollars)

	Underwear	Blouses	Shirts	Pants	Skirts	Dresses	Leather Shoes	Total Clothing
1963	4.15	0.52	1.92	2.95	0.44	0.73	6.52	17.61
1964	5.29	0.60	2.05	2.95	0.51	0.94	7.02	20.05
1965	4.29	0.50	2.11	2.80	0.51	0.68	5.89	17.37
1966	3.95	0.50	1.78	2.57	0.48	0.49	6.60	16.78
1967	4.36	0.50	1.87	3.37	0.48	0.51	7.02	18.52
1968	3.15	0.41	1.63	4.47	0.44	0.44	6.90	17.78
1969	3.15	0.37	1.59	4.13	0.61	0.28	6.56	16.88
1970	3.08	0.28	1.31	3.28	0.48	0.12	5.89	14.47
1971	3.69	0.37	1.50	3.61	0.54	0.18	6.86	16.91
1972	3.89	0.41	1.89	4.94	0.68	0.22	6.77	18.99
1973	4.09	0.52	2.15	5.89	0.54	0.26	6.81	20.48
1974	4.56	0.41	1.98	5.32	0.75	0.24	6.14	19.65
1975	4.82	0.43	2.52	6.08	0.82	0.30	6.94	22.16
1976	4.29	0.50	2.37	5.84	0.48	0.25	6.60	20.58
1977	4.09	0.50	2.52	6.18	0.61	0.33	5.43	19.91
1978	4.62	0.49	2.33	5.13	0.65	0.37	6.40	20.15
1979	4.56	0.60	3.00	7.03	0.82	0.28	5.89	22.31
1980	4.42	0.45	2.78	5.75	0.48	0.28	5.56	19.85

Sources: Appendix 2, Tables 19 and 22.

Table A2.24. Basic needs indicators, clothing, 1963-1980 (number of items per thousand persons purchased in the year)

	Under-wear	Blouses	Shirts	Pants	Skirts	Suits	Dresses	Shoes (leather)	Cotton Cloth*	Rayon Cloth*
1963	6,180	280	1,040	620	130	12	108	1,560	7,300	1,070
1964	7,880	320	1,110	620	150	22	139	1,680	7,980	1,610
1965	6,410	270	1,140	590	150	19	101	1,410	7,360	2,420
1966	5,900	270	960	540	140	13	73	1,580	4,980	790
1967	6,460	270	1,010	710	140	13	75	1,680	3,950	450
1968	5,660	220	880	940	130	11	65	1,650	2,900	380
1969	4,710	200	860	870	180	6	42	1,570	1,890	170
1970	4,600	150	710	690	140	1	17	1,410	2,010	800
1971	5,500	200	810	760	160	5	26	1,640	2,430	1,128
1972	5,850	220	1,020	1,040	200	6	32	1,620	2,900	1,340
1973	6,100	280	1,160	1,240	160	7	39	1,630	2,620	920
1974	6,820	220	1,070	1,120	220	8	35	1,470	1,520	750
1975	7,170	230	1,360	1,280	240	8	44	1,660	2,850	970
1976	6,440	270	1,280	1,230	140	8	37	1,580	2,570	1,450
1977	6,080	270	1,360	1,300	180	8	49	1,300	2,770	1,640
1978	6,870	260	1,260	1,080	190	5	54	1,530	2,780	1,230
1979	6,800	320	1,620	1,480	240	4	41	1,410	3,900	2,060
1980	6,580	240	1,500	1,210	140	4	41	1,330	4,130	2,060

* = m^2 per thousand persons

Sources: BEC (1968, 1970, 1971), AEC (1974, 1979), and BEM (March 1981).

Table A2.25. Basic needs indicators, housing, 1958-1980

	Total Number of Dwellings (000s)	Estimated Dwellings with Basic Facilities			
		Electricity (%)	Flush Toilet (%)	Piped Water (%)	Quality Index*
1958	1,763.7	59.1	29.4	36.4	0.416
1959	1,771.7	60.5	30.3	37.6	0.428
1960	1,799.9	62.5	32.0	39.4	0.446
1961	1,821.3	63.4	32.8	40.4	0.455
1962	1,837.6	64.0	33.1	40.8	0.460
1963	1,849.1	64.9	33.6	41.5	0.467
1964	1,856.2	65.8	34.0	42.1	0.473
1965	1,861.3	66.7	34.5	42.7	0.480
1966	1,867.6	67.9	35.1	43.6	0.489
1967	1,877.8	68.6	35.5	44.1	0.494
1968	1,884.3	69.5	35.9	44.7	0.500
1969	1,889.1	70.3	36.2	45.2	0.506
1970	1,893.1	70.7	36.7	45.7	0.510
1971	1,898.1	70.8	36.9	45.8	0.512
1972	1,914.9	71.0	37.4	46.3	0.516
1973	1,935.6	71.3	38.1	46.9	0.521
1974	1,954.2	71.6	38.7	47.4	0.526
1975	1,972.8	71.9	39.3	47.9	0.530
1976	1,988.1	72.1	39.7	48.3	0.534
1977	2,008.1	72.4	40.3	48.8	0.538
1978	2,025.2	72.6	40.8	49.2	0.542
1979	2,039.4	72.8	41.3	49.8	0.546
1980	2,054.2	73.0	41.8	50.2	0.550

* = unweighted average of the three basic facilities indicators divided by 100

Sources: Censo de población y viviendas 1970 (1975), Censo de población, viviendas y electoral 1953 (1953), and Table 4.2; estimates explained in text.

Table A2.26. Estimated per capita expenditures on housing, 1958-1980 (constant prices)

	Unadjusted Values		Values Adjusted for Quality*	
	Cuban prices	Canadian prices	Cuban prices	Canadian prices
1958	118.47	273.31	49.28	113.70
1959	116.96	269.41	50.06	115.44
1960	116.46	267.00	51.94	119.83
1961	116.05	267.42	52.80	121.77
1962	115.15	265.93	52.97	122.15
1963	113.24	261.36	52.86	122.06
1964	110.73	255.57	52.38	120.88
1965	108.22	249.77	51.95	119.89
1966	106.21	245.11	51.93	119.86
1967	104.80	241.80	51.77	119.45
1968	103.29	238.40	51.65	119.20
1969	101.89	235.11	51.56	118.97
1970	100.48	231.81	51.24	118.22
1971	99.17	228.88	50.78	117.19
1972	98.17	226.47	50.66	116.86
1973	97.37	224.52	50.73	116.97
1974	96.56	222.76	50.79	117.17
1975	96.06	221.56	50.91	117.47
1976	95.36	220.00	50.92	117.48
1977	95.26	219.65	51.25	118.17
1978	94.85	218.73	51.41	118.55
1979	94.85	218.75	51.98	119.44
1980	96.46	222.47	53.05	122.36

* = unadjusted values times quality index

Source: Explained in text.

Table A2.27. Enrollments by level of education, 1958-1980* (in thousands)

	Primary	Secondary	Higher	Adult	Total
1958	717.4	88.1	25.6	7.0	838.1
1959	1,092.3	90.2	19.5	73.0	1,275.0
1960	1,136.3	122.9	19.9	66.6	1,345.7
1961	1,166.9	151.0	17.9	436.4	1,772.2
1962	1,217.3	166.9	17.3	496.5	1,898.0
1963	1,316.0	201.4	20.4	483.6	2,021.4
1964	1,370.7	196.7	26.3	848.0	2,441.7
1965	1,332.1	202.7	26.2	581.7	2,142.7
1966	1,367.3	234.4	28.2	451.5	2,081.4
1967	1,397.7	234.4	29.2	500.0	2,161.3
1968	1,466.3	250.7	32.3	417.7	2,167.0
1969	1,558.1	255.9	34.5	360.6	2,209.1
1970	1,664.6	237.7	35.1	365.3	2,302.7
1971	1,759.2	282.3	36.9	354.1	2,432.5
1972	1,852.7	324.4	48.7	431.3	2,657.1
1973	1,899.3	395.5	55.6	444.5	2,794.9
1974	1,923.3	520.3	68.5	412.0	2,924.1
1975	1,922.3	629.2	84.7	594.0	3,230.2
1976	1,899.0	806.0	107.1	701.3	3,513.4
1977	1,845.2	963.3	122.5	605.2	3,536.2
1978	1,761.2	1,074.3	133.0	500.9	3,469.4
1979	1,672.9	1,150.3	146.2	392.0	3,361.4
1980	1,592.3	1,167.4	151.7	277.0	3,188.4

* = enrollments during the school year--1958 thus refers to school year 1958-1959 etc.

Sources: BEC (1968, 1970, 1971); AEC (1974, 1979, 1981); and Ministerio de Educación (1980).

Table A2.28. Estimated basic needs expenditures per capita in Cuba, 1958-1980

	Constant Cuban Pesos					
	Food & Beverages	Clothing	Housing	Education	Health	Total
1958	178.51	74.23	49.28	18.70	18.63	339.35
1959	192.36	89.40	50.06	21.14	19.76	372.72
1960	189.50	70.84	51.94	22.79	19.38	354.45
1961	186.79	50.80	52.80	29.55	18.67	338.61
1962	168.32	65.69	52.97	31.17	19.19	337.34
1963	159.24	70.56	52.86	32.98	19.13	334.77
1964	175.17	83.08	52.38	38.32	19.63	368.58
1965	176.42	83.11	51.95	34.17	19.95	365.60
1966	182.09	61.99	51.93	33.61	20.78	350.40
1967	197.41	62.09	51.77	34.10	21.64	367.01
1968	191.77	60.35	51.65	33.64	21.12	358.53
1969	186.80	52.43	51.56	33.90	22.08	346.77
1970	191.33	52.00	51.24	34.37	19.99	348.93
1971	207.08	62.54	50.78	36.31	20.34	377.05
1972	217.40	71.39	50.66	45.25	21.00	405.70
1973	217.22	71.39	50.73	52.70	23.51	415.55
1974	220.01	64.84	50.79	63.22	25.98	424.84
1975	226.89	76.29	50.91	76.15	27.89	458.13
1976	225.75	76.81	50.92	98.81	30.30	482.59
1977	210.91	76.83	51.25	107.45	33.82	480.26
1978	226.07	72.94	51.41	111.21	34.82	496.45
1979	229.81	84.37	51.98	115.30	35.41	516.87
1980	245.40	82.81	53.05	115.69	36.21	533.16

Table A2.28 (continued)

	Constant Canadian Dollars					
	Food & Beverages	Clothing	Housing	Education	Health	Total
1958	175.62	18.53	113.70	66.61	65.13	439.59
1959	187.61	22.31	115.44	81.74	69.12	476.22
1960	186.08	17.68	119.83	89.52	68.46	481.57
1961	184.54	12.68	121.77	110.25	66.46	495.70
1962	171.29	16.39	122.15	116.30	68.19	494.32
1963	162.17	17.61	122.06	126.29	68.16	496.29
1964	175.72	20.05	120.88	141.15	71.21	529.01
1965	178.63	17.37	119.89	127.37	73.10	516.36
1966	186.29	16.78	119.86	127.91	76.23	527.07
1967	198.29	18.52	119.45	128.99	80.56	545.81
1968	194.97	17.78	119.20	130.76	79.03	541.74
1969	183.97	16.88	118.97	131.70	82.61	534.13
1970	187.06	14.47	118.22	130.48	73.89	524.12
1971	199.02	16.91	117.19	140.05	76.23	549.40
1972	203.55	18.99	116.86	155.74	78.52	573.66
1973	206.20	20.48	116.97	170.24	88.82	602.71
1974	215.64	19.65	117.17	193.80	97.00	643.26
1975	222.54	22.16	117.47	221.41	105.15	688.73
1976	224.00	20.58	117.48	259.23	114.34	735.63
1977	207.28	19.91	118.17	285.10	126.56	757.02
1978	218.83	20.15	118.55	291.64	130.61	779.78
1979	218.64	22.31	119.44	305.92	132.55	798.90
1980	244.34	19.85	122.36	306.16	135.19	827.90

Sources: Tables 4.6, 4.7, and 4.8; Appendix 2, Tables 20-23 and 26-27.

Appendix 2

Table A2.29. Estimated distribution of wages and salaries in 1953

Number of Persons	%	Cumulative %	Annual Average Income (pesos)	Total Income (000 pesos)	%	Cumulative %
82,512	4.0	4.0	0	0	0	0
197,911	9.6	13.6	100	19,791	0.9	0.9
321,374	15.6	29.2	200	62,475	3.0	3.9
271,939	13.2	42.4	300	81,582	3.9	7.8
168,779	8.2	50.6	400	67,512	3.2	11.0
85,573	4.2	54.8	600	51,344	2.4	13.4
80,000	3.9	58.7	900	72,000	3.4	16.8
112,070	5.4	64.1	1,000	112,070	5.3	22.1
197,391	9.6	73.7	1,200	236,869	11.3	33.4
223,940	10.9	84.6	1,500	335,910	16.0	49.4
15,546	0.8	85.4	1,812	28,169	1.3	50.7
35,000	1.7	87.1	2,000	70,000	3.3	54.0
12,720	0.6	87.7	2,244	28,544	1.4	55.4
74,974	3.6	91.3	2,352	176,338	8.4	63.8
26,134	1.3	92.6	2,784	72,757	3.5	67.3
43,346	2.1	94.7	2,808	121,716	5.8	73.1
30,000	1.5	96.2	3,000	90,000	4.3	77.4
2,827	0.1	96.3	3,552	10,042	0.5	77.9
22,613	1.1	97.3	3,696	83,578	4.0	81.9
10,302	0.5	97.8	5,424	55,878	2.7	84.6
39,208	1.9	99.7	8,230	322,682	15.4	100.0
Total 2,059,659	99.7		1,019	2,099,257	100.0	

Sources: Censos de población, viviendas y electoral 1953 (1953), U.S. Department of Commerce (1956), Tables 95, 96, Padula (1974), C. R. Rodríguez (1979), Blackburn (1963), FAO (1966), IBRD (1952), p. 142, Nelson (1950), p. 170.

Table A2.30. Estimated distribution of wages and salaries in 1962

Number of Persons (000s)	%	Cumulative %	Annual Average Income (pesos)	Total Income (000 pesos)	%	Cumulative %
136	7.7	7.7	250	34,000	1.5	1.5
75	4.2	11.9	382	28,650	1.3	2.8
136	7.7	19.6	500	68,000	3.1	5.9
11	0.6	20.2	538	5,918	0.3	6.2
33	1.9	22.1	544	17,952	0.8	7.0
24	1.4	23.5	576	13,824	0.6	7.6
26	1.5	25.0	680	17,680	0.8	8.4
53	3.0	28.0	682	36,146	1.6	10.0
136	7.7	35.7	750	102,000	4.6	14.6
74	4.2	39.9	763	58,462	2.6	17.2
66	3.7	43.6	776	51,216	2.3	19.5
3	0.2	43.8	793	2,379	0.1	19.6
15	0.8	44.4	891	13,365	0.6	20.2
1	0.06	44.5	955	955	0.04	20.2
136	7.7	52.1	1,000	136,000	6.1	26.3
33	1.9	54.7	1,088	35,904	1.6	28.5
74	4.2	58.9	1,145	84,730	3.8	32.3
24	1.4	60.3	1,152	27,648	1.2	33.5
25	1.4	61.7	1,360	34,000	1.5	35.0
52	2.9	64.6	1,363	70,876	3.2	38.2
74	4.2	68.8	1,526	112,924	5.1	43.3
67	3.8	72.6	1,553	104,051	4.7	48.0
3	0.2	72.8	1,586	4,758	0.2	48.2
11	0.6	73.4	1,613	17,743	0.8	49.0
33	1.9	75.3	1,632	53,856	2.4	51.4
24	1.4	76.7	1,728	41,472	1.9	53.3
16	0.9	77.6	1,782	28,512	1.3	54.6
1	0.06	77.7	1,910	1,910	0.1	54.7

Table A2.30 (continued)

Number of Persons (000s)	%	Cumulative %	Annual Average Income (pesos)	Total Income (000 pesos)	%	Cumulative %
25	1.4	79.0	2,040	51,000	2.3	57.0
52	2.9	81.9	2,045	106,340	4.8	61.8
11	0.6	82.5	2,150	23,650	1.1	62.9
33	1.9	84.4	2,176	71,808	3.2	66.1
24	1.4	85.8	2,304	55,296	2.5	68.6
67	3.8	39.6	2,329	156,043	7.0	75.6
3	0.2	89.8	2,380	7,140	0.3	75.9
15	0.8	90.6	2,672	40,080	1.8	77.7
25	1.4	92.0	2,720	68,000	3.1	80.8
52	2.9	94.9	2,726	141,752	6.4	87.2
1	0.06	95.0	2,866	2,866	0.1	87.3
67	3.8	98.7	3,106	208,102	9.4	96.6
3	0.2	98.9	3,173	9,519	0.4	97.0
16	0.9	99.8	3,563	57,008	2.6	99.6
1	0.06	99.9	3,820	3,820	0.2	99.8
Total 1,769	99.9		1,255	2,220,255	99.8	

Sources: AEC (1968); O'Connor (1970), Table 4, p. 210; Minrex (1966), p. 58.

Table A2.31. Estimated distribution of wages and salaries in 1973

Number of Persons (000s)	%	Cumulative %	Annual Average Income (pesos)	Total Income (000 pesos)	%	Cumulative %
45	2.1	2.1	561	25,245	0.8	0.8
165	7.7	9.8	566	94,522	2.9	3.7
131	6.0	15.8	578	75,718	2.3	6.0
6	0.3	16.1	637	3,822	0.1	6.1
114	5.2	21.3	641	73,074	2.2	8.3
44	2.0	23.3	693	30,492	0.9	9.2
39	1.8	25.1	726	28,314	0.9	10.1
44	2.0	27.1	1,122	49,368	1.5	11.6
168	7.7	34.8	1,133	190,344	5.8	17.4
131	6.0	40.8	1,155	151,305	4.6	22.0
6	0.3	41.1	1,274	7,644	0.2	22.2
113	5.2	46.3	1,282	144,866	4.4	26.6
44	2.0	48.3	1,386	60,984	1.8	28.4
40	1.8	50.1	1,452	58,080	1.8	30.2
44	2.0	52.1	1,682	74,008	2.2	32.4
167	7.7	59.8	1,699	283,733	8.6	41.0
131	6.0	65.8	1,733	227,023	6.9	47.9
6	0.3	66.1	1,910	11,460	0.3	48.2
113	5.2	71.3	1,924	217,412	6.6	54.8
44	2.0	73.3	2,080	91,520	2.8	57.6
40	1.8	75.1	2,178	87,120	2.6	60.2
44	2.0	77.1	2,243	98,692	3.0	63.2
168	7.7	84.8	2,266	380,688	11.5	74.7
131	6.0	90.8	2,310	302,610	9.1	83.8
5	0.2	91.1	2,547	12,735	0.4	84.2
113	5.2	96.2	2,565	289,845	8.8	93.0
44	2.0	98.2	2,773	122,012	3.7	96.7
40	1.8	100.0	2,904	116,160	3.5	100.2
Total 2,182	100.0		1,516	3,308,795	100.2	

Source: AEC (1974), pp. 40–42.

Table A2.32. Estimated distribution of wages and salaries in 1978

Number of Persons (000s)	%	Cumulative %	Annual Average Income (pesos)	Total Income (000 pesos)	%	Cumulative %
216	7.4	7.4	543	117,424	2.4	2.4
74	2.5	9.9	626	46,340	0.9	3.3
179	6.1	16.0	684	122,368	2.5	5.8
5	0.2	16.2	690	3,657	0.1	5.9
80	2.7	18.9	737	58,757	1.2	7.1
138	4.7	23.6	742	102,563	2.1	9.2
40	1.4	25.0	838	33,813	0.7	9.9
216	7.4	32.4	1,086	234,848	4.8	14.7
74	2.5	34.9	1,251	92,605	1.9	16.6
179	6.1	41.0	1,368	244,735	5.0	21.6
5	0.2	41.2	1,381	7,319	0.2	21.8
80	2.7	43.9	1,474	117,515	2.4	24.2
138	4.7	48.6	1,483	204,988	4.2	28.4
216	7.4	56.0	1,678	352,055	7.2	35.6
40	1.4	57.4	1,675	67,586	1.4	37.0
74	2.5	59.9	1,877	138,945	2.8	39.8
179	6.1	66.0	2,052	367,103	7.5	47.3
5	0.2	66.2	2,071	10,976	0.2	47.5
7	0.2	66.4	2,103	14,800	0.3	47.8
216	7.4	73.8	2,171	469,479	9.6	57.4
80	2.7	76.5	2,212	176,352	3.6	61.0
138	4.7	81.2	2,225	307,551	6.3	67.3
74	2.5	83.7	2,502	185,211	3.8	71.1
40	1.4	85.1	2,513	135,173	2.8	73.9
179	6.1	91.1	2,736	489,470	10.0	83.9
5	0.2	91.4	2,762	14,639	0.3	84.2
80	2.7	94.1	2,949	235,109	4.8	89.0
138	4.7	98.8	2,966	409,975	8.4	97.4
40	1.4	100.2	3,350	135,173	2.8	100.2
Total 2,938	100.2		1,667	4,896,529	100.2	

Source: AEC (1979), p. 57.

Notes

Introduction

1. For a discussion on the development debate in Latin America after World War II and an evaluation of various country experiences, see Brundenius and Lundahl, eds. (1982).
2. See Streeten (1982).
3. Ibid.
4. Second national developing plan of Brazil, quoted in Brundenius and Lundahl, eds. (1982), p. 7.
5. Streeten (1982), p. 17; Myrdal (1968), vol. 3, chap. 21; and International Labour Office (1977), pp. 16–17.
6. The Cocoyoc Declaration, UNCTAD document 74-10536. Among the prominent people signing this declaration were Barbara Ward, Wassily Leontieff, Enrique Iglesias, Johan Galtung, Maurice Strong, Samir Amin, Mahbub ul-Haq, Juan Somavia, Ignacy Sachs, and Shigeto Tsuru.
7. See, for instance, Adelman and Robinson (1978) and Fei, Ranis, and Kuo (1979).
8. Morawetz (1980).
9. See, for instance ECLA/CEPAL (1978).

Chapter 1

1. Ginsberg (1961), p. 18.
2. Oshima (1961), p. 214.
3. O'Connor (1970), p. 17.
4. Ibid.
5. Alienes (1950), Table 17, p. 52.
6. International Bank for Reconstruction and Development (1951), p. 1046.
7. Cost of food index taken from Zanetti and García (1976), p. 441; U.S. wholesale price index inferred from Alienes's figures on nominal and real income.
8. Thomas (1971), p. 546.
9. Aguilar (1972), p. 40.
10. Black et al. (1976), p. 40.
11. Domínguez (1978), p. 21.
12. Le Riverend (1965), chap. 22.

13. Aguilar (1972), pp. 41–42.
14. Le Riverend (1965), chap. 23.
15. U.S. Department of Commerce (1956), p. 9.
16. Ibid.
17. Thomas (1971), p. 466.
18. Lewis (1938), p. 616.
19. Ibid.
20. Ritter (1974), p. 18.
21. U.S. Department of Commerce (1956), p. 37; and Seers et al. (1964), p. 398 n.19.
22. Thomas (1971), chap. 45, and Aguilar (1972), p. 41.
23. Moreno Fraginals (1978), 2:157–163.
24. Thomas (1971), p. 245.
25. Aguilar (1972), p. 44.
26. Cuban Economic Research Project (CERP) (1965), p. 199.
27. Alonso and Chavez (1978), p. 74.
28. Lundahl (1979), pp. 625–626; and Lundahl (1981), pp. 11–16.
29. O'Connor (1970), p. 25.
30. Thomas (1971), p. 1536.
31. Seers et al. (1964), pp. 12–14.
32. Calculated from data given in L. Soto (1977), 1:240–243.
33. Ibid.
34. O'Connor (1970), p. 13.
35. Furtado (1976), p. 283.
36. Tabares del Real (1975); and Farber (1969), chap. 3.
37. Furtado (1976), p. 284.
38. Acosta (1976), p. 55.
39. U.S. Department of Commerce (1956), p. 6.
40. United Nations (1965), p. 15.
41. Another estimate of U.S. investments in Cuba in 1927 (Lewis [1938], p. 616) gives a figure of $1,140 million, of which 52.6 percent was sugar, 10.5 percent in railways, 10 percent in other public utilities, 4.3 percent in mining, 1.7 percent in tobacco, and only 1.3 percent in other manufacturing.
42. Between 1934 and 1951, forty-seven sugar mills, worth $48 million, passed back into Cuban hands (Padula [1974], p. 48).
43. U.S. Department of Commerce (1956), p. 37.
44. Ibid., p. 65.
45. Ibid., p. 62.
46. Ibid.
47. Ibid., p. 63; and Brundenius (1968), pp. 94–95.
48. Brundenius (1968), p. 95.
49. Estimates by the author based on Pérez-López (1974) and CERP (1965), p. 556, for sector production data; and Pizer and Cutler (1960), p. 113, for production of U.S. subsidiaries established in Cuba in 1957.
50. Padula (1974), pp. 592–599.
51. Ibid.

52. Pérez-López (1974).
53. "Food," of course, only represents part of the "cost of living." Unfortunately, there is no official cost of living index before 1953, but in that year, an official survey showed that food accounted for 43.1 percent of the total average living expenditures; rents accounted for 27.4 percent; clothing and footwear, for 8.4 percent; and other items, for 21.1 percent—see Seers et al. (1964), p. 33.
54. Domínguez (1978), p. 74.
55. Seers et al. (1964), p. 13; O'Connor (1970), p. 17; CERP (1965), pp. 568–570; and J.-L. Rodríguez (1980), pp. 184–185.
56. Mesa-Lago (1971c), p. 278.
57. This concept is explained in the section in Chapter 2 on "An Index of Total Material Production, 1946–1961."
58. CERP (1965), Table 409, p. 555.
59. G. M. Rodríguez (1980), pp. 148–150.
60. Mesa-Lago (1971c), p. 277.
61. Ibid.
62. Mesa-Lago (1968b), Table 40, p. 382.
63. Mesa-Lago (1971c), p. 279.
64. Ibid.
65. Agrupación Católica (1972), p. 198.

Chapter 2

1. As regards the Soviet Union, see for instance Bergson (1961), Hodgman (1954), Boorstein (1968), Gerschenkron (1951), Grossman (1960), Nutter (1962); for China, see for instance A. Eckstein (1961), Chao (1965), Li (1959), Ishikawa (1965); for GDR, Hungary, Czechoslovakia, and Poland, see Alton (1962, 1963, 1965), and Zauberman (1964).
2. The 1975 statistical yearbook (*Annario estadístico de Cuba* [AEC] 1975) was published in 1978, AEC 1976 and 1977 were published in 1979, and AEC 1978 and 1979 were published in 1980.
3. The author was told in November 1980 by CEE officials that the labor force section will be substantially improved and enlarged in the future.
4. Mesa-Lago (1969), both issues.
5. Nove (1965), p. 267.
6. Mesa-Lago (1969), 4:1, p. 70.
7. Ibid., p. 71.
8. Ibid., p. 72.
9. Boorstein (1968), p. 160.
10. Economic Commission for Latin America (ECLA) (1965).
11. This reconstruction of the Cuban national accounting system was published in an earlier study by the author—see Brundenius (1979a)—and it was verified by officials at the CEE in an interview with the author on 4 November 1980.
12. It seems that there were intentions to change this system in 1968—see Juceplan (1968), p. 17 n.6—but as far as is known, the basic principles of the system were still being practiced in 1981.

13. For a summary and criticism of the Soviet practice, see Kaser (1957), pp. 83–104.

14. United Nations (1971a); see also Li (1959), p. 75.

15. Regalado (1981), p. 51, and Comité Estatal de Precios (CEP) (1979). The budgetary system of finance was based on the principle of a single state enterprise within which each group of industries constituted a consolidated enterprise (*empresa consolidada*), for instance, the sugar industry. All revenues went to the state, depriving the enterprises of an independent source of financing, and all financing also came from the central budget—thus the name.

16. ECLA/CEPAL (1978), p. 325.

17. Regalado (1981), p. 52.

18. Bettelheim (1975), pp. 124–127, Kantorovich (1963), and Liberman (1966a).

19. Between 1962 and 1966, the self-finance system was only applied in the areas of agriculture and foreign trade—see Valdés (1979), p. 14.

20. See Pérez-López (1974), chap. 3.

21. At the beginning of 1981, a new price system was introduced in Cuba, but the effects of this system are not known.

22. Chao (1965), p. 26.

23. Ibid., pp. 26 and 27.

24. The weighting problem is not, however, related only to relative prices as such but also depends on the actual basket of goods produced—see Nutter (1962), p. 110.

25. Pérez-López (1974).

26. Cuban Economic Research Project (CERP) (1965), p. 568.

27. Pérez-López (1974), p. 58.

28. It is not known why Pérez-López decided to include "fishing," which is hardly an industrial activity according to his definition. At any rate, since fishing only accounts for 0.63 percent of the gross value added (of the branches considered by Pérez-López), it does not affect the overall index in any significant way.

29. Pérez-López (1974), p. 58.

30. Ibid., pp. 121–128.

31. Acosta (1973a), p. 76.

32. As recorded by Ritter (1974), p. 215, for the years 1949–1961. Estimates for the period 1946–1948 have been added and are based on data on agricultural sector income given in International Bank for Reconstruction and Development (1952), p. 1043.

33. CERP (1965), p. 568.

34. O'Connor (1970), p. 271, and Noyola (1961), p. 416. The 29 percent growth rate given by O'Connor is probably a misprint since he is actually referring to the Noyola article.

35. Panorama Económico Latinoamericano (PEL) (1968), p. 16.

36. J.-L. Rodríguez (1979), p. 151.

37. The newly created Statistical Research Institute of the CEE is currently working on a complete revision of the national accounts of Cuba since 1950.

38. Mesa-Lago (1971c), p. 329, gives the following output index for agriculture and industry combined (1959=100): 1957=94.6; 1958=94.7; 1960=98.5; and 1961=105.5. It is not explained, however, how this index was constructed or which products were included.
39. Hodgman (1954).
40. Chao (1965).
41. Ministerio de Relaciones Exteriores (1966), p. 58.
42. Ibid.
43. Estimate by Juceplan quoted in O'Connor (1970), p. 210.
44. This is the share in Peruvian agriculture—see Brundenius (1976c), Appendix. In Poland in 1956, the corresponding share was no less than 98 percent—see Alton (1965), p. 58—which may indicate that the 85 percent figure is a minimum.
45. Juceplan (1966), p. 110.
46. Growth indicators by sector given in *Boletín estadístico de Cuba* (1968).
47. Mesa-Lago (1969).
48. Nove (1965), Gerschenkron (1951), and Ishikawa (1965), p. 35.
49. Peter Wiles finds this problem so serious that he suggests that a Laspeyre-type index is wholly misleading in less developed economies and that "for welfare purposes only the Pasche index applies" (that is, using present year weights)—see Wiles (1963), p. 250. Perhaps a Divisia-type chain index would be even better, but such an index would require price and output data, which are usually unavailable for these countries.
50. Comité Estatal de Precios (1981).
51. The dollar was officially at par with the peso in 1965, and the decline in the value of the dollar between 1965 and 1980 could thus be seen as an implicit deflator of the 1980 dollar. A similar method was used by the Interamerican Development Bank in its estimates of GDP in member countries measured in 1980 U.S. dollar equivalents—see Banco Interamericano de Desarrollo (BID) (1982), Methodological Notes, p. 378.
52. Mesa-Lago and Pérez-López (1982).
53. Ibid., p. 38.
54. Ibid.
55. Ibid., p. 26.

Chapter 3

1. "Program Manifesto" in Bonachea and Valdés (1972b); see also O'Connor (1970), p. 44.
2. Morray (1962), p. 20.
3. O'Connor (1970), p. 49; and Morray (1962), p. 24.
4. Ministerio de Relaciones Exteriores (Minrex) (1966), p. 201; and J.-L. Rodríguez (1979), p. 114.
5. Morray (1962), p. 25.
6. Huberman and Sweezy (1961), p. 135.
7. Morray (1962), p. 26.

8. Gutelman (1967); Aranda (1968); C. R. Rodríguez (1979); Acosta (1972a, 1973b); Barkin (1970); MacEwan (1981); Chonchol (1963).

9. Minrex (1966), p. 63. The cane cooperatives were incorporated in the state sector in 1962.

10. Ibid.

11. Ibid.

12. Gutelman (1967), p. 54.

13. The law Recuperation of Ill-Gained Wealth (22 December 1959) allowed for the confiscation of the wealth of Batista and his family as well as of people who had enriched themselves notoriously under the dictatorship (Gutelman [1967], p. 37).

14. Marinello and Pertsev (1963), cited in Gutelman (1967), p. 54.

15. Chonchol (1963), p. 75.

16. Bonsal was U.S. ambassador to Cuba at the time, and he feared that the result would be to give the Cuban revolution a shot in the arm comparable to that which Egypt had received when it was demonstrated that the Suez Canal could be operated in spite of the withdrawal of Western pilots (Bonsal [1972], p. 150).

17. Che Guevara in an interview with Laura Berggvist in *Look*, 8 November 1960, quoted in Huberman and Sweezy (1961), p. 175.

18. J.-L. Rodríguez (1979), p. 145.

19. Seers et al. (1964), p. 377.

20. For a detailed account of the "October revolution" and its aftermath, see Morray (1962).

21. The effects of the U.S. embargo against Cuba are discussed in Adler-Karlsson (1968), chap. 17.

22. Ritter (1974), p. 101; and Mesa-Lago (1971c), p. 283.

23. Mesa-Lago (1971c).

24. Kenner and Petras, eds. (1970), p. 114.

25. Martínez-Alier (1977), p. 114.

26. Noyola (1961), p. 414.

27. Pazos (1962), p. 8.

28. Chonchol (1963), p. 139.

29. INRA Report quoted in Seers et al. (1964), p. 113.

30. Pazos (1962), p. 7.

31. Noyola (1961), p. 415.

32. Huberman and Sweezy (1961), p. 140.

33. Dumont in the French weekly *L'Express* of 22 September 1960; quoted in Huberman and Sweezy (1961), p. 195.

34. Ibid., p. 196.

35. Charles Bettelheim, "Memorandum sobre la planificación económica en Cuba," 19 September 1960, quoted in Huberman and Sweezy (1961), p. 196.

36. Kalecki in 1960; English translation in Kalecki (1976).

37. U.S. Department of Commerce (1956), Table 4, p. 7.

38. Boorstein (1968), p. 90.

39. Ibid., p. 91.

Notes to Chapter 3   191

40. Guevara (1977d), p. 63.
41. Quoted in Boorstein (1968), p. 93.
42. Ibid., p. 92.
43. J.-L. Rodríguez (1979), p. 145.
44. Ritter (1974), chap. 4.
45. Seers et al. (1964), pp. 384-389.
46. Ritter (1974), p. 135.
47. Boorstein (1968), p. 129.
48. García and Noyola (1962).
49. Adler-Karlsson (1968), p. 210.
50. Boorstein (1968), p. 130.
51. Ibid., p. 208.
52. Guevara (1977b), p. 39.
53. Feldman (1965). Feldman's model and some of its unrealistic assumptions are discussed in Domar (1957).
54. Wheelwright and McFarlane (1970), p. 54.
55. Mora (1971b), p. 225.
56. Ibid., p. 227.
57. Bettelheim (1964), p. 55.
58. One of the participants, Alberto Mora, did refer to the debate briefly, quoting Erlich's study (Erlich [1960]).
59. The "scissor's crisis" got its name from movements of agricultural and industrial prices. When price differences increased, the "scissor" opened; when they became smaller, the "scissor" closed (Dobb [1960], chap. 7).
60. Ibid., p. 162.
61. The new economic policy was the "tactical retreat" endorsed by Lenin after the period of "war communism" (1918-1920). The retreat implied a revitalization of the market, incentives to the private sector, increasing salary differentials, and using profit as a means to increase efficiencies—all measures considered necessary for the reactivation of the economy (see Dobb [1960], chap. 6; and Erlich [1960], chap. 1).
62. Shanin (1965a), pp. 208 and 209.
63. Mesa-Lago (1972b).
64. Guevara (1977b), pp. 134-135.
65. Mesa-Lago (1972b), p. 67.
66. Wheelwright and McFarlane (1970), p. 74.
67. The Liberman discussions in the Soviet Union are reprinted in Sharpe (1966).
68. Castro (1968b).
69. Mesa-Lago (1972a).
70. C. R. Rodríguez (1979), p. 146.
71. Gutelman (1967), p. 64.
72. C. R. Rodríguez (1979), p. 147, and Gilly (1964), p. 22.
73. *Boletín estadístico de Cuba* (1971), p. 173.
74. Ibid., p. 31.
75. Mesa-Lago (1979c), and Torres (1981), p. 289.

76. Torres (1981).
77. MacEwan (1978), p. 17.
78. Kenner and Petras, eds. (1970), p. 327.
79. Ibid.
80. *Latin America Regional Report (Caribbean)*, 21 August 1981, p. 11.
81. Denisovy and Yodkovski (1957), p. 37, and Grinko (1931).
82. View expressed to the author by Dr. Carlos Rafael Rodríguez, vice-president of the Council of Ministers and the Council of State, Havana, 4 November 1980.
83. Chonchol (1963), p. 80.
84. Edquist (1981); Roca (1976); Pollist (1981); MacEwan (1978, 1981); Aranda (1968), pp. 63–68.
85. Mesa-Lago (1981), p. 59.
86. Ibid.
87. Edquist (1981), p. 80.
88. Ibid.
89. Pollitt (1973), p. 257.
90. Pollitt (1981), p. 8.
91. Mesa-Lago (1981), pp. 176–177.
92. The definition of capital and consumer goods follows Gonzalo Rodríguez's definitions (see G. M. Rodríguez [1980], p. 214):

Capital Goods Sector (A) [heavy industry]	Consumer Goods Sector (B)
Metallurgy & mechanical ind.	Food & beverages
Petro-chemical industry	Textiles & leather
Construction materials	Sugar
Electricity	Rest of industries
Mining	

93. See G. M. Rodríguez (1980), p. 258.
94. See Dumont and Mottin (1981), pp. 213–218.
95. Mesa-Lago (1981), p. 70.
96. Ibid.
97. Ibid., p. 72.
98. Moran (1979), p. 205.
99. Mesa-Lago (1981), p. 46.
100. Banco Nacional de Cuba (1979), p. 2.
101. Mesa-Lago (1981), p. 129.
102. Ibid., p. 131.
103. Ibid., Table 32.
104. See Appendix 1.
105. Mesa-Lago (1981), p. 61.
106. Ibid.
107. Edquist (1981), p. 100.
108. Comité Estatal de Estadisticas (1981), p. 67.

109. Pollitt (1981), p. 7.
110. Castro (1971a).
111. Mesa-Lago (1981), p. 130.
112. Quoted in Pérez-Stable (1975), p. 68.
113. Dupuy and Yrchik (1978), p. 56.
114. Leo Grande (1979), Table 1.
115. Ibid. and Mesa-Lago (1981), chap. 5.
116. Leo Grande (1979), p. 6.
117. Ibid., p. 8.
118. Mesa-Lago (1981), Table 15.
119. Mesa-Lago (1979b), p. 187.
120. *Granma Weekly*, 8 January 1973.
121. U.S. Congress (1982), Table 4.
122. *Financial Times* (London), 17 September 1982.
123. Banco Nacional de Cuba, August 1982.
124. Ibid.
125. Iglesias (1983), Tables 6 and 15.
126. *Latin America Regional Report (Caribbean)*, 1 October 1982.
127. *Latin America Regional Report (Caribbean)*, 31 March 1983.
128. *New York Times*, 9 and 10 January 1984.
129. U.S. Congress (1982), Table 4.
130. Mesa-Lago (1981), chap. 2.
131. Castro (1980), chap. 4.

Chapter 4

1. See, for instance, Amaro and Mesa-Lago (1971) and Barkin (1980).
2. Seers (1974).
3. Hicks and Streeten (1979).
4. International Labour Office (1977), pp. 191–192.
5. Hicks and Streeten (1979).
6. See, for instance, Beckerman (1966).
7. Clark (1960); Gilbert and Kravis (1954); Beckerman (1966); and Kravis, Heston, and Summers (1978).
8. Stone (1975).
9. Seers (1972).
10. Morris (1979).
11. See, for instance, Larson and Wilford (1979).
12. Morris (1979), pp. 138–145.
13. Larson and Wilford (1979), p. 576.
14. Hicks and Streeten (1979), p. 598.
15. Ibid., p. 577.
16. Ibid., p. 578.
17. See Usher (1980), p. 186.
18. "Distribución total del comercio al por mayor de productos alimenticios" and "Distribución total del comercio al por mayor de productos industriales,"

Anuario estadístico de Cuba (AEC) (1979), pp. 135, 137, 138; AEC (1974), pp. 177–179; *Boletín estadístico de Cuba* (BEC) (1971), pp. 200–209.

19. A check with one of the rare official Cuban references to the availability of food indicates that my estimates might be somewhat underestimated. A report by the Cuban National Bank in 1975 has some figures showing per capita availability of selected food products for 1970 and 1974 (Banco Nacional de Cuba [1975]). These figures coincide more or less with my own estimates with respect to meat and fish but are about 20 percent higher in the case of cereals, fruits, vegetables, and tubers. I do not know the exact reason for these discrepancies, but one likely reason is that my figures do not include estimates for consumption by the independent farmers and their families, who accounted for about 10 percent of the population in 1974.

20. Comité Estatal de Precios (1981).

21. For a comparison of prices on the rationed, parallel, and black markets, see Mesa-Lago (1981), p. 163.

22. Cuban Economic Research Project (CERP) (1965), pp. 536–537.

23. BEC (1968).

24. AEC (1979).

25. Castro (1976).

26. Knippers Black (1976), p. 405.

27. CERP (1965), p. 185.

28. The area planted with cotton increased from fewer than 150 hectares in 1958 to 3,600 hectares in 1959 in an effort to allocate new areas to import-substituting crops (Seers et al. [1964], p. 116). The peak was reached in 1967 when the cotton-planted area embraced 13,970 hectares, yielding an output of 3,660 tons of cotton compared with an import in the same year of 16,730 tons of cotton fibers (BEC [1968], pp. 29–30, and BEC [1971], p. 227). There are no figures on domestic output of cotton after 1968, which presumably means that there has been no increase, and an indicator of that fact is that some 38,000 tons of cotton fibers were being imported as late as 1977 (AEC [1979], p. 172).

29. Usher (1980), p. 129.

30. The president of Juceplan, Humberto Pérez, said in an interview in February 1979 that about 25,000 dwellings a year were falling apart due to lack of repair (Pérez [1979]). I have been told, however, that this situation does not mean that these dwellings are demolished (interview with Dr. Fidel Vascos, president of CEE, Havana, 28 April 1981).

31. When this index was drawn up, I had no access to the results of the Cuban 1981 population and housing census. However, preliminary figures from this census (CEE [1981a], Table 10) claim that there were no fewer than 2,364,778 dwellings in September of that year, of which 1,658,302 (70.1 percent) were in urban areas and 706,476 were in rural areas. These figures would indicate that my figure of 2,054,200 dwellings is grossly underestimated, but on the other hand, it is hard to believe that the stock of dwellings increased by 471,700 between 1970 and 1981 (the difference between the two censuses) when accumulated figures of annual housing construction for the same period only amount to 189,000. The only conclusion is that the 1970 and 1981 censuses are not comparable as to the number of dwellings.

32. Mace (1979), p. 121.
33. CERP (1965), p. 476.
34. Mace (1979), p. 122.
35. Ibid.
36. Mesa-Lago (1981), p. 173.
37. Ibid.
38. Castro (1980). According to Humberto Pérez, president of Juceplan, 24,000 dwellings were completed in 1981, and about 30,000 were completed in 1982 (*Granma Weekly*, 10 January 1982, and 16 January 1983).
39. Mace (1979), p. 127.
40. *Latin American Economic Report* (April 1979).
41. CERP (1965), p. 477.
42. Usher (1980), p. 130.
43. Ministerio de Relaciones Exteriores (1966), p. 120.
44. Mesa-Lago (Summer 1969), p. 76.
45. Mesa-Lago (1981), p. 164.
46. Chadwick (1975), p. 91.
47. Ibid.
48. Seers et al. (1964), p. 204.
49. According to Mesa-Lago (1981), p. 164.
50. Figure given to the author by Dr. Fidel Vascos, president of CEE, Havana, 28 April 1981.
51. Valdés (1972), p. 429.
52. Castro (1980), p. 26. This achievement is even more impressive if one considers the fact that only 25.6 percent of the adult population had had six years of schooling or more in 1953 (Seers et al. [1964], p. 328).
53. Usher (1980), p. 195.
54. Ibid.
55. Karl (1975), p. 33.
56. AEC (1981), Table 8, and World Bank (1981a), Table 21.
57. Ministerio de Salud (1980); pp. 25–26.
58. Castro (1975), p. 130.
59. Leyva (1972), p. 495.
60. Kravis, Heston, and Summers (1978), p. 248.

Chapter 5

1. Seers (1974), p. 262.
2. Bernardo (1971b), p. ix.
3. MacEwan (1981), p. 229.
4. *Censo de población, viviendas y electoral 1953* (1953).
5. Survey by the U.S. embassy in Havana, quoted in U.S. Department of Commerce (1956), Tables 95 and 96.
6. Brundenius (1979a).
7. I am greatly indebted to Oscar Pino-Santos, former director of the Institute of Studies of the World Economy in Havana, for drawing my attention to important documents on the income situation in prerevolutionary Cuba.

8. U.S. Department of Commerce (1956), p. 167.
9. Mesa-Lago (1968b), p. 375.
10. Agrupación Católica (1972), p. 191.
11. Jacques Chonchol, "Memorandum sobre el proceso de la reforma agraria en Cuba," quoted in Ritter (1974), p. 32.
12. According to a report on the Cuban land reformation presented to the FAO, there were 894 *latifundistas* (landowners) before the revolution who had an average annual income of 40,000 pesos (Food and Agriculture Organization of the United Nations [1966], p. 4).
13. Castro (1975), p. 145.
14. O'Connor (1970), p. 245.
15. J.-L. Rodríguez (1979), p. 148.
16. Dumont (1964), p. 43.
17. Guevara (1977b), p. 91.
18. Ministerio de Relaciones Exteriores (Minrex) (1966), p. 60.
19. Similar problems were encountered by Janet Chapman and Alec Nove in their studies on real wages and income distribution in the USSR and Eastern Europe (Chapman [1963] and Nove [1974], pp. 164–195).
20. See Appendix 2, Table 17.
21. "Proyecto de Anuario Estadístico 1962," quoted in O'Connor (1970), Table 4, p. 210.
22. Minrex (1966), p. 58.
23. See Bernardo (1971b), pp. 69–71, and Seers (1974), p. 265.
24. Bernardo (1971b), pp. 69–71.
25. O'Connor (1970), p. 246.
26. Seers et al. (1964), p. 23.
27. O'Connor (1970), p. 247.
28. Ibid., p. 245.
29. Pazos (1962), p. 7.
30. See Mesa-Lago (1972a), pp. 392–396.
31. The private sector accounted for only 11 percent of the civilian labor force in 1973, and its inclusion in the estimate probably would not affect the result very much.
32. Brundenius (1979b), Table 3.
33. Mesa-Lago (1968a), p. 94.
34. I was told in November 1980 by people at the CEE that there were very few people in Cuba earning less than 85 pesos per month by the end of the 1970s, and this fact is also confirmed by the new wage scales (see Table 5.5).
35. The idea behind the historical wage was that wage or salary earners should lose with the introduction of the new wage scales in 1962, but the historical wage was attributed to the individual as such, not to any particular occupational group.
36. Castro (1975), p. 149.
37. A survey of household budgets was conducted in Havana in April 1979, but the income distribution results were not available when this study was finished.

38. The typical lunch in a workers' canteen costs 0.50 pesos.
39. Information given to the author by Dr. Carlos Rafael Rodríguez, vice-president of the Council of State and the Council of Ministers in Havana, 4 November 1980.
40. Nelson (1950), p. 217.
41. There was a new territorial division in 1976 with fourteen provinces.
42. Seers et al. (1964), p. 23.

Chapter 6

1. See Inglesias (1983), Table 3; Table 2.8; and Tables 6.1 and 2.7.

Appendix 1

1. *Boletín estadístico de Cuba* (1964–1971) and *Anuario estadístico de Cuba* (1972–1980).
2. Such as occasional reports by the Banco Nacional de Cuba.
3. See, for instance, his latest book, *The Economy of Socialist Cuba: A Two-Decade Appraisal* (Albuquerque, 1981), chap. 6.
4. Comité Estatal de Estadísticas, Dirección de Demografía, *Encuesta demográfica nacional de 1979—metodología y tablas seleccionadas* (Havana, April 1981).
5. Comité Estatal de Estadísticas, *Principales características laborales de población de Cuba—encuesta demográfica nacional de 1979* (Havana, 1981).
6. Ministerio de Relaciones Exteriores (1966), p. 58.
7. Mesa-Lago (1981), Table 32, p. 122.
8. Ibid.
9. Of the 146,965 Cubans who emigrated in 1980 ("the Mariel exodus"), it is estimated that 75.5 percent were of working age, of which 80.2 percent were men. Of the total number of emigrants, however, only 57.7 percent were men. Thus, it can be concluded that relatively fewer women of working age left Cuba.
10. Mesa-Lago (1981), Table 26, p. 111.

Bibliography

Official Cuban Sources

Anuario estadístico de Cuba (AEC). Havana, 1968, 1972, 1974–1981.
Boletín estadístico de Cuba (BEC). Havana, 1964, 1968, 1970, 1971.
Boletín estadístico mensual de Cuba (BEM). Havana, March 1981–May 1983.
Censo de población, viviendas y electoral 1953. Havana, 1953.
Censo de población y viviendas 1970. Havana: Juceplan, 1975.
Comité Estatal de Estadísticas (CEE). *Atlas demográfico de Cuba.* Havana, 1979.
──────. *Boletín estadístico mensual.* Havana, May 1983.
──────. *Comunicado de los resultados preliminares del Censo Nacional de Población y Viviendas de 1981.* Havana, 1981a.
──────. "Cuba—conversión de los principales indicadores macroeconómicos del sistema de balances de la economía nacional (SBEN) al Sistema de Cuentas Nacionales (SCN) 1974." Paper presented to Latin American Seminar on National Accounts and Economic Balances, Havana, May 1982b.
──────. *Cuba—desarrollo económico y social durante el período 1958–80.* Havana, 1981b.
──────. *Cuba en cifras 1981.* Havana, 1982e.
──────. *Estadísticas quinquenales de Cuba, 1965–80.* Havana, 1982d.
──────. *Organización de la estadística en Cuba.* Havana, 1982a.
──────. *Principales características laborales de la población de Cuba—encuesta demográfica nacional de 1979.* Havana, 1982c.
──────. *Resumen estadístico, sector campesino.* Havana, 1977. Comité Estatal de Precios (CEP). *Lista oficial de precios.* 5 vols. Havana, 1981d.

Other Sources

Acosta, José. "Cuba: de la neo-colonia a la construcción del socialismo." *Economía y desarrollo* no. 19, 1973a.
──────. "La Estructura agraria en el sector agropecuario al triumfo de la Revolución." *Economía y desarrollo* no. 9, 1972a.
──────. "Las Leyes de reforma agraria en Cuba y el sector privado campesino." *Economoía y desarrollo* no. 12, 1972b.
──────. "La Revolución agraria en Cuba y el desarrollo económico." *Economía y desarrollo* no. 17, 1973b.

Adelman, Irma, and Robinson, Sherman. *Income Distribution Policy in Developing Countries: A Case Study of Korea.* Oxford, 1978.

Adelman, Irma, and Taft Morris, Cynthia. *Economic Growth and Social Equity in Developing Countries.* Stanford, 1973.

Adler-Karlsson, Gunnar. *Kuba Report: Sieg oder Niederlage.* Vienna, 1973.

―――. *Western Economic Warfare 1947–1967.* Uppsala, 1968.

Agrupación Católica Universitaria. "Encuesta de trabajadores rurales 1956–1957 realizada por la Agrupación Católica Universitaria." *Economía y desarrollo* no. 12, 1972.

Aguilar, Luis E. *Cuba 1933: Prologue to Revolution.* Ithaca, 1972.

Alienes, Julian. *Características fundamentales de la economía cubana.* Havana, 1950.

Alonso, Gladys, and Chavez A., Ernesto. *Memorias inéditas del censo de 1931.* Havana, 1978.

Alphandery, J. J. *Cuba, l'autre révolution.* Paris, 1970.

Alton, Thad Paul, et al. *Czechoslovak National Income and Product, 1947-1948 and 1955-1956.* New York, 1962.

―――. *Hungarian National Income and Product in 1955.* New York, 1963.

―――. *Polish National Income and Product in 1954, 1955, and 1956.* New York, 1965.

―――. *The Structure of Gross National Product in Eastern Europe.* Occasional Paper no. 64, Research Project on National Income in Eastern Europe. New York, 1981.

Amaro, Nelson, and Mesa-Lago, Carmelo. "Inequality and Classes." In Carmelo Mesa-Lago, ed., *Revolutionary Change in Cuba.* Pittsburgh, 1971.

Amat, Carlos, and Leon, Hector. *Estructura y nivels de ingreso familiar en Perú.* Lima, 1979.

Appleman Williams, William. *The United States, Cuba and Castro.* New York, 1962.

Aranda, Sergio. *La Revolución en Cuba.* Mexico City, 1968.

Arrinda, Alberto. "El Problema de la vivienda en Cuba." *Cuba socialista,* December 1964.

Balari, Eugenio, and Ramírez, Luis. "Eficiencia y calidad en la investigación económica en el Instituto de la Demanda Interna," *Areito* (New York) 6:23, 1980.

Banco Interamericano de Desarrollo (BID). *Progreso económico y social en América Latina, informe 1982.* Washington, D.C., 1982.

Banco Nacional de Cuba. *Cuba: Economic Development and Prospects.* Havana, 1978.

―――. *The Cuban Economy in 1979 and Prospects for 1980.* Havana, 1979.

―――. *Development and Prospects of the Cuban Economy.* Havana, 1975.

―――. *Highlights of Cuban Economic and Social Development 1976–80 and Main Targets for 1981–85.* Havana, 1981.

―――. *Informe económico.* Havana, August 1982.

Baran, Paul. "Reflexiones sobre la Revolución Cubana." *Trimestre económico* (Mexico) 28:3, July–September 1961.

Barkin, David. "Agricultura: el sector clave del desarrollo de Cuba." *Economía y desarrollo* no. 3, 1970.
———. *Confronting the Separations of Town and Village in Cuba*. Research Paper, UNAM. Xochimilco, 1980.
———. "Popular Participation and the Dialectics of Cuban Development." *Latin American Perspectives* 2:4 (Supplement), 1975.
———. "La redistribución del consumo en Cuba." *Comercio exterior* (Mexico), July 1972.
Baudis, Dieter; García, Gloria; Kuczynski, Jürgen; and Piñera, J. A. "Aus den Geheimarchiven amerikanischer Monopole in Kuba: Die Planung bei Standard Oil (1957 bis 1960)." *Jahrbuch für Wirtschaftsgeschichte* (Berlin), 1966.
Beckerman, W. *International Comparisons of Real Incomes*. Paris, 1966.
Benavides, Joaquín. "La Ley de la distribucion con arreglo al trabajo y la reforma de salarios en Cuba." *Cuba socialista*, March 1982.
Bergson, Abram. *The Real National Income of Soviet Russia Since 1928*. Cambridge, Mass., 1961.
Bernardo, Robert. "Managing and Financing the Firm." In Carmelo Mesa-Lago, ed., *Revolutionary Change in Cuba*. Pittsburgh, 1971a.
———. *The Theory of Moral Incentives in Cuba*. Alabama, 1971b.
Bernis, G. Destanne de. "Deux stratégies pour l'industrialisation du Tiers Monde: les industries industrialisantes et les options algériennes." *Revue Tiers Monde* no. 12, 1971.
———. "Industrializing Industries and the Economic Integration of Less Developed Countries." In L. E. di Marco, ed., *International Economics and Development*. Essays in honor of Raul Prebisch. London, 1972.
Bettelheim, Charles. *Economic Calculation and Forms of Property*. New York, 1975.
———. "Formas y métodos de planificación socialista y nivel de desarrollo de las fuerzas productivas." *Cuba socialista*, April 1964.
———. *La transition vers l'économie socialiste*. Paris, 1968.
Blackburn, Robin. "The Economics of the Cuban Revolution." *Veliz*, 1968.
———. "Prologue to the Cuban Revolution." *New Left Review* (London), October 1963.
Blasier, Cole. "Comecon in Cuban Development." In Cole Blasier and Carmelo Mesa-Lago, eds., *Cuba in the World*. Pittsburgh, 1979.
———. "The Elimination of United States Influence." In Carmelo Mesa-Lago, ed., *Revolutionary Change in Cuba*. Pittsburgh, 1971.
Blasier, Cole, and Mesa-Lago, Carmelo, eds. *Cuba in the World*. Pittsburgh, 1979.
Bonachea, Rolando E., and Valdés, Nelson P., eds. *Cuba in Revolution*. New York, 1972a.
———. "Program Manifesto of the 26th of July Movement." In *Cuba in Revolution*. New York, 1972b.
Bonsal, Philip W. *Cuba, Castro, and the United States*. Pittsburgh, 1972.
Boorstein, Edward. *The Economic Transformation of Cuba: A First-Hand Account*. New York, 1968.
Boti, Regino. "El Plan de desarrollo económico." *Cuba socialista*, December 1961.

———. "El Plan de la economía nacional para 1963." *Cuba socialista*, April 1963.
Breuer, Wilhelm M. *Sozialismus in Kuba—Zur politischen Ökonomi*. Cologne, 1973.
Brundenius, Claes. "An Assessment of Basic Needs Satisfaction in Cuba 1958–1978." Mimeographed, Research Policy Institute, University of Lund, Sweden, 1980.
———. "Development Strategies and Basic Needs in Revolutionary Cuba." In Claes Brundenius and Mats Lundahl, eds., *Development Strategies and Basic Needs in Latin America: Challenges for the 1980s*. Boulder, 1982.
———. *Gaps in Technology Between Member Countries—Non-Ferrous Metals*. Sector Report to Third Ministerial Meeting on Science, 11–12 March 1968. Paris, 1968.
———. *Measuring Economic Growth and Income Distribution in Revolutionary Cuba*. Research Policy Institute, University of Lund, Sweden, Discussion paper no. 130, July 1979.
———. "Measuring Income Distribution in Pre- and Postrevolutionary Cuba." *Cuban Studies*. Pittsburgh, vol. 2, 1979b.
———. *Patron de crecimiento de la economía peruana 1950–1975*. Lima, 1976a.
———. *Renumeraciones y redistribución de ingresos en el Perú 1960–1975*. Lima, 1976b.
———. *Structural Changes in the Peruvian Economy 1968–75*. Lund, 1976c.
Brundenius, Claes, and Lundahl, Mats, eds., *Development Strategies and Basic Needs in Latin America: Challenges for the 1980s*. Boulder, 1982.
Brunner, H. *Cuban Sugar Policy from 1963 to 1970*. Pittsburgh, 1977.
Buttari, Juan J., ed. *Employment and Labor Force in Latin America: A Review at National and Regional Levels*. Rio de Janeiro, 1979.
Casal, Lourdes. "Cuba, abril-mayo 1980: la historia y la histeria." *Areito* (New York) 6:23, 1980.
———. "On Popular Power: The Organization of the Cuban State During the Period of Transition." *Latin American Perspectives* 2:4 (Supplement), 1975.
Castro, Fidel. "Criterios de nuestra revolución." *Cuba socialista*, September 1965.
———. "Cuba's Agrarian Reform." Speech on 18 August 1961 in M. Kenner and J. Petras, eds., *Fidel Castro Speeches*. Middlesex, 1970a.
———. "Discurso el 26 de julio de 1970." *Pensamiento crítico* no. 45, 1970b.
———. "Discurso en el acto de clausura del XIII Congreso CTC (11–15 November 1973)." *Granma*, 25 November 1973a.
———. "Discurso en la clausura del II Congreso de la Federación de Mujeres Cubanas." Speech on 29 November 1974 in *Discursos*, vol. 2. Havana, 1976.
———. "Discurso en la clausura del V Congreso de la Asociación Nacional de Agricultores Pequeños (ANAP)." Speech on 17 May 1977 in *Discursos*, vol. 3. Havana, 1979a.
———. *Discursos del Dr. Fidel Castro Ruz*. 3 vols. Havana, 1976–1979b.
———. *History Will Absolve Me*. Havana, 1968a.
———. *Informe central al I Congreso del Partido Comunista de Cuba*. Havana, 1975.
———. *Informe central al II Congreso del Partido Comunista de Cuba*. Havana, 1980.

———. "Report on the Sugar Harvest." Speech on 20 May 1970 in Rolando E. Bonachea and Nelson P. Valdés, eds., *Cuba in Revolution*. New York, 1972.
———. "The Second Declaration of Havana." Speech on 4 February 1962 in M. Kenner and J. Petras, eds., *Fidel Castro Speeches*. Middlesex, 1970c.
———. Speech on 19 October 1959 in M. Kenner and J. Petras, eds., *Fidel Castro Speeches*. Middlesex, 1970d.
———. Speech on 26 September 1960 at the United Nations, in M. Kenner and J. Petras, eds., *Fidel Castro Speeches*. Middlesex, 1970c.
———. Speech on 1 May 1961 in M. Kenner and J. Petras, eds., *Fidel Castro Speeches*. Middlesex, 1970f.
———. Speech on 1 May 1966, Partido Comunista de Cuba, in *Speeches Made by Major Fidel Castro Ruz*. Havana, 1968b.
———. Speech on 28 September 1966 in M. Kenner and J. Petras, eds., *Fidel Castro Speeches*. Middlesex, 1970g.
———. Speech on March 13, 1968, Partido Comunista de Cuba, *Speeches Made by Major Fidel Castro Ruz*. Havana, 1968c.
———. "To Create Wealth with Social Conscience." In Bertram Silverman, ed., *Man and Socialism in Cuba*. New York, 1971.
Castro, Fidel, et al. *Un Quinquenio de desarrollo socio-económico, 1976-80*. Various speeches by the Cuban leaders. Havana, 1973.
Chadwick, Lee. *Cuba Today*. Westport, 1975.
Chao, Kang. *The Rate and Pattern of Industrial Growth in Communist China*. Ann Arbor, 1965.
Chapman, Janet. "Consumption in the Soviet Union." In Morris Bornstein and Daniel R. Fusfeld, eds., *The Soviet Economy—A Book of Readings*. Homewood, 1966.
———. *Real Wages in Soviet Russia Since 1928*. Cambridge, Mass., 1963.
Charadán López, Fernando. *La Industria azucarera en Cuba*. Havana, 1982.
Chavez, Ernesto. *La Población de Cuba*. Havana, 1976.
Chenery, H., et al. *Redistribution with Growth*. Oxford, 1974.
Chía, Jesús, et al. *Monopolios norteamericanos en Cuba: contribución al estudio de la penetración imperialista*. Havana, 1973.
Chonchol, Jacques. "Análisis cúlico de la Reforma Agraria Cubana." *Trimestre económico* (Mexico) no. 117, March 1963.
Clark, Colin. *The Conditions of Economic Progress*. Third ed. London, 1960.
Comité Central del Partido Comunista de Cuba. *Constitución de la República de Cuba*. Havana, 1976a.
———. *Directivas para el desarrollo económico y social del país en el quinquenio 1976-1980*. Havana, 1976b.
———. *Plataforma programática del Partido Comunista de Cuba*. Havana, 1976c.
———. *Sobre el pleno ejercicio de la igualdad de la mujer*. Havana, 1976d.
———. *Sobre el sistema de dirección y planificación de la economía*. Havana, 1976e.
———. *Sobre la cuestión agraria y las relaciones con el campesinado*. Havana, 1976f.
———. *Sobre los órganos del poder popular*. Havana, 1976g.

Comité Estatal de Precios (CEP). "Antecedentes, situación actual y perspectiva de la formación de precios en Cuba." *Teoría y práctica de los precios* no. 5, 1979.
Cossio, Miguel. "Contribution to the Debate on the Law of Value." In Bertram Silverman, ed., *Man and Socialism in Cuba.* New York, 1971.
Council for Mutual Economic Assistance (COMECON). *Resumen del desarrollo de las economías de los países miembros del CAME en condiciones de su colaboración económica multilateral y solución del problema de igualación de los niveles del desarrollo económico.* Moscow, 1980.
Croner, Claes. "Labor Force Utilization and Mobilization in Cuba, 1959–80." Manuscript, Department of Economic History, University of Uppsala, Sweden, 1981.
Cuban Economic Research Project (CERP). *A Study of Cuba.* Miami, 1965.
Delegación de Cuba. "Una Evaluación de la reforma agraria en Cuba." Paper presented to FAO seminar in Peru on agrarian reform, November 1971. *Economía y desarrollo* no. 11, 1972.
Denison, Edward. "Welfare Measurement and GNP." *Survey of Current Business* 51:5, January 1971.
Denisovy, A. I., and Yodkovski, A. N. *SSSR—gosudarstuo trudyashchikhsya* [USSR—state of the working people]. Moscow, 1957.
de Santis, Sergio. "The Economic Debate in Cuba." *International Socialist Review,* August 1965.
Diaz, Elena, and Villar, Elia. *Nivel de vida.* Havana, 1978.
Diaz Balaguer, Rafael. "Apuntes metodológicos para el cálculo del nivel de vida." *Economía y desarrollo* no. 39, 1977.
Dobb, Maurice. *An Essay on Economic Growth and Planning.* New York, 1964.
———. *Soviet Economic Development Since 1917.* Fifth ed. London, 1960.
Dorticós, Osvaldo. "Análisis y perspectivas del desarrollo de la economía cubana." *Economía y desarrollo* no. 12, 1972.
Domar, Evsey. "A Soviet Model of Growth." In *Essays in the Theory of Economic Growth.* New York, 1957.
Domínguez, Jorge I. *Cuba—Order and Revolution.* Cambridge, Mass., 1978.
Drechsler, Horst, ed., *Studien zum Aufbau des Sozialismus in Kuba.* Berlin, 1979.
Dubois, Jules. *Fidel Castro—Rebel, Liberator, or Dictator?* New York, 1959.
Dumont, René. *Cuba, est-il socialiste?* Paris, 1970.
———. *Cuba—socialisme et développement.* Paris, 1964.
Dumont, René, and Mottin, Marie-France. *Le Mal Développement en Amérique Latine.* Paris, 1981.
Dupuy, Alex, and Yrchik, John. "Socialist Planning and Social Transformation in Cuba: A Contribution to the Debate." *Review of Radical Political Economics* 10:4, 1978.
Eckstein, Alexander. *The National Income of Communist China.* New York, 1961.
Eckstein, Susan. "Capitalist Constraints on Cuban Socialist Development." *Comparative Politics,* April 1980.
———. "Cuba and the World Economy: The Limits of Socialism in One Country." Paper presented to the World Congress of Sociology, Uppsala, 1978.

———. "Long Live Wallerstein's World Economy: Lessons from Cuba." Manuscript, 1981a.
———. "Socialist Internationalism, the Capitalist World Economy, and the Cuban Revolution." Paper presented at the International Studies Association Annual Convention, Philadelphia, 18–21 March, 1981b.
Economic Commission for Latin America (ECLA). *Economic Survey of Latin America 1963*. New York, 1965.
———. "The Measurement of Latin American Real Incomes in US Dollars." *Economic Bulletin for Latin America* 12:2, 1967.
———. *Statistical Bulletin for Latin America*. 6:1–2, 1969.
ECLA/Comisión Económica Para América Latina (CEPAL). *Apreciaciones sobre el estilo de desarrollo y sobre las principales políticas sociales en Cuba*. Mexico City, 1978.
———. *Comparabilidad de los sistemas de cuentas nacionales y del producto material en América Latina*. E/CEPAL/SEM5/L.2. Mexico City, 13 April 1982b.
———. *Cuba: notas para el estudio de América Latina 1980*. Mexico City, 1981.
———. *Cuba: notas para el estudio de América Latina 1981*. Mexico City, 1982a.
Editorial Oriente. *Provincia granma*. Santiago de Cuba, 1977.
Edquist, Charles. *Technical Change in Sugar Cane Harvesting: A Comparison of Cuba and Jamaica (1958–1980)*. Working paper presented to the International Labour Organization (Geneva: ILO, July 1982).
Eich, Dieter. "Ein Kampf an hundert Fronten." *Dritte Welt* nos. 11–12, 1977.
Erlich, Alexander. *The Soviet Industrialization Debate, 1924–1928*. Cambridge, Mass., 1960.
Fabian, Horst. *Der Kubanische Entwicklungsweg: Ein Beitrag zum Konzept autozentrierter Entwicklung*. Opladen, 1981.
Fagen, Richard. *The Transformation of Political Culture in Cuba*. Stanford, 1969.
Farber, Samuel. *Revolution and Social Structure in Cuba, 1933–1959*. Ph.D. dissertation, University of California, 1969.
Fei, John; Ranis, Gustav; and Kuo, Shirley. *Growth and Equity: The Taiwan Case*. New York, 1979.
Feldman, G. A. "On the Theory of Growth Rates of National Income." In Nicolas Spulber, ed., *Foundations of Soviet Strategy for Economic Growth*. Bloomington, 1965.
Fermoselle, Rafael. "Cuba's Energy Balances and Future Energy Picture." *Cuban Studies* no. 2, 1979.
Fernández Font, Marcelo. "Development and Operation of Socialist Banking in Cuba." In Bertram Silverman, ed., *Man and Socialism in Cuba*. New York, 1971.
Fernández Núñez, José Manuel. *La Vivienda en Cuba*. Havana, 1976.
Ferrán, Juan. "Cuántos trabajadores necesita un Central?" *Economía y desarrollo* no. 11, 1972a.
———. "Las Microinversiones y la productividad en la industria azucarera." *Economía y desarrollo* no. 14, 1972b.
Food and Agriculture Organization of the United Nations (FAO). *Cuba—Report on Land Reform*. World Land Reform Conference, 20 June–2 July 1966. Rome, June 1966.

———. *The State of Food and Agriculture in 1968.* Rome, 1968.
Forster, Nancy. "Cuban Agricultural Productivity: A Comparison of State and Private Farm Sectors." *Cuban Studies,* July 1981/January 1982.
Foxley, Alejandro, ed., *Distribución del ingreso.* Santiago, Chile, 1974.
Frank, Charles, and Webb, Richard, eds. *Income Distribution and Growth in the Less-Developed Countries.* Washington, D.C., 1977.
Furtado, Celso. *Economic Development in Latin America: Historical Background and Contemporary Problems.* Second ed. London, 1976.
García, Francisco, and Noyola, Juan. "Principales objectivos de nuestro plan económico hasta 1965." *Cuba socialista,* September 1962.
García Capoto, Emilio. *Generación y transferencia de technología en Cuba después de 1959.* Havana, 1980.
Gerschenkron, Alexander. *A Dollar Index of Soviet Machinery Output.* Santa Monica, 1951.
———. *Economic Backwardness in Historical Perspective.* New York, 1962.
Gilbert, Milton, and Associates. *Comparative National Products and Price Levels.* Paris, 1958.
Gilbert, Milton, and Kravis, Irving B. *An International Comparison of National Products.* Paris, 1954.
Gilly, Adolfo. "Inside the Cuban Revolution." *Monthly Review,* October 1964.
Ginsberg, Norton. *Atlas of Economic Development.* Chicago, 1961.
González Vergara, Ramón. "Acerca de la vinculación del comercio exterior con el sistema de precios de la economía nacional." *Teoría y práctica de los precios* no. 1, 1979.
Griffiths, John, and Griffiths, Peter, eds. *Cuba—The Second Decade.* London, 1979.
Griffiths, Peter. "Fidel Castro's Report on Education, 1976." In John Griffiths and Peter Griffiths, eds., *Cuba—The Second Decade.* London, 1979.
Grinko, G. *El Plan quinquenal de los soviets.* Madrid, 1931.
Grossman, Gregory. *Soviet Statistics of Physical Output of Industrial Commodities—Their Compilation and Quality.* Princeton, 1960.
Guerra, Ramiro. *Azúcar y población en las Antillas.* Havana, 1976.
Guevara, Ernesto Che. "Banking, Credit and Socialism." In Bertram Silverman, ed., *Man and Socialism in Cuba.* New York, 1971a.
———. "Consideraciones sobre los costos, junio de 1963." *Escritos y discursos* vol. 7, 1977a.
———. "Discurso en el seminario sobre planificación en Argelia, 13 de julio de 1963." *Escritos y discursos* vol. 7, 1977b.
———. "Discurso en la primera reunión nacional de producción, 27 de agosto de 1961." *Escritos y discursos* vol. 5, 1977c.
———. "Discurso en la quinta sesión plenaria del Consejo Interamericano Economico y Social, Punta del Este, 8 de agosto de 1961." *Escritos y discursos* vol. 9, 1977d.
———. "Man and Socialism." In Bertram Silverman, ed., *Man and Socialism in Cuba.* New York, 1971b.

---. "The Meaning of Socialist Planning." In Bertram Silverman, ed., *Man and Socialism in Cuba*. New York, 1971c.

---. "On Production Costs and the Budgetary System." In Bertram Silverman, ed., *Man and Socialism in Cuba*. New York, 1971d.

---. "Participación en programa televisada acerca de la implantación de normas de trabajo y escala salarial en los sectores industriales, 26 de diciembre de 1963." *Escritos y discursos* vol. 7, 1977e.

---. "Sobre el sistema presupuestario de financiamiento, febrero de 1964." *Escritos y discursos* vol. 8, 1977f.

---. "Sobre la concepción del valor, octubre de 1963." *Escritos y discursos* vol. 7, 1977g.

Gutelman, Michel. *L'agriculture socialisée á Cuba*. Paris, 1967.

Hagelberg, C. B. "Cuba's Sugar Policy." In Martin Weinstein, ed., *Revolutionary Cuba in the World Arena*. Philadelphia, 1959.

Handelman, Howard. "Cuban Food Policy and Popular Nutritional Levels." *Cuban Studies*, July 1981/January 1982.

Hansen, Joseph. *Dynamics of the Cuban Revolution—The Trotskyist View*. New York, 1978.

Harnecker, Marta. *Cuba: dictadura o democracia?* Mexico, 1975.

---. *Cuba—los protagonistas de un nuevo poder*. Havana, 1979.

---. "Operación Camarioca." *Areito* (New York) 6:23, 1980.

Havana Book Institute. *Cuba '67—Image of a Country*. Havana, 1967.

Hernández, Rafael. "La Política imigratoria de Estados Unidos y la Revolución Cubana." Report prepared for the Centro de Estudios sobre America. Havana, 1980.

Herrera, Juan, and González, Angel. "Normas y escala salarial en la agricultura." *Cuba socialista*, March 1966.

Herrera, Raúl. "Problemas que plantea a la agricultura una zafra de 10 millones de toneladas." *Cuba socialista*, March 1965.

Hicks, Norman. "Growth vs. Basic Needs: Is There a Trade-off?" *World Development* no. 7, 1979.

Hicks, Norman, and Streeten, Paul. "Indicators of Development: The Search for a Basic Needs Yardstick." *World Development* no. 6, 1979.

Hodgman, Donald R. *Soviet Industrial Production, 1928–1951*. Cambridge, 1954.

Hollister, W. W. *China's Gross National Product and Social Accounts 1950–1957*. Glencoe, 1958.

Huberman, Leo, and Sweezy, Paul. *Cuba: Anatomy of a Revolution*. 2nd ed. New York, 1961.

---. *Socialism in Cuba*. New York, 1969.

Iglesias, Enrique. *Balance preliminar de la economía latinoamericana en 1982*. Santiago, Chile, January 1983.

Illán, José. *Cuba—Facts and Figures of an Economy in Ruins*. Miami, 1964.

Infante, Joaquín. "On the Operation of the Auto-Financed Enterprise." In Bertram Silverman, ed., *Man and Socialism in Cuba*. New York, 1971.

Instituto Brasileiro de Geografia e Estatística (IBGE). *Tabulacoes avancadas do censo demográfico 1980 (Resultados preliminares)*. Rio de Janeiro, 1981.

International Bank for Reconstruction and Development (IBRD). *Report on Cuba.* Washington, D.C., 1952.
International Labor Office (ILO). *Employment, Growth, and Basic Needs: A One-World Problem.* New York, 1977.
Ishikawa, Shigeru. *National Income and Capital Formation in China—An Examination of Official Statistics.* Tokyo, 1965.
Jain, Shail. *Size Distribution of Income: A Compilation of Data.* Washington, D.C., 1975.
Jegen, Mary Evelyn, and Wilbur, Charles K., eds. *Growth with Equity: Strategies for Meeting Human Needs.* New York, 1971.
Jenks, Leland. *Our Cuban Colony.* New York, 1928.
Jørgensen, Bård. *Folkemakt og politisk deltakelse—en studie av Cubas utvikling efter revolusjonen* [People's power and participation—a study of Cuba's development after the revolution]. Bergen, 1980.
Juceplan. *Cuba—cifras estadísticas.* Havana, 1980a.
———. *Densidad de población y urbanización.* Havana, 1975.
———. "El Desarrollo industrial de Cuba, I and II." *Cuba socialista,* April and May 1966.
———. *Experiencias sobre la planificación en la República de Cuba.* Havana, 1976.
———. *Indicaciones metodológicas para la elaboración del plan anual de la economía nacional.* Havana, 1978.
———. *Lineamientos económicos y sociales para el quinquenio 1981–85.* Havana, 1981.
———. *La Planificación económica en Cuba.* Havana, 1968.
———. *Segunda plenaria nacional de chequeo de la implantación del sistema de dirección y planificación de la economía.* Havana, 1980b.
———. *El Sistema de dirección y planificación de la economía en las empresas.* Havana, 1980c.
Kalecki, Michal. "Hypothetical Outline of the Five Year Plan 1961–65 for the Cuban Economy." In Michal Kalecki, *Essays on Developing Economies.* Hassocks, 1976.
Kantorovitch, L. V. *Calcul économique et utilisation des ressources.* Paris, 1963.
Karl, Terry. "Work Incentives in Cuba," *Latin American Perspectives* 2:4 (Supplement), 1975.
Karol, K. S. *Les guérilleros au pouvoir.* Paris, 1970.
Kaser, M. C. "Estimating the Soviet National Income." *Economic Journal,* March 1957.
Kenner, M., and Petras, J., eds. *Fidel Castro Speeches.* Middlesex, 1970.
Knippers Black, Jan, ed. *Area Handbook for Cuba.* Second ed. Washington, D.C., 1976.
Kornai, János. *Overcentralization in Economic Administration: A Critical Analysis Based on Experience in Hungarian Light Industry.* Oxford, 1959.
Krantz, Olle. *Struktur och strukturförändring som ekonomisk-historiska begrepp* [Structure and structural change as economic historical concepts]. Lund, 1979.

Kravis, Irving; Heston, Alan; and Summers, Robert. *International Comparisons of Real Product and Purchasing Power.* Baltimore, 1978.
Kumm, Björn. *Cuba sí.* Stockholm, 1963.
Kuznets, Simon. "Economic Growth and Income Inequality." *American Economic Review,* March 1955.
———. *Modern Economic Growth: Rate, Structure, and Spread.* Clinton, 1966.
Landstreet, Barent, and Mundigo, Axel. "Development Policies and Demographic Change in Socialist Cuba." In Louis Lefeber and Lisa North, *Democracy and Development in Latin America.* Toronto, 1981.
———. "Migraciones internas y cambios en las tendencias de urbanización en Cuba." Working Paper no. 13, Population Council. Mexico City, 1982.
Langoni, Carlos. *Distribucão de renda e desenvolvimento econômico no Brasil.* Rio de Janeiro, 1973.
Larson, D., and Wilford, W. T. "The Physical Quality of Life Index: A Useful Indicator?" *World Development* no. 6, 1979.
Lataste, Alban. *Cuba: hacia una nueva economía politica del socialismo?* Santiago, Chile, 1968.
———. "1964: Año de la economía." *Cuba socialista,* February 1964.
Leeman, Wayne A., ed. *Capitalism, Market Socialism, and Central Planning.* Boston, 1963.
Leo Grande, William M. "Cuban Dependency: A Comparison of Pre-Revolutionary and Post-Revolutionary International Economic Relations." *Cuban Studies* no. 2, 1979.
Leontieff, Wassily. "Notes on a Visit to Cuba." *New York Review of Books,* 21 August 1969.
———. "The Trouble with Cuban Socialism." *New York Review of Books,* 7 January 1971.
Le Riverend, Julio. *Historia económica de Cuba.* Havana, 1965.
Lewis, Cleona. *America's Stake in International Investments.* New York, 1938.
Leyva, Ricardo. "Health and Revolution in Cuba." In Rolando E. Bonachea and Nelson P. Valdés, eds., *Cuba in Revolution.* New York, 1972.
Li, Choh-Ming. *Economic Development of Communist China—An Appraisal of the First Five Years of Industrialization.* Berkeley, 1959.
Liberman, E. G. "Cost Accounting and Material Encouragement of Industrial Personnel." In Myron E. Sharpe, ed., *Planning, Profit, and Incentives in the USSR,* vol. 1. New York, 1966.
———. "Profitability of Socialist Enterprises." In Myron E. Sharpe, ed., *Planning, Profit, and Incentives in the USSR,* vol. 2. New York, 1966.
Little, Ian; Scitovsky, Tibor; and Scott, Maurice. *Industry and Trade in Some Developing Countries: A Comparative Study.* London, 1970.
Lopez Segrera, Francisco. *Cuba: capitalismo dependiente y subdesarrollo (1510–1959).* Havana, 1972.
Lowy, Michael. *The Marxism of Che Guevara.* New York, 1973.
Lundahl, Mats. "A Note on Haitian Migration to Cuba." Prepared for the Department of Economics, University of Lund, Sweden, 1981.
———. *Peasants and Poverty: A Study of Haiti.* London, 1979.

Mace, Rodney. "Housing." In John Griffiths and Peter Griffiths, *Cuba in the Second Decade*. London, 1979.
MacEwan, Arthur. *Cuban Agriculture and Development: Contradictions and Progress*. Geneva, June 1978.
──────. *Revolution and Economic Development in Cuba*. Hong Kong, 1981.
McGreevey, William Paul. *Third World Poverty—New Strategies for Measuring Development Progress*. Lexington, Mass., 1980.
Mandel, Ernest. "Le Grand Débat." *Partisans* (Paris) no. 37, 1967.
──────. "Mercantile Categories in the Period of Transition." In Bertram Silverman, ed., *Man and Socialism in Cuba*. New York, 1971.
Marinello, Juan, and Pertsev, Nikolai. *Los Rasgos principales del período de transición del capitalismo al socialismo*. Havana, 1963.
Martínez, Alberto. "El Plan de la economía nacional para 1964." *Cuba socialista*, March 1964.
Martínez-Alier, Juan. "La Burguesía nacionalista en Cuba en la década de 1950." *Boletín Americanista* (University of Barcelona) no. 29, 1979.
──────. *Haciendas, Plantations, and Collective Farms—Agrarian Class Societies: Cuba and Peru*. London, 1977.
Martínez Junco, H. *Los Avances de la salud pública en Cuba*. Havana, 1968.
Martínez-Sanchez, Augusto. "La Implantación del nuevo sistema salarial en las industrias." *Cuba socialista*, October 1963.
Martínez-Soler, Francisco. *Hacia una estrategia de desarrollo económico y social de Cuba hasta el año 2000*. Second Congress of Third World Economists. Havana, 1981.
Mayo, José. *Dos Décadas de lucha contra el latifundismo: breve historia de la Asociación Nacional Campesina*. Havana, 1980.
Mesa-Lago, Carmelo. "Availability and Reliability of Statistics in Socialist Cuba." *Latin American Research Review* 4:1, Spring 1969, and 4:2, Summer 1969.
──────. "Building Socialism in Cuba: Romantic versus Realistic Approach. (Reply to Terry Karl)." *Latin American Perspectives* 3:4, 1976.
──────. "Central Planning." In Carmelo Mesa-Lago, ed., *Revolutionary Change in Cuba*. Pittsburgh, 1971a.
──────. *Cuba in the 1970s: Pragmatism and Institutionalization*. Albuquerque, 1971b.
──────. "Cuban Statistics Revisited." *Cuban Studies* no. 2, 1979a.
──────. "Economic Policies and Growth." In Carmelo Mesa-Lago, ed., *Revolutionary Change in Cuba*. Pittsburgh, 1971c.
──────. "Economic Significance of Unpaid Labor in Socialist Cuba." In Rolando E. Bonachea and Nelson P. Valdés, eds., *Cuba in Revolution*, New York, 1972a.
──────. "The Economics of US-Cuban Rapprochement." In Cole Blasier and Carmelo Mesa-Lago, eds., *Cuba in the World*. Pittsburgh, 1979b.
──────. "The Economy and International Economic Relations." In Cole Blasier and Carmelo Mesa-Lago, eds., *Cuba in the World*. Pittsburgh, 1979c.
──────. *The Economy of Socialist Cuba: A Two-Decade Appraisal*. Albuquerque, 1981.

———. "Ideological, Political, and Economic Factors in the Cuban Controversy on Material vs. Moral Incentives." *Journal of Inter-American Studies and World Affairs* no. 14, 1972b.

———. *The Labor Force, Employment, Unemployment, and Underemployment in Cuba 1899–1970.* Beverly Hills, 1972c.

———. *The Labour Sector and Socialist Distribution in Cuba.* New York, 1968a.

———. *Unemployment in Socialist Countries: Soviet Union, East Europe, China, and Cuba.* Ph.D. dissertation, Cornell University, 1968b.

Mesa-Lago, Carmelo, ed. *Revolutionary Change in Cuba.* Pittsburgh, 1971.

Mesa-Lago, Carmelo, and Pérez-López, Jorge. *Study of Cuba's MPS, Its Conversion to SNA, and Estimation of GDP/Capita and Growth Rates.* Washington, D.C., November 1982.

Mills, C. Wright, *Castro's Cuba—The Revolution in Cuba.* London, 1960.

Ministerio de Educación. *Algunos Datos de la educación cubana.* Havana, 1980.

———. *El Plan de perfeccionamiento y desarrollo del sistema nacional de educación en Cuba.* Havana, 1976.

Ministerio de Relaciones Exteriores (MNREX). *Profile of Cuba.* Havana, 1966.

Ministerio de Salud. *Informe anual 1979.* Havana, 1980.

Montaner, Carlos Alberto. *Secret Report on the Cuban Revolution.* New Brunswick, 1981.

Mora, Alberto. "On Certain Problems of Building Socialism." In Bertram Silverman, ed., *Man and Socialism in Cuba.* New York, 1971a.

———. "On the Operation of the Law of Value in the Cuban Economy." In Bertram Silverman, ed., *Man and Socialism in Cuba.* New York, 1971b.

Moran, Theodore H. "The International Political Economy of Cuban Nickel Development." In Cole Blasier and Carmelo Mesa-Lago, eds., *Cuba in the World.* Pittsburgh, 1979.

Morawetz, David. "Economic Lessons from Some Small Socialist Countries." *World Development*, May–June 1980.

Moreno Fraginals, Manuel. *El Ingenio: complejo economico social cubano del azúcar.* 2 vols. Havana, 1978.

Morray, J. P. "Cuba and Communism." *Monthly Review*, July–August 1961.

———. *The Second Revolution in Cuba.* New York, 1962.

Morris, Morris David. *Measuring the Conditions of the World's Poor: The Physical Quality of Life Index.* New York, 1979.

Mottin, Marie-France. *Cuba quand même: vies quotidiennes dans la Révolution.* Paris, 1980.

Müller, W., ed. *Wertgesetz, Plannung, und Bewusstsein: Die Planungsdebatte in Cuba.* Frankfurt, 1969.

Myrdal, Gunnar. *Asian Drama. An Inquiry into the Poverty of Nations.* New York, 1968.

Nelson, Lowry. *Cuba—The Measure of a Revolution.* St. Paul, 1972.

———. *Rural Cuba.* Minneapolis, 1950.

Nove, Alex. "Distribución del ingreso en la Union Soviética y Europa Oriental." In Alejandro Foxley, ed., *Distribución del ingreso.* Santiago, Chile, 1974.

———. "A Note on the Availability and Reliability of Soviet Statistics." In Morris Bornstein and Daniel R. Fusfeld, *The Soviet Economy—A Book of Readings*. Homewood, 1966.

Noyola, Juan. "La Revolución cubana y sus efectos en el desarrollo económico." *Trimestre económico* (Mexico) 28:3, July–September 1961.

Nuñez Jimenez, Antonio. *La Reforma agraria en la revolución cubana*. Havana, 1960.

Nurkse, Ragnar. "The Case of Balanced Growth." In Gerald Meier, ed., *Leading Issues in Economic Development*, 2nd ed. New York, 1970.

Nutter, Warren. *Growth of Industrial Production in the Soviet Union*. Princeton, 1962.

———. "Industrial Growth in the Soviet Union." *American Economic Review, Papers and Proceedings*, May 1958.

———. "On Measuring Economic Growth." *Journal of Political Economy*, February 1957.

O'Connor, James. "On Cuban Political Economy." In E. Bernstein, ed., *Underdevelopment and Development*. Middlesex, 1973.

———. *The Origins of Socialism in Cuba*. New York, 1970.

Oshima, Harry T. "A New Estimate of the National Income and Product of Cuba in 1953." *Food Research Institute Studies* (Stanford University) 2:3, November 1961.

Padula, Alfred. *The Fall of the Bourgeoisie: Cuba, 1959–1961*. Ph.D. dissertation, University of New Mexico, 1974.

Panorama Económico Latinoamericano (PEL). *Síntesis Económica—Cuba*. PEL, no. 295. Havana, 1968.

Partido Comunista de Cuba (PCC). *Lineamientos económicos y sociales para el quinquenio 1981–85*. Havana, 1981.

Pazos, Felipe. "Comentarios a dos artículos sobre la revolución cubana." *Trimestre económico* (Mexico) 29:1, January–March 1962.

Pérez, Humberto. "La Plataforma Programatica y el desarrollo de Cuba." *Cuba socialista*, June 1982.

———. "Problemas objetivos de nuestra revolución—lo que el pueblo debe saber." Interview with Marta Harnecker. *Bohemia*, 16 February 1979.

———. "Sobre la implantación del sistema de la dirección y planificación de la economía de la provincia Ciudad de la Havana." *Cuestiones de la economía planificada* no. 2, 1980.

Pérez-López, Jorge. "The Cuban Nuclear Power Program." *Cuban Studies* no. 1, 1979a.

———. *An Index of Cuban Industrial Output, 1930–1958*. Ph.D. dissertation, State University of New York at Albany, 1974.

———. "Sugar and Petroleum in Cuban-Soviet Terms of Trade." In Cole Blasier and Carmelo Mesa-Lago, eds., *Cuba in the World*. Pittsburgh, 1979b.

Pérez-Stable, Mareifeli. "Whither the Cuban Working Class." *Latin American Perspectives* 2:4 (Supplement), 1975.

Petushko, Ivan. "Desarrollo integral de la industria azucarera de Cuba." *America Latina* (Moscow) no. 1, 1975.

Pino-Santos, Oscar. *El Asalto a Cuba por la oligarquía financiera yanqui.* Havana, 1973.

———. *Historia de Cuba.* Havana, 1964.

———. *El Imperialismo Norteamericano en la economía de Cuba.* Havana, 1960.

Pizer, Samuel, and Cutler, Frederick. *U.S. Business Investments in Foreign Countries.* Washington, D.C., 1960.

Pollitt, Brian. "Employment Plans, Performance, and Future Prospects in Cuba." In Richard Jolley et al., eds., *Third World Employment.* London, 1973.

———. "Revolution in the Mode of Production in the Sugar Cane Sector of the Cuban Economy, 1959–1980." Paper presented to the fifth annual conference of a society for Caribbean studies, High Leigh, U.K., 17–18 May 1981.

Regalado, Alfonso. "El Establecimiento de un sistema de precios planificados en la economía nacional como parte de implantación gradual del sistema de dirección y planificación de la economía." *Teoría y práctica de los precios* no. 1, 1981.

Riera, Santiago. "Presencia y vigencia del pensamiento económico del Comandante Ernesto Che Guevara en la creación de un sistema de precios." *Teoría y práctica de los precios* no. 4, 1979.

Ritter, Archibald. *The Economic Development of Revolutionary Cuba.* New York, 1974.

———. "The Transferability of Cuba's Revolutionary Development Models." In Cole Blasier and Carmelo Mesa-Lago, eds., *Cuba in the World.* Pittsburgh, 1979.

Rivero, Nicolas. *Castro's Cuba: An American Dilemma.* Washington, D.C., 1962.

Roberts, C. Paul, ed. *Cuba 1968—Supplement to the Statistical Abstract of Latin America.* Berkeley, 1970.

Roca, Sergio. *Cuban Economic Policy and Ideology: The Ten Million Ton Sugar Harvest.* London, 1976.

Rodríguez, Basilio. "La Seguridad social en Cuba." *Cuba socialista,* December 1966.

Rodríguez, Carlos Rafael. "Las Bases del desarrollo económico de Cuba." *Economía y desarrollo* no. 56, 1980a.

———. "Cuatro años de reforma agraria." *Cuba socialista,* May 1963.

———. *Cuba—ejemplo de América: diez años del poder revolucionario.* Lima, 1969.

———. *Cuba en el tránsito al socialismo (1959–1963).* Havana, 1979.

———. "Interview with Marta Harnecker." *Chile Hoy* no. 9, 1972.

———. "Problemas prácticas de la planificación centralizada." *Comercio exterior* (Mexico), November 1980b.

———. "A Proposito de 'El empleo en Cuba.'" *Economía y desarrollo* no. 56, 1980c.

Rodríguez, Gonzalo M. *El Proceso de industrialización de economía cubana.* Havana, 1980.

Rodríguez, José-Luis. "La Economía de Cuba socialista." *Economía y desarrollo* no. 2, 1981.

———. "Politica económica de la revolución cubana, 1959–60," *Economía y desarrollo* no. 54, 1979.

———. "La Política Económica en Cuba prerevolucionaria." *Economía y desarrollo* no. 56, 1980.

Romeo, Carlos. "Acerca del desarrollo económico de Cuba." *Cuba socialista*, December 1965.

Seers, Dudley. "The Cuban experience." In H. Chenery et al. *Redistribution with Growth*. Oxford, 1974.

———. "What Are We Trying to Measure?" *Journal of Development Studies*, April 1972.

Seers, Dudley, et al. *Cuba—The Economic and Social Revolution*. Durham, 1964.

Selser, Gregorio, ed. *La Revolución Cubana*. Buenos Aires, 1960.

Shanin, Lev. "The Economic Nature of Our Commodity Shortage." In Nicolas Spulber, ed., *Foundations of Soviet Strategy for Economic Growth*. Bloomington, 1965a.

———. "Questions of the Economic Course." In Nicolas Spulber, ed., *Foundations of Soviet Strategy for Economic Growth*. Bloomington, 1965b.

Sharpe, Myron E., ed. *Planning, Profit, and Incentives in the USSR*. vol. 1, *The Liberman Discussion;* vol. 2, *Reform of Soviet Economic Management*. New York, 1966.

Šik, Ota. *Plan and Market Under Socialism*. Prague, 1967.

Silva Leon, Arnaldo. *Cuba y el mercado internacional azucarero*. Havana, 1975.

Silverman, Bertram, ed. *Man and Socialism in Cuba: The Great Debate*. New York, 1971.

Solimano, Giorgio, and Taylor, Lance, eds. *Food Price Policies and Nutrition in Latin America*. Tokyo, 1980.

Soto, Adrián. *The United States Latin American Policy During the Great Depression, 1929–1933—A Historical Study on Dependency*. Helsinki, 1981.

Soto, Lionel. *La Revolución del 33*. 2 vols. Havana, 1977.

Soviet Ekonomischeskoy Vzaimopomoschchi (SEV). *Statisticheskiy ezhegodnik stran-chlenov SEV*. Moscow, 1979.

Spulbur, Nicolas, ed. *Foundations of Soviet Strategy for Economic Growth*. Bloomington, 1965.

Stojanović, Radmila, ed. *Yugoslav Economists on Problems of a Socialist Economy*. New York, 1964.

Stone, Richard. *Toward a System of Social and Demographic Statistics*. New York, 1975.

Streeten, Paul. "Balanced Versus Unbalanced Growth." In Gerald Meier, ed., *Leading Issues in Economic Development*, 2d. ed. New York, 1970.

———. "Growth, Redistribution, and Basic Human Needs." In Claes Brundenius and Mats Lundahl, eds., *Development Strategies and Basic Needs in Latin America: Challenges for the 1980s*. Boulder, 1982.

Sundell, Jan-Olaf. *Revolutionens Kuba*. Stockholm, 1970.

Tabares del Real, José A. *La Revolución del 30: sus dos ultimos años*. Havana, 1975.

Taylor, Lance, ed. *Models of Growth and Distribution for Brazil*. Washington, D.C., 1980.

Theriot, Lawrence. *Cuba Faces the Economic Realities of the 1980s*. Washington, D.C., 1981.

Thomas, Hugh. *Cuba. The Pursuit of Freedom*. New York, 1971.

Torres, Olga. "El desarrollo de la economía cubana a partir de 1959." *Comercio exterior* (Mexico), March 1981.

Tutino, Severio. *Den Kubanska Oktoberrevolutionen*. Uddevalla, 1971. Originally published under the title *L'Ottobre Cubano*. Torino, 1968.

United Nations. "Basic Principles of the System of Balances of the National Economy." In *Studies in Methods*. Series F/No. 17. New York, 1971a.

———. *The Economic Development of Latin America in the Post-War Period*. New York, 1964.

———. *External Financing in Latin America*. New York, 1965.

———. *Income Distribution in Latin America*. New York, 1971b.

———. *Statistical Yearbook 1962*. New York, 1963.

———. *Statistical Yearbook 1978*. New York, 1979.

United Nations Educational, Scientific, and Cultural Organization (UNESCO). *Methods and Means Utilized in Cuba to Eliminate Illiteracy*. Paris, 1965.

U.S. Congress. *Cuba Faces the Economic Realities of the 1980s*. Washington, D.C., 1982.

U.S. Department of Commerce. *Historical Statistics of the United States—Colonial Times to 1957*. Washington, D.C., 1960.

———. *Investment in Cuba*. Washington, D.C., 1956.

Usher, Dan. *The Measurement of Economic Growth*. Oxford, 1980.

———. "Measuring Real Consumption from Quantity Data, Canada 1935–1968." In Nestor E. Terleckyj, ed., *Studies in Income and Wealth*, vol. 40. New York, 1976.

———. *The Price Mechanism and the Meaning of National Income Statistics*. Oxford, 1968.

Valdés, Nelson. "The Cuban Revolution: Economic Organization and Bureaucracy." *Latin American Perspectives* no. 1, 1979.

———. "The Radical Transformation of the Cuban Education." In Rolando E. Bonachea and Nelson P. Valdés, eds., *Cuba in Revolution*. New York, 1972.

Valdés, Nelson, and Liewen, Edwin. *The Cuban Revolution: A Research Guide (1959–1969)*. Albuquerque, 1971.

Vázquez Galego, Antonio. *La Consolidación de los monopolios en Camagüey en la década del 20*. Havana, 1975.

Veliz, Claudio, ed. *Latin America and the Caribbean: A Handbook*. London, 1968.

Walker, K. R. "A Chinese Discussion on Planning for Balanced Growth—A Summary of the Views of Ma Yin-Ch'u and His Critics." In C. D. Cowan, ed., *The Economic Development of China and Japan*. London, 1964.

Wallich, Henry. *Monetary Problems of an Export Economy*. Cambridge, Mass., 1950.

Wheelwright, E. L., and McFarlane, Bruce. *The Chinese Road to Socialism—Economics of the Cultural Revolution*. New York, 1970.

Wiles, Peter. *Distribution of Income: East and West*. Amsterdam, 1974.

———. "Growth vs. Choice." In Wayne A. Leeman, ed., *Capitalism, Market Socialism, and Central Planning.* Boston, 1963.
Winocur, Marcos. *Las Clases olvidadas en la revolución cubana.* Barcelona, 1979.
World Bank. *World Development Report 1981.* Washington, D.C., 1981a.
———. *Staff Paper on Peru (1980).* Washington, D.C., 1980.
Würtz-Sørensen, Jørgen. *Det socialistiske Cuba: ekonomi og politik* [Socialist Cuba: economy and politics]. Aarhus, 1982.
Yanowitch, Murray. "The Soviet Income Revolution." In Morris Bornstein and Daniel R. Fusfeld, eds., *The Soviet Economy—A Book of Readings.* Homewood, 1966.
Yglesias, José. *In the Fist of the Revolution.* New York, 1969.
Zanetti, Oscar, and García, Alejandro. *United Fruit Co.: un caso del dominio imperialista en Cuba.* Havana, 1976.
Zauberman, Alfred. *Industrial Progress in Poland, Czechoslovakia, and East Germany, 1937–1962.* London, 1964.
Zeitlin, Maurice. *Revolutionary Politics and the Cuban Working Class.* New York, 1970.
Zórina, Adelaida. "On the Genesis of Capitalism in Nineteenth-Century Cuba." *Latin American Perspectives* 2:4 (Supplement), 1975.

Index

Acid leaching process, 11
Acosta, José, 25
AEC. *See Anuario estadístico de Cuba*
African swine fever, 58
Aggregates, 22
Agrarian Reform Bonds, 43
Agrarian Reform Institute (INRA), 45, 46, 53, 69(table)
Agrarian Reform Law, 69(table)
  1959, 42–43, 45, 106
  1963, 54
Alienes, Julian, 5, 6, 12, 143–144(table)
American Express Company, 66
American Metals Company, 11
American Tobacco Company, 8
ANAP. *See* Small Farmers' Association
Anemia, 14
Anuario estadístico de Cuba (AEC), 125
Argentina, 5, 123(tables)
Asian Drama; An Inquiry into the Poverty of Nations (Myrdal), 2
Atlas (World Bank), 30
Automobile assembly plant, 49

Bagasse, 57
Basic needs, 79–82, 91–92, 103(tables), 104(fig.), 120, 166–167(table), 174–175(tables), 178–179(table). *See also* Cuba, education/health services/housing; Food and beverages, basic needs; Textiles and leather, basic needs
Batista, Fulgencio, 41

Bay of Pigs invasion (1961), 45
Beckerman, W., 80
Beef, 46, 159(table), 162–165(table)
Beet production (Europe), 9
Bernardo, Robert, 105
Bettelheim, Charles, 47, 52
Black market, 55, 56, 83
Bohío, 14
Boletín estadístico de Cuba, 21
Bonsal, Philip, 43
Bonuses, 109, 110, 120
Boorstein, Edward, 21, 50
Boti, Regino, 48, 49
Bourgeoisie, 54
Braceros, 9, 13, 56, 74(table), 106
Brazil, 2, 57, 81, 122, 123–124(tables)

Cane cutters. *See Braceros*
Capital accumulation, 67
Capital goods, 53, 57, 67, 76–77(tables), 192(n92)
Caribbean, 123(tables)
Carter, Jimmy, 44
Castro, Fidel, 19, 48
  and employment, 60
  and housing, 86
  and industrialization, 53
  and nationalization, 55
  reforms, 41, 42
  socialist revolution, 45, 54
Castro, Raúl, 55
Cattle, 7, 42, 43, 46
CEE. *See* Comité Estatal de Estadísticas
Cement, 7, 25, 67, 158(table)
Censo de población y electoral 1953, 86

Censo de población y viviendas 1970, 86
Central America, 121, 123(tables)
Centrales. See Sugar, mills
Central Intelligence Agency, U.S., 45
Centralized budgetary system, 22, 54
Chao, Kang, 23, 26
Chemicals industry, 11, 13, 37–38(tables), 49. *See also* Cuba, manufacturing
Chonchol, Jacques, 46, 106
Cigars, 8
Clark, Colin, 80
Clay, Henry, cigar manufacturing combine, 8
Clothing. *See* Textiles and leather, basic needs
Cobalt, 11
Coca Cola plant, 44
Cocoyoc (Mexico) symposium (1974), 2, 185(n6)
Coffee, 7, 8, 9
Collectivization, 55, 71(table)
Colonos. See Sugar, growers
Comercio exterior, 51
Comité Estatal de Estadísticas (CEE), 19, 22, 28
Committees for the Defense of the Revolution, 91
Construction industry, 18(table), 23, 24, 25, 34–38(tables), 42, 67, 70(fig.), 71(tables), 77–78(tables), 86–87, 95(tables), 131–133(tables), 136(table), 146–153(tables), 158(table), 160–161(table)
Consumer goods, 47–48, 49, 59, 192(n92)
  consumption, 14(table), 112
  imports, 9, 65
  prices, 28, 118(table)
  production, 61, 127, 158–159(tables)
  rationing, 51
Cooperatives, 42
Copper, 8, 11
Costigan-Jones Act, U.S. (1932), 10
Cotton, 85
Credit, 9

Cuba
  agriculture, 18(table), 23, 24, 25, 26, 36–38(tables), 45–47, 49, 50, 51, 54–55, 58, 60, 70(fig.), 71(tables), 77–78(tables), 126, 131–133(tables), 136(table), 138(table), 146–153(tables), 160–161(table)
  armed forces, 160–161(table)
  baby boom (1960s), 59, 126
  balance of payments, 50
  banking, 9, 36(table), 44, 71(table)
  caloric intake, 14, 50
  Communist Party, 48, 90
  Constitution, 45
  consumption, per capita, 6–7, 14(table), 27, 47, 162–165(table)
  consumption total, 31(fig.), 32–33(table)
  consumption distribution, 111–112, 118(table)
  cost of living, 6, 12, 187(n53)
  currency, 6, 30
  and Czechoslovakia, 49
  debt, 65–66
  development, 3, 67, 68. *See also* Basic needs
  disease, 14, 91
  domestic market, 9
  economic growth, 57, 119–120, 121, 122, 124(table), 143–144(table)
  economic reform (1976), 22
  economic statistics, 19–23
  economy, pre-1959, 5–7, 9, 10, 12–13, 18(table), 19
  economy, post-1959, 19, 20, 21, 25–28, 45, 48, 50–51, 54, 57
  education, 29, 59, 71(table), 78(table), 79, 88–90, 97–98(tables), 99–100(figs.), 103(tables), 120, 121, 126, 129–130, 137(table), 177–179(tables)
  Education, Ministry of, 89
  expenditures, per capita, 91, 93–94(figs.), 96(fig.), 100(fig.), 102(fig.), 111–112, 117(table), 168–173(tables), 176–179(tables)
  exports, 5, 32–33(table), 57–58, 62–64, 75–76(tables), 120. *See also under* Sugar

Finance, Ministry of, 22
Five Year Plan (1961-1965), 20
Five Year Plan (1976-1980), 58, 67, 84, 120
Five Year Plan (1981-1985), 86
Five Year Plan (1986-1990), 65
foreign trade, 22, 62-67, 71(table), 72(fig.)
Foreign Trade, Ministry of, 53
forests, 8
Four Year Plan (1962-1965), 49, 50, 51
GDP, 5, 29-30, 39-40(tables), 62, 63, 64, 67, 75(table), 77(table), 92, 123(table)
GDP, per capita, 40(table), 121, 123-124(tables)
and German Democratic Republic, 49
and Great Britain, 8, 43
growth with equity, 4, 121
and Haiti, 9
health services, 29, 78(table), 79, 90-91, 101-102(tables), 102(fig.), 103(tables), 120, 126, 178-179(table)
housing, 42, 54, 85-88, 95-96(tables, fig.), 103(tables), 120, 175-176(tables), 178-179(table). *See also* Bohío
immigrant workers, 9
imports, 32-33(table), 53, 58, 65, 76(table), 84
income, national, 5-6, 7, 12, 13, 15(fig.), 17(fig.), 18(table), 21, 140(table), 143-145(tables)
income, net domestic, 24, 36(table)
income, per capita, 7, 119, 122, 124(table), 145(table)
income, real, per capita, 5, 10
income distribution, 4, 105-110, 112, 113-118(tables, fig.), 120, 180-184(tables)
income redistribution, 41, 46, 107, 108, 109-110, 120, 122
industrialization, 9, 49, 51, 57, 119
industrial output, 23-24, 25, 28, 34-36(tables), 57, 67, 70(fig.), 71(table), 121-122, 143-144(table)
industrial sector, 22, 50, 71(table), 77-78(tables), 126

Industries, Ministry of, 45, 53
infant mortality, 90
infrastructure, 68
investment, 5, 32-33(table), 59, 71(table), 78(table). *See also under* Sugar
and Jamaica, 9
labor force, 9, 13-14, 57, 58-60, 61, 73(table), 87, 113(table), 125-130, 131-138(tables), 160-161(table). *See also* Braceros; Wages
literacy rate, 89, 129
manufacturing, 11, 13, 18(table), 23, 26, 27, 36-38(tables), 131-132(table), 146-153(tables)
manufacturing output, 9, 12, 25, 67, 77(table)
material product, 21, 30. *See also* Net material product
national accounting system, 31(fig.)
nationalizations in, 41, 44, 45, 55
natural resources. *See* Copper; Nickel
and Netherlands, 43
oil refineries, 43-44
and People's Republic of China, 54
planning office. *See* Juceplan
population, 7, 9, 86, 126
PQLI, 81
private sector, 55-56, 116(table)
railways, 8
revolution (1933), 10
revolution (1959), 5, 41
revolutionary government, 41-43, 45, 79, 106-107, 120
rural, 13, 14, 41-43, 49-50, 79, 88, 89, 96(table), 108, 112, 113(table), 118(table), 120-121
service sector, 129, 131-133(tables), 136(table), 160-161(table)
and Soviet Union, 44, 49, 55, 56, 57, 58, 61, 64, 65, 66-67, 71(table), 72(fig.), 75-76(tables), 85
and Spain, 1, 9
standard of living, 13, 14, 46, 106, 111, 121. *See also* Basic needs
State Committee on Prices, 28

terms of trade, 58, 71(table), 72(fig.)
total material production (TMP), 13, 18(table), 23, 24–28, 29, 31(fig.), 36–38(tables), 40(table), 48, 49, 50, 69(fig.), 70(fig.), 71(table), 77(table), 92, 104(table), 146–153(tables)
underemployment, 13, 59
unemployment, 10, 13, 58–60, 61, 113(table), 127–128, 130, 134–135(tables), 138(table), 160–161(table)
unemployment, seasonal, 13
urban, 13, 50, 88, 89, 96(table), 113(table), 118(table), 120
and U.S., 10, 41, 43, 44, 64, 66, 85
and U.S. embargo (1960), 44, 50, 57
U.S. investment in, 7, 8, 9, 10, 11–12, 17(table), 186(n41)
and U.S. occupation, 7
women, 59, 60, 61, 73(table), 126, 127–129, 130, 134–137(tables)
Cuba-American Sugar Company, 8
Cuban Electric Company, 11, 41
Cuban missile crisis (1962), 50
Cuban Telephone Company, 8
Cuba Railroad, 8
Cuba socialista, 51
Czechoslovakia. *See under* Cuba

Dams, 68
Development, 2–3. *See also under* Cuba
Diario de la marina, 42
Diphtheria, 91
Disponibles, 61
Disposable product, 27, 32–33(table)
Distilleries, 44
Domínguez, Jorge I., 12, 143–144(table)
Drought (1962), 49
Dumont, René, 46–47, 107

ECLA. *See* United Nations Economic Commission for Latin America
Economic calculation. *See* Self-finance system

EDN. *See Encuesta demográfica nacional de 1979*
Eisenhower, Dwight D., 44
El Cobre mine, 8, 11
Electricity and gas, 11, 12, 23, 24, 34–38(tables), 41–42, 88, 96(table), 120, 148–153(tables), 155(table), 175(table)
Empresas consolidadas. *See* Cuba, industrial sector
Encuesta demográfica nacional de 1979 (EDN), 125
Escuelas en el campo, 89
Ethanol, 57

Factor cost, 24, 27, 146–153(tables)
FAO. *See* Food and Agriculture Organization
Feldman models, 51
Fertilizer, 56, 57, 157(table)
Fishing industry, 24, 57, 188(n28). *See also* Cuba, agriculture
Food
cost of, index, 6, 12
imports, 76(table), 84
Food and Agriculture Organization (FAO), 25
Food and beverages, 11, 24, 34–35(table), 37–38(tables), 159(table)
basic needs, 82–84, 103–104(tables), 120, 178–179(table)
consumption, 93(table), 162–165(table)
expenditures, per capita, 93(fig.), 112, 117(table), 168–171(tables), 178–179(table)
prices, 166–167(table)
rationed, 118(table)
shortages, 47–48, 49
subsidies, 112
See also Cuba, manufacturing
Forestry. *See* Cuba, agriculture/forests
Freeport Nickel (U.S. company), 11

Gambling, 107
GDP (gross domestic product). *See under* Cuba

German Democratic Republic. *See under* Cuba
Gilbert, Milton, 80
Global social product (GSP), 22, 26, 27, 29, 31(fig.), 32–33(table), 38(table), 67
GMP. *See* Gross material product
GNP. *See* Gross national product
Good Neighbor Policy, 10
Granma Province, 112, 118(table)
Great Britain. *See under* Cuba
Gross material product (GMP), 27, 29, 31(fig.), 32–33(table), 38(table), 40(table), 47, 62, 63, 75(table), 77(table)
Gross national product (GNP), 80. *See also under* Cuba
Gross value added, 24, 26, 27, 31(table)
Growth and equality, 1–2
Growth with equity, 3. *See also under* Cuba
GSP. *See* Global social product
Guajiro, 14
Guantánamo base, U.S. (Cuba), 10
Guantánamo Province, 112, 118(table)
Guevara, Che, 43, 44, 45, 48, 50, 51, 52, 53, 54, 107

Habana Province, La, 112, 118(table)
Hacendados, 10
Haiti. *See under* Cuba
Harvest period. *See Zafra*
Havana (Cuba), 46, 112, 117–118(tables)
Havana Hilton, 44
Havana Railways, 8
Hawley-Smoot Tariff Act, U.S. (1930), 10, 12
Hicks, Norman, 80, 81, 82
Hodgman, Donald R., 26
Huberman, Leo, 46
"Hungerkiller." *See* Matahambre copper mine

IBRD. *See* International Bank for Reconstruction and Development
Idle capacity, 49
ILO. *See* International Labour Organization
Import substitution, 13, 49, 120
Income distribution, 2, 3. *See also under* Cuba
Income tax, 108
Industrial output index, 12
INRA. *See* Agrarian Reform Institute
Integrated Revolutionary Organization (ORI), 48
Interamerican Bank, 121
Interest rates, 66
International Bank for Reconstruction and Development (IBRD), 6, 12, 143–144(table)
International Labour Organization (ILO), 2
International Sugar Agreement (ISA), 64
Iron, 7
Irrigation, 56, 68
ISA. *See* International Sugar Agreement

Jamaica. *See under* Cuba
Jolly, Richard, 89
Juceplan, 27, 28, 48, 51, 58, 107

Kalecki, Michal, 47
Khozrazchet, 22
Korea, 3
Kravis, Irving B., 80
KTP-1 harvester, 60
Kuznets, Simon, 1

Land ownership, 68(table). *See also* Agrarian Reform Law; Latifundios
Larson, D., 81
Laspeyre index, 24, 28, 82
Latifundios, 7, 43
Latin America, 5, 121, 122, 123(tables)
Law 851 (1960), 44
Law 890 (1960), 44
Leo Grande, William M., 62, 63, 64
Liberman, E. G., 53
Liu Shao-chi, 53
Lorenz curves, 110, 116(fig.)
Lottery, 42
Lovisa Bay nickel deposits, 11

MacEwan, Arthur, 105, 109

Machado, Gerardo, 10
Machinery industry, 13, 49, 154–155(tables)
  farm, 57, 60, 68, 74(table), 154(table)
Macroeconomic variables, 21, 22
Malaria, 91
Mariel exodus (1980), 128, 197(n9)
Massey-Ferguson harvesters, 60
Matahambre copper mine, 11
Material product system (MPS), 30
Mesa-Lago, Carmelo, 13, 19, 25, 30, 36(table), 53, 57, 59, 62, 63, 64, 67, 110, 127, 130
Metallurgy, 49, 156(table). *See also* Cuba, manufacturing
Methanol, 57
Mexico, 123(tables)
Microbrigades, 87
Mining, 12, 13, 23, 24, 28, 34–38(tables), 146–153(tables), 155(table). *See also* Copper; Nickel
Moa Bay nickel deposit, 11, 58
Mora, Alberto, 51, 53
Morris, Morris D., 81
MPS. *See* Material product system
Myrdal, Gunnar, 2

National Bank, 23, 24, 25, 43, 65
National City Bank of New York, 8
National Production Conference, 48, 52
Nelson, Lowry, 112
Netherlands. *See under* Cuba
Net material product (NMP), 27, 32–33(table)
Net of depreciation value added, 24–25, 26, 31(fig.), 32–33(table)
Nicaro nickel deposit, 11, 44
Nickel, 5, 11, 57–58, 63, 66
NMP. *See* Net material product
NMS. *See* Nonmaterial services
Nonmaterial services (NMS), 29, 40(table), 77(table)
Nove, Alex, 20
Noyola, Juan, 25, 36(table), 45, 46
Nuestra industria, 51

OAS. *See* Organization of American States

O'Connor, James, 5, 9, 25, 108
"October revolution" (1960), 44, 45
OECD. *See* Organization for Economic Cooperation and Development
Organization for Economic Cooperation and Development (OECD), 80
Organization of American States (OAS), 48
ORI. *See* Integrated Revolutionary Organization
Oriente Province, 112
Oshima, Harry T., 5, 24, 25
Output indexes, 23–24

Panorama Económico Latinamericano (PEL), 36(table)
Paper industry, 24, 34–35(table), 157(table)
Parallel market, 83, 118(table)
Parasitic diseases, 14, 91
Pazos, Felipe, 46, 109
Patterns of Resource Use, Environment, and Development Strategies symposium. *See* Cocoyoc symposium
PEL. *See* Panorama Económico Latinamericano
People's Republic of China, 23, 26, 47, 51, 53. *See also under* Cuba
Pérez-López, Jorge, 12, 23, 24, 25, 30, 143–144(table)
Peru, 81, 122, 123–124(tables)
Pesticides, 57, 157(table)
Petroleum, 37–38(tables), 66, 76(table), 156(table). *See also* Cuba, manufacturing/oil refineries
Physical quality of life index (PQLI), 81
Plantation owners. *See Hacendados*
Platt Amendment, U.S. (1901), 7, 10
Poliomyelitis, 91
PQLI. *See* Physical quality of life index
Preobrazhenskii, Eugeni, 52
Price index, 6
Prices
  constant, 22, 23, 26, 28, 29, 63, 64, 75(tables), 87, 176(table)

current, 22, 23, 29, 67, 75(tables), 149(table), 151–152(table)
export, 24, 28
factory, 28
fixed, 28
retail, 22, 24, 28, 83, 84, 118(table)
shadow, 84
subsidies, 62, 63, 66, 112
wholesale, 24, 28
See also under Sugar
Program Manifesto of the 26th of July Movement, 41
Prospective Sugar Plan (1965), 55, 56
Puerto Rico, 5

Rationing, 49, 50, 51, 118(table)
Recuperation of Ill-Gained Wealth law (1959), 43, 69(table), 190(n13)
Redistribution with Growth, 3
Rent Law (1959), 42
Rice
mills, 44
production, 54–55, 84, 159(table)
Risquet, Jorge, 61
Rodríguez, Carlos Rafael, 53
Rodríguez, José-Luis, 25
Roosevelt, Franklin D., 10
Rubber industry, 11, 34–35(table), 157(table)
Rural worker. *See Guajiro*

Sanitation, 87–88, 96(table), 120, 175(table)
Santiago de Cuba Province, 112, 118(table)
Savings, 117(table)
Sears (U.S. company), 44
Seers, Dudley, 80, 105
Self-finance system, 22, 52, 53
Shanin, Lev, 53
Shipbuilding, 57
Shoemaking. *See* Textiles and leather
Small Farmers' Association (ANAP), 54
SNA. *See* System of national accounts
Social accounts, 80
Social indicators, 80–81

Soviet Union, 20, 22, 26, 43, 44, 47, 52–53, 55. *See also under* Cuba
Spain. *See under* Cuba
Stalin, Joseph, 53
Statistical yearbooks. *See* Comité Estatal de Estadísticas
Stone, Richard, 80
Streeten, Paul, 80, 81, 82
Sugar
by-products, 57
cane burning, 60
exports, 5, 47, 55, 63, 67, 75–76(tables), 120
growers, 7, 9, 43
income, 141–142(table)
investment in, 8, 10, 11, 13, 56, 78(table)
mechanization, 55, 56, 60, 74(table)
mills, 8, 9, 10–11, 13, 44
plantations, 8, 42
prices, 7, 8–9, 10, 15–16(figs.), 55, 57, 58, 62, 63, 64, 65, 66, 71(table), 76(table), 120
production, 7, 8, 9, 12–13, 14(table), 15(fig.), 18(table), 24, 25, 34–38(tables), 45, 46, 55, 56, 67, 74(table), 77(table), 141–142(table), 146–147(table), 156(table). *See also Zafra*
quotas, 10, 44
rust, 58
workers. *See Braceros*
Sussex Institute of Development Studies, 3
Sweezy, Paul, 46
System of national accounts (SNA), 30

Taiwan, 3
Tariff protection, 9
Tax Reform Law (1959), 108
Telephone service, 54
Textiles and leather, 11, 13, 24, 34–35(table), 37–38(tables), 44, 67, 85, 159(table)
basic needs, 84–85, 103–104(tables), 166–167(table), 178–179(table)
expenditure, per capita, 94(fig.), 172–174(tables), 178–179(table)

See also Cuba, manufacturing
TMP. *See* Cuba, total material production
Tobacco, 5, 7, 8, 9, 24, 34–35(table), 37–38(tables), 58. *See also* Cuba, manufacturing
Trade dependency, 61–67, 75(table)
Trade Development Bank, 66
Transportation and communication, 36(table), 56, 71(table), 78(table), 131–133(tables), 136(table), 154(table), 160–161(table)
Tribunal de cuentas, 24
Trickle-down policies, 122
Trotsky, Leon, 52
Tuberculosis, 14, 91
26th of July Movement, 41, 42

U-curve, 1
UNCTAD. *See* United Nations Conference on Trade and Development
UNESCO. *See* United Nations Educational, Scientific, and Cultural Organization
Unions, 61
United Fruit Company, 8
United Nations Conference on Trade and Development (UNCTAD), 2
United Nations Development Decades, 1
United Nations Economic Commission for Latin America (ECLA), 21, 26, 27
United Nations Educational, Scientific, and Cultural Organization (UNESCO), 80, 89
United States, 5, 6, 10, 12, 47, 81. *See also under* Cuba
Urban Reform Law (1960), 86
Uruguay, 5
Usher, Dan, 84, 85, 87, 88, 90

Vacant Lot Law, 42
Value, law of, 51–52
Value added. *See* Gross value added; Net of depreciation value added
Venezuela, 5, 43
Voluntary mobilization campaigns, 109

Wages
 for health professionals, 90, 117(table)
 historical, 110
 and moral incentives, 54, 120
 1953, 106, 113(table), 180(table)
 1960s, 106–109, 115(table), 181–182(table)
 1970s, 109–110, 115(table), 117(table), 183–184(tables)
 1980, 111, 115(table), 120
 overtime, 109, 110, 120
 real, 18(table)
 by sector, 27, 115(table)
 weights, 26
Wall Street crash (1929), 9, 10
War of Independence (1895–1898), 7, 9
Weights, 23, 24, 25, 26, 28, 82, 83–84, 87
Wilford, W. T., 81
Woolworth (U.S. company), 44
Workers' Congress
 Twelfth (1966), 54, 109
 Thirteenth (1973), 61, 109
World Bank, 3, 30
World Employment Conference (1976), 79

Year of planning (1962), 49

Zafra, 8, 9, 74(table)
 duration, 13
 1961, 45
 1962, 49
 1967, 55
 1970, 56, 57, 119